Feminist Poetics

In *Feminist Poetics*, Terry Threadgold looks at the influence of poststructuralism and feminism on poetics, the study of ready-made textual forms. She argues that these movements have changed poetics into a study of the 'making' (poiesis) or 'performing' of textual forms.

Threadgold uses the infamous Australian 'Governor murders' of 1900 as a case study and looks at an extensive group of texts produced over a century. These texts come from a wide range of different genres and social spheres, written by men and women, all telling or reacting to the story of these murders. She uses these texts to answer the questions raised by feminist theory: who writes for whom; who reads; and how and why? And what does embodiment, sexuality and race have to do with these processes?

Feminist Poetics draws on a wealth of research in linguistics, discourse analysis, structuralism and poststructuralism, feminisms including psychoanalytic and linguistic versions, film studies, critical theory and cultural studies, and discusses the work of theorists from Kuhn to de Lauretis, Foucault and de Certeau, and from Bourdieu and Habermas to Halliday. This work is informed by insights gained from feminist theory, especially from the work of Grosz, Butler and Dorothy Smith. Its aim is to reconnect the study of grammatical forms to understandings of the body.

Terry Threadgold is Professor of English at Monash University, Victoria, Australia. Her publications include *Language Topics*, edited with Ross Steele (1988) and *Feminine/Masculine and Representation*, edited with Anne Cranny-Francis (1990).

Feminist Poetics

Poiesis, performance, histories

Terry Threadgold

London and New York

First published 1997
by Routledge
11 New Fetter Lane, London EC4P 4EE

Simultaneously published in the USA and Canada
by Routledge
29 West 35th Street, New York, NY 10001

© 1997 Terry Threadgold

Typeset in Times by Routledge
Printed and bound in Great Britain by
Mackays of Chatham PLC, Chatham, Kent

British Library Cataloguing in Publication Data
A catalogue record for this book is available from the British Library

Library of Congress Cataloguing in Publication Data
Threadgold, Terry.
 Feminist poetics: poiesis, performance, histories / Terry
 Threadgold.
 Includes bibliographical references and index.
 1. Australian literature–Women authors–History and criticism–
 Theory, etc. 2. Feminism and literature–Australia–History.
 3. Serial murders–Australia–Historiography. 4. Women and
 literature–Australia–History. 5. Australian aborigines–
 Historiography. 6. Literature and history–Australia.
 7. Authorship–Sex differences. 8. Intertextuality. 9. Literary
 form. 10. Poetics. I. Title
 PR9608.T47   1997
 820.9′9287′0994–dc20   96–28384
                                                              CIP

 ISBN 0–415–06291–8(hbk)
 ISBN 0–415–02939–2(pbk)

For my mother and father
Bess and Merv Wilson

Contents

Acknowledgements

This book has been a long time in the making. When things go on for so long, many people become implicated in, and part of, the continuing process that is and is not the writing of it. I will never manage to thank you all, but thanks are due to many people. The early research for the book was completed at Sydney University. I owe thanks to a number of people who supported the project in the early stages and encouraged me, despite all the ups and downs of my life at the time – the death of a first husband, a daughter challenging a will and a farm full of inherited animals – to keep working. I would like to thank Margaret Clunies Ross, Rosemary Huisman, Marie de Lepervanche, Gay McAuley, Tim Fitzpatrick, Ross Steele and Anne Cranny-Francis for their support and friendship. To the members of what was The Newtown Semiotic Circle in Sydney there is a special debt, for it was at those meetings that many of the ideas for this book were first argued and debated. I am especially grateful to Gunther Kress, Theo van Leeuwen, Paul Thibault, Michael Halliday and others too many to name, for long hours of productive argument, searching questions, encouragement and good company. I want to thank my students at Sydney and Monash Universities who have taught me more than I can say about the things this book became. Special thanks are due to Susan Yell, Jan Wright, Elizabeth Wilson, David McInnes, Bridget Bainbridge, Kate Cregan, Ian Roderick and Nina Puren, whose projects have challenged and developed mine. A list is hardly adequate, but I cannot begin to say how much I owe, intellectually and personally, to the following people. I am especially grateful to Elizabeth Grosz, Anna Yeatman, Carmen Luke, Allan Luke, Cate Poynton, Alison Lee, Barbara Kamler, Geoff Williams, Ross Steele, Christine Walton, Anneliese Kramer-Dahl, Norman Fairclough, Michael O'Toole, David Birch, Barbara Godard, Yola de Lusenet and Penny Pether. Thanks, too, to Robert Pargetter who believed, when it mattered, that the book would happen. The greatest debt of all, however, is to Ron Carter who commissioned the book a long time ago and went on believing in it, and in me, despite all the odds. Thanks to the succession of patient editors at Routledge whom this project has outlasted, but especially to Claire l'Enfant, Julia Hall,

Alison Foyle, Louisa Semlyen and Miranda Filbee. My sincere thanks to Pam Williams for her support, and for her calm and meticulous assistance in the last weeks of the project. Thank you to my family who have always been there for me; and finally to Peter who has gone on with patience and good cheer making cups of tea far into the night and missing Christmas holidays so that the book would finally happen – all my love and thanks.

Chapter 1

Feminist poetics

METALANGUAGE AND REWRITING

It is now both a feminist and a poststructuralist/postmodernist catch-cry, in some places, that one does not analyse texts, one rewrites them, one does not have an objective metalanguage, one does not use a theory, one *performs* one's critique. Critique is itself a *poiesis*, a making. In feminist theories and practices what has been at issue is the rewriting of patriarchal knowledges (Caine et al. 1988). I want to suggest that there are also seductions involved in allowing oneself to be positioned totally by the discourses and genres of rewriting and refusal of metalanguages, the seductions of an anti-science metaphysics (Haraway 1991b). If we have accepted, in the postmodernist context in which we now work in the humanities, that science and modernist theory are stories told from some *body's* position, stories that can be rewritten, then I think we must also accept that stories are theories, and that they always involve a metalinguistic critique of the stories they rewrite.

To accept this means to rewrite the notion of metalanguage, and perhaps to reconsider some modernist theory, in ways that may make it useful again for an explicit feminist critique. Any such undertaking also forces a rethinking of the politics and '*poiesis* of rewriting'. That politics and *poiesis* is, after all, at least in part derived from the work of male theorists. And it owes much more than it ever admits to the histories and disjunctions of its production in relation to an older poetics, rhetoric and hermeneutics. Nor does it ever actually function without a metalanguage as it claims to do. There is much that a feminist poetics – by which I mean here a feminist work on and with texts – can learn from rereading and rewriting the theories and practices of poetics and *poiesis* against one another. To rethink poetics in these ways suggests a variety of other possible strategies and metaphors for making new feminist theories which will speak and write what the older poetics 'does not know it says'. It will also transform the aporias of masculinist 'rewriting', what Foucault called commentary, into new concepts of metalanguage and theory for use in a feminist poetics of explicit textual analysis and critique.

That is why in this book I want to question the patriarchal nature of the linguistic/structuralist contexts in which the production and reception of texts has been understood historically, but also to suggest that aspects of linguistics and structuralism can again be made functional for an embodied feminist textual practice. This involves rethinking a version of linguistics to challenge also the current feminist and theoretical anxiety about metalanguage. It also involves challenging the (by now) almost institutionalised belief in some quarters that women are oppressed *by language* (Threadgold 1988).

Why then does the title of a book calling itself feminist poetics juxtapose the terms *poiesis*, performance and history?

If we take the term 'poetics' to mean 'work on and with texts' then there have been a number of generalised movements or intellectual frameworks in the twentieth century that qualify as poetics in this very general sense. All of them share an interest in some of the following questions: What is a text? How is it internally structured? How do texts mean? What is a writer? What is a reader? What is the relationship between verbal and non-verbal, ordinary and aesthetic texts, and so on? What do these things have to do with the social world, with culture, with history, and with subjectivity and the body? There has been a general, but uneven, progression in the twentieth century, from theories which have concentrated on the first two of these questions to theories which have gradually tried to grapple with all of them. Russian formalism and Roman Jakobson's poetics, narrative poetics in its standard forms, and structuralism generally, concentrated on the problem of understanding the internal structure and nature of verbal (and aesthetic) texts. Theories like those of Prague School poetics, ethnographic, sociolinguistic, pragmatic and anthropological theories, dominant modes of semiotics, and poststructuralist and deconstructive approaches, as well as reader-response theory and certain kinds of social semiotic perspectives (Kress and van Leeuwen 1990; O'Toole 1994) and feminist theory (de Lauretis 1984; Gatens 1989; Butler 1990; Grosz 1994), have gradually extended the meaning of text to include, for example, the visual, the filmic, the spatial, the corporeal. The source of textual meaning has been relocated in negotiations between readers, writers and texts. That has necessitated a theorisation of the subjects who read and write, first a deconstruction of the humanist knowing subject (Henriques et al. 1984), then a gendering and sexing of the subject, and finally a recognition of the importance of her colour. In the process the older construct of social class has been radically rewritten (Bourdieu 1980/1990; Finch 1993), and the metaphor of performativity has emerged to focus attention on the subject's (compulsory) performance of gender and the possibilities for performing gender differently (Butler 1993).

As the understanding of these processes became more processual, less focused on cultural and semiotic products and more on cultural and semiotic processes, the dynamic term *'poiesis'*, making, seemed for a time more appropriate than the static term 'poetics'. But that very focus on the dynamics of the processes of cultural making also foregrounded the need for *histories*, histories of the making of texts and of the subjects who, in negotiation with textual processes, made or were made themselves. Various terms have been coined for the products of those histories. They have been conceptualised, among other terms, as accumulated cultural, economic or symbolic capital (Bourdieu 1980/1990), 'members' resources' (Fairclough 1989), 'linguistic potential' (Halliday 1978), codes (Eco 1979), intertextuality and interdiscursivity (Bakhtin 1981; Kristeva 1970; Pêcheux 1975/1982). In general terms these theoretical categories have been to do with explaining the semiotic and discursive possibility of cultural exchanges between networks of bodies and networks of texts, although Bakhtin, Kristeva and Bourdieu are the only theorists among these who deal with the body in any explicit way. In a good deal of poststructuralist work the categories of genre (Derrida 1980), narrative (Lyotard 1979/1984), discourse (Foucault 1973), myth (Barthes 1973) and metaphor (Ricoeur 1978) have also been privileged as constituting some combination of the resources subjects use to make texts with. These are resources derived from experience in and with other texts, large chunks of ready-made text to be used again as the occasion arises. The references I have just given are at least the source of my own use of this terminology (Kress and Threadgold 1988) but the terms, along with 'subjectivity' and 'intertextuality', have become a kind of poststructuralist metalanguage for focused work on language and textuality in a whole range of interdisciplinary places – women's studies, cultural studies, literary studies, and radical and feminist pedagogy to name only the most obvious. A system of intertextual resources – multi-medial, understood to be differentiated according to the subject's location in the social and cultural space, limited or constrained by the habitus of daily life, by class, race and gender – is put in the place of the linguist's system of language. Texts are now understood to be constructed chunk by chunk, intertextually, not word by word, and there can thus be no link between text and context except through the intertextual resources of this discursively produced subjectivity.

What this has accomplished is a radical deconstruction of many of the tenets of the older structuralist poetics and associated theories of text/context relations which depended on a prioritising of the verbal (and often also the literary) text in relation to a non-verbal context. In the process, in a number of poststructuralist and interdisciplinary contexts, including academic feminisms, linguistics as a discipline and as a methodology for the analysis of cultural processes and products has been largely discredited, along with many other specific forms of textual analysis and criticism. Paradoxically, at the same time there has been a general acceptance of the fundamental importance of language and other semiotic processes in the constitution of the social world, the culture and subjectivity.

Both moves have been aspects of the radical critique of the disciplines which followed Foucault's (1969/1972, 1975/1982) identification of disciplinary structures as technologies of power and subjection (in both senses, control and the making of subjects). Derrida's (1967/1976b, 1978) deconstruction of the languages of the social sciences and of the binary narrative structure of Western epistemology provided a second focus for this critique. Almost contemporary with this work was the struggle within semiotics over the verbal/non-verbal binary which resulted in the discursive routing of a linguistics that was perceived to be a colonising discourse. Linguistics was for a time the dominant discourse in the field of semiotics, but at the point where the 'non-verbal' (context) was recognised as semiotic in its own right (culture as systems of interrelated semiotics), linguistics was decisively rejected in a series of protracted discursive encounters. My accounts of Foucault and de Lauretis in this book record some aspects of the complexities of these encounters.

This conjunction of often disjunctive theoretical agendas has had profound effects, not least on feminist theory and the work now done in Women's Studies and Cultural Studies. Linguistics, like all the other major disciplines, has come to be 'read' as a particular construction of knowledge, of a specifically modernist, patriarchal and gender or sex-specific kind, an objectifying metalanguage. This is, of course, not true of the work that continues in linguistics itself, or of the work of feminist linguists, which has taken much of this poststructuralist work on board and made good use of it (Mills 1995). Elsewhere, though, it has implicated all the older forms of poetics and textual analysis, which derived many of their fundamental arguments and modes of analysis from specific kinds of linguistics. It has also produced new forms of interdisciplinary and cross-disciplinary alliances, and focused textual work on almost every kind of textual semiotic but the specifically linguistic.

SUBJECTIVITY, BODY, PERFORMATIVITY

From the discursively produced body we have moved to a focus on the body as signifying practice, branded by the other signifying practices with which it engages. This concept of the body has come to be among the most powerful resources for feminist work in certain contexts in recent years. Much of that work is strongly influenced by psychoanalysis. At various points in this book I have also questioned that dependency, quite deliberately engaging with other theories of the body, derived from different paradigms, in order to try to write back in some of the materialist and sociological focus (the focus on the semiotic apparatus) that it seems to me some of these more recent theories (or at least their current uses) have lost touch with. That is why in

Chapter 3 I have used de Lauretis's Peircean semiotic of habit-change, linked it with Bourdieu's work on habitus, and then gone looking in Chapter 5 for a linguist/semiotician (Rossi-Landi) whose work would say some of these things again from somewhere else.

I have also been concerned, however, to trace the feminist concern with subjectivity, with identity and location, and to trace it as a rhetorical and theoretical response to scientific and masculinist pretensions to objectivity and impartiality, and to attempts to elide the self, the body and sexuality, not only in the making of texts and in theorising about that making, but also in the everyday practices through which certain types of masculinity and femininity are constructed. This dialogic response of feminist theory to the scientific metalanguages of patriarchal theory, and the fictional objectivity of patriarchal textual productions (including masculinities of various kinds), results in attempts in feminist writings and theories to name and specify identities and the positions from which texts are written, read and made. These recognise that 'identity' is discursively produced, and that it is *not one*; that it is a network of multiple positions, constructed in and through many chains of signification, always realised in texts, enacted and performed, read and written, heard and spoken, in verbal, visual, graphic, photographic, filmic, televisual and embodied forms, to name just some. In Chapter 2 I historicise these concerns, explore the multiple identities of Newton making science. I look at the ways in which his texts and his selves are discursively constructed in complex dialogic and institutional contexts and the way his texts and the textual generic practice they give rise to are disembodied. I want to de-reify the subject of patriarchal science, and use feminist theory to do it with.

I also want, in this book, to use feminist understandings of biology and sexual difference as themselves discursive and textual constructions. The difficulties associated with the understanding of 'construction' and the relation of 'construction' to biology or sex have been carefully articulated by recent feminist work, which has tried to relocate sex as performance, iterable and normative, and always constitutively unstable:

> Crucially then, construction is neither a single act nor a causal process initiated by a subject and culminating in a set of fixed effects. Construction not only takes place *in* time, but is itself a temporal process which operates through the reiteration of norms; sex is both produced and destabilized in the course of this reiteration. As a sedimented effect of a reiterative or ritual practice, sex acquires its naturalized effect, and, yet, it is also by virtue of this reiteration that gaps and fissures are opened up as the constitutive instabilities in such constructions, as that which escapes or exceeds the norm, as that which cannot be wholly defined or fixed by the repetitive labor of that norm. This instability is the *de*constituting possibility in the very process of repetition, the power that undoes

the very effects by which 'sex' is stabilized, the possibility to put the con-
solidation of the norms of 'sex' into a potentially productive crisis.

(Butler 1993: 10)

Sexuality, then, is not a fixed biological origin, but nor is it as primary as
much psychoanalytical feminism has argued. Freud argued that the super-
ego was the psychic agency which regulated sexuality, the interiorised judge,
which produced socially ideal 'men' and 'women'. Lacan intervened at this
point to argue that it was the symbolic itself, the set of laws that are language, which compel the performance of socially ratified versions of 'masculinity' and 'femininity'. Much psychoanalytic feminism has taken this
position as a starting point, arguing that sexual difference is as primary as
language, that there is no speaking, no writing, no listening, no reading
without the mediation and the presupposition of sexual difference. This has
also tended to produce the claim that sexual difference is somehow more
fundamental than other kinds of difference. Butler (1993: 181) suggests that
this has led to the assumption that there is something called 'sexual difference' that is itself unmarked by race, so that white sexual difference becomes
the norm, and whiteness itself fails to be categorised as a form of racial difference. Butler's radical rewriting of the Lacanian symbolic to include
'*racializing norms*' is in fact central to some of my arguments about race in
the later part of this book, but it is also crucial to a feminism or a feminist
poetics which wants to understand and to represent categories such as race,
class and gender as something more than simply a litany of politically correct concerns:

> If, as Norma Alarcon has insisted, women of colour are 'multiply inter-
> pellated', called by many names, constituted in and by that multiple call-
> ing, then this implies that the symbolic domain, the domain of socially
> instituted norms, is composed of *racializing norms*, and that they exist
> not merely alongside gender norms, but are articulated through one
> another. Hence, it is no longer possible to make sexual difference prior to
> racial difference or, for that matter, to make them fully sexual axes of
> social regulation and power.
>
> (Butler 1993: 182)

Thus it is that the discourses of sexuality, biology and race transgress (and
intersect with) the discourses of 'position' and social categorisation. They do
this according to a whole range of additional discursive and narrative practices which locate these already complex intersections in relation to other
positions, both in the texts of everyday life in late-twentieth-century societies
(being a mother or a housewife, being a citizen who applies for jobs, takes
out insurance, borrows money for a home, pays rent, applies for the dole,
being a middle-aged unemployed man, and so on) and in relation to the
texts of explicitly disciplinary or vocational knowledges, skills and practices

(being a linguist, a sociologist, a teacher, being a computer programmer or a laboratory technician, being a secretary or a boss, a process worker or a part-time or home-worker of some kind).

These discourses participate in and help to construct yet other discourses and narratives about the nature of the social and cultural worlds, their typical 'sectors' and 'divisions' or 'spheres' – divisions between public and private, economic and cultural, social and individual, everyday and institutional, politics and knowledge, and so on. And for every individual these multiple positionings and constructions must be seen as forms of identity and experience which frame and constitute the sexed, classed and raced human subject's life history, which give it both its narrative coherence and its discursive and narrative multiplicity.

To understand even some of these complexities is to provide the scope for much more acute empirical and theoretical accounts of the intersections through which what used to be called the categories of class, race and gender – or of ethnicity and age – might actually be produced as changing and constantly processual forms of subjectivity, subjects who are both synchronically and diachronically in process. It is also to provide important insights into the fragile dynamics of subjectivity and identity, and into the nature of the production of the gendered and ethnic body (and of other kinds of bodies), of the embodied and emotional attachments we have to beliefs and stories about social and cultural difference, and of the production of the ethics of beliefs about, and attitudes towards, those who embody different sexual and cultural realities to ourselves. These feminist interventions have been important and powerful as new knowledges and they inform much of what I do in this book. But I have also wanted to stand back from them and look again at what we may have lost in the making of them.

Part of my agenda in this book, then, is to trace the way these changes occurred, to look at the often entirely fortuitous ways in which linguistics has been written out as other kinds of 'rewriting' for change have gone on, to question the assumption that we can do without it, and indeed to argue that the chunking system of poststructuralism needs to be put back together with a rewritten version of linguistics, and that both need to be accompanied by much more detailed and well-theorised accounts of 'context' than is usually the case. Newton's making of a genre (Chapter 2), de Lauretis's semiotics of the cinematic apparatus (Chapter 3) and Foucault's rewriting of the semiotic relations between discursive and non-discursive realities (Chapter 4) are all examples of the kinds of complexities that are involved in any such attempt at contextualisation. In Chapter 6 I use the insights gained in these chapters to contextualise two very different texts. The framing of the performance text in that chapter is also in some ways an argument about feminist theories of performativity, trying to take the metaphor back to the empirical space of theatrical rehearsal and to the actual difficulties of 'remaking selves', performing them differently, in that context.

I also want to argue that, as the newer terminology of intertextuality has become institutionalised (substituted for textual analysis of a linguistic or older rhetorical kind), it has rarely been either recognised or analysed as being *in itself* a metalanguage. Indeed, having critiqued everybody else's metalanguage in order to begin rewriting, we seem to have then allowed the whole important issue of metalanguage to slip off the agenda. That is something I take up in Chapters 4 and 5.

Parallel with these concerns I want to raise again the issue of rewriting and rereading, or the relation between the two. Recent theorising of readership and the general uncritical acceptance of a version of the death of the author that Barthes did not write (Morris 1988) have suggested a kind of freedom for the reader which is I think not always borne out within the academy or outside it, at least in the theoretical/doctrinal and cultural texts I have explored in this book. It is too easily assumed that strategies and tactics of rereading and rewriting *necessarily* effect change in disciplinary and other social systems. That is why I have reread and rewritten the theoretical texts covered in Chapters 2, 3 and 4, and why my feminist reading of the Governor murders in Chapters 7 and 8 is so intent on showing how certain racist and sexist discourses, and certain kinds of masculine author forms, remain stable across a century of what looks like constant change and variety. In Chapter 8 I have added Dorothy Smith's (1990) account of cumulative reading relations and their recuperative effects to extend the concept of reading formation introduced in Chapter 2.

My re-use of linguistics in this context is part of an argument that it has been precisely because of our commitment to 'rewriting' not 'analysing' that we have failed to analyse just how it is that 'rewriting' occurs and what different rhetorical and linguistic strategies it might involve. Chapters 2, 3 and 4 are centrally concerned with these questions, but they use 'rewriting' and 'intertextuality' of the kind Foucault taught us (Chapter 2), not linguistics, as textual strategies. In this part of the book I have also used recent feminist theories of sexuality and performativity to focus attention on some of the less well-researched aspects of the way knowledges are transmitted or changed, now, in the kinds of gendered interactions that constitute the major modes of transmission or transformation of knowledges in the academy. Among these, postgraduate supervision or discipleship, the need, still, to constitute oneself as 'being in the true' of the discipline (or now interdiscipline), and writing for publication, continue to be the most significant.

Chapters 2, 3 and 4 also recursively take up the question of the definition of the 'popular', watching the concept emerge in Bennett, become gendered in de Lauretis and then arrive fully fledged in metaphors in de Certeau. Chapters 7 and 8 attempt to relocate the concept in a complex and ambivalent textual and discursive scenario.

TELLING INTERTEXTUAL HISTORIES

Chapter 2 is thus largely about genre, the way a genre is constructed historically and intertextually through negotiations with a doctrinal group or field
(in this case, Newton's field), the way it can be used to contain and constrain
the production of knowledge, and the ways it can be contested, rewritten to
effect change. I use Foucault's rewriting of the academic genre Newton's
work established because Foucault has been so extraordinarily influential in
feminism as elsewhere. I explore de Certeau's attempt to understand how
Foucault did what he did because I think we have not paid nearly enough
critical attention to that 'how'. In the same chapter I have introduced
Roland Barthes' early separation of the subject who writes from the subject
who is written, the linguistics-based account of the 'death of the author' that
feminism has been contesting ever since, in order to find an author form for
feminist interventions. Tony Bennett's work on intertextuality and reading
formations is juxtaposed with this to raise crucial issues about the writing
and the reading subject, the subjects who were Newton, Foucault and de
Certeau, and the subjects who were not – Bennett's miller and his heretical
stories. I conclude the chapter with an account, a very provisional one, of
some of the issues of sexuality, erotics and the body which more recent work
by Jane Gallop and others has suggested needs to be addressed in any discussion of the processes of writing and rewriting that constitute and thus
reproduce or change the disciplines. My aim here has also been to show how
the historical making of an academic genre, the genre of the research article,
wrote those issues of embodiment out of the academic story.

In Chapter 3 I turn from that account of disembodiment to the feminist
subject, and to the sexing of the subject of semiosis – a process which
already questioned Barthes' and Benveniste's separation of the subject who
writes from the subject who is written. But the chapter is also about narrative. I chose de Lauretis because she is one of the few feminist theorists of
semiotics itself, because she uses the semiotic metalanguage, because her
work engages with Eco and Kristeva, and because it contributes a semiotically based account of the sexed subject of perception and signification. It is
sophisticated and difficult work which is, yes, about cinema and film, not
language, but it says things that are entirely relevant to any work one might
want to do with any semiotic system, including language. It has the advan-
tage of working with the semiotics of C. S. Peirce and Umberto Eco, both of
whom offer advances on the semiotics of de Saussure, and provides an
example of a successful and influential feminist rewriting of a field – that of
film studies within semiotics.

I have therefore paid particular attention to the feminist strategies of
rewriting that de Lauretis adopts, the way she positions herself *vis-à-vis* the
canonical patriarchal texts of structuralism, her narrative strategies, and her
in-depth and scholarly knowledge of the field of semiotics itself. It is the

latter which gives her the intertextual resources to rewrite Eco and Kristeva. She also makes two other critical contributions. She debates, from a position of semiotic and theoretical sophistication, Laura Mulvey's foundational Oedipal reading of visual narrative, demonstrating the oversimplification, in terms of the complexity of the 'cinematic apparatus', of imagining that deconstructions of realist narrative either can or will change the world, and providing a critique of the idea that the female body is always and necessarily the object of the male gaze. This was a crucial intervention, from a position within a materialist feminist semiotics, into debates that emerged in feminist psychoanalysis. It is still exemplary. So, too, was her very early intervention into debates about high and popular culture within semiotics itself. Her debate with Kristeva and Eco argued that both were still working within an older aesthetic framework that needed to be contested. I have briefly, at the end of this chapter, made an excursion into much more recent feminist theory and de Lauretis's latest book in order to question the continued use of psychoanalysis to theorise the lesbian experience and to point to the limits of any one version of feminism.

I see de Lauretis's work as an important feminist commentary on the kinds of desexing of rewriting I have discussed in Chapter 1, and as an anticipation of the account of Foucault's rewriting of semiotics and structuralism that I deal with in Chapter 3. She is, I think, so important precisely because she had developed with others in film theory at the time – contemporaneously with and not dependent on Foucault's work – a very sophisticated understanding of the cinematic apparatus, of the intersecting assemblages of semiotic practices, of institutions and power relations that frame and contextualise the making and the embodied reading of filmic and other representations.

In Chapter 4 I focus on Foucault and on 'discourse'. This, it seems to me, is the third term in that metalanguage for textual analysis that is now so taken for granted – genre, narrative and discourse. You can analyse anything with them – or can you? I want to explore just what it was that Foucault argued discourse to be. My aim was to explore Foucault's relations with linguistics and structuralism, to see what it was we gained and lost when (after Foucault) we began to read the world as discourse. I wanted to suggest that the arguments about the speaking position of the enounced and the enunciation, and indeed genre (both discussed above), have somehow been elided or confused here, and to explore the way the notions of intertextuality and interdiscursivity were developed in Foucault's work by looking at the uses of these ideas in the work of Bakhtin and Kristeva. In focusing on Deleuze's reading of Foucault on the linguistic and the Visible, I attempt to relocate Foucault's work within the tradition of semiotics and structuralist linguistics from which it has generally become disconnected. Foucault's understanding of the relations between what he called the discursive and the non-discursive was a crucial contribution to what could subsequently be said about text–context relations. It totally changed the ways in which that relationship could be conceptualised, rewriting hierarchies as networks, and making it possible, as de Lauretis also did, to think much larger sets of textual relations, working across different semiotic systems, than had ever been the case with linguistic accounts of those relations which construed the verbal and the non-verbal as distinct and separate realms. My own work on the Governor murders in Chapters 7 and 8 is inevitably informed by this work, as are the textual analyses in Chapter 6.

My other concerns in Chapter 4 are to consider the contributions Foucault made to the way feminist (and, indeed, poststructuralist theory) now understands the disciplined and discursively produced body and the ethical production of the self. This is another theorisation of these questions that should be read against Bennett's concept of reading formations, de Lauretis's understandings, from Peirce, of semiotic habit-change and the sexed subject of semiosis, and the connections I have made there with Bourdieu's work on the habitus. Feminist critique of Foucault's failure to theorise female sexuality has been abundant. But the work has remained central to a great deal of feminist theorising and has motivated a series of attempts to reconstruct a position of resistance to discipline within social and cultural theory. I have used here de Certeau's account of the popular and of resistance as an exemplar, not least (again) because it has been so influential a text. But I have also used it because of the textual and rhetorical strategies it employs to deal with Foucault. My most important arguments here are that it works metaphorically, that it constructs metaphors of the social and of 'popular' resistance to disciplinary and institutional structures which must always therefore be fictions, projections of the popular from the space of the academy, which actually do some violence to 'the people' they claim to represent. In this respect it should be contrasted to the very different work of Bennett in Chapter 2 on reading formations and of de Lauretis in Chapter 3 on the technological apparatus of cinema and the popular. Both actually engage in some ethnographic, historical and textual work to locate the 'people' they talk about. My point here is that the avoidance of 'objectifying metalanguages' may result in what can only be described as dangerous, if suggestive and evocative, metaphors which are themselves metalanguages – the return of the repressed.

I have also been concerned in this chapter to point to the tendency to reproduction of the same (what Foucault called commentary) even in the most radical texts of the moment. This, it seems to me, is an intertextual phenomenon and results from shared reading formations. The 'same' I have chosen to look briefly at is the representation of the evil of linguistics in these texts, the way these representations reproduce themselves intertextually, confusing the social realities of linguistic oppression with linguists' accounts of these, generalising from some linguistic traditions to all linguistics, and failing to connect with the realities of at least some linguistic positions. Here, at last, I have been able to quote a feminist linguist, Deborah Cameron, and the linguist Michael Halliday, as counter-examples. This was an important way, for me, of contextualising Judith Butler's work, which is becoming a canonical text in Women's Studies and Cultural Studies at the present time, but which also has an intertextual history in psycho-analysis, Derrida, Foucault and American speech act theory. Her concept of performativity, the performativity of gender, is a powerful and productive new metaphor, but I think it too has limits and I want to signal those.

REWRITING LINGUISTICS

One of the single most difficult aspects of any attempt to rewrite linguistics, to make it usable again within the kinds of contexts I have been describing above, centres around the question of metalanguage. The strategy I have adopted here is that of attempting to show that that which claims not to be metalanguage in fact still is (Chapter 4), and that that which has been denounced as metalanguage may not be what it seems (Chapter 5). I have quite deliberately in Chapter 5 used the theories of a select group of lin-guists whose work is related to that of Halliday. I have used Halliday and Hjelmslev (the same linguist Deleuze used to explain what Foucault does with the Visible) to rewrite the notion of metalanguage in ways which bring it much closer to poststructuralist and feminist understandings of *poiesis* and performativity. It too is a set of metaphors, ineffable and having no meaning at all until they are located within some complex, contextualising system and performed by some body for some reason. I have also in this chapter, because of the disrepute into which the term 'system' has also fall-en, used the Firthian and Hallidayan rewritings of the linguistic system to argue that we need to look again at the complexities of so-called 'systems', in much the way that de Lauretis does when she questions the possibility of reading all narrative as Oedipal by relocating the issue of filmic narrative within the complexities of the cinematic apparatus.

It is, I think, also impossible to simply read linguistics and linguists' understandings of systems as patriarchal if one takes into account the com-plexities and multiple levels and networks at which, and within which, that particular apparatus can and does work. So Chapter 5 also questions some feminist positions on language, using the work of Elizabeth Grosz and Derrida on the signature, the corporeal trace and the text which goes astray, to suggest that all texts, even linguistics, should be able to be useful for a feminist poetics. I have also used Grosz here to refer back to the work of Barthes and Benveniste on the writing subject (Chapter 2), to rewrite that separation of subject of enounced and enunciation as a Derridean enfolding of one with the other, and thus to reassert the possibility of the author form as the trace of corporeality in texts. I have also here considerably reworked the notion of the textual function of language in Halliday and Hasan, foregrounding that as the place where the corporeality of reading and writing may be located in a functionalist linguistics. This is the function of language which allows specifically for metaphoric and metonymic exchanges with the semiotic networks of other texts and other contexts. Those exchanges are specifically not accomplished *among and by texts*. They must move through the corporeality of those who read and write, those who make and remake texts, and they must leave corporeal traces in the texts they make and mark the readers and writers who make them. The textual function is the space of intertextuality and of subjectivity and the habituated body. It is a space which also suggests that the interpersonal function of language must be the driving rhetorical function. I have left that discussion to the beginning of Chapter 8 where I have wanted to actually use the functions of language to analyse a number of texts.

I have given as straightforward an account of Halliday's linguistics as I can in Chapter 5, and have avoided certain of the complexities of the kinds of developments in systemic-functional linguistics that have gone on in Australia and elsewhere since Halliday's original contributions. These silences have two functions. On the one hand, it is difficult enough in a context not used to linguistic argument to make oneself understood. On the other, much of the work that has taken up Halliday within linguistics has been masculinist, technicist and not very helpful to a feminist poetics. My silence on some of these issues in this book may well be one of the most feminist choices I have made. Halliday's work was itself a remarkable inter-disciplinary enterprise, drawing on the work of linguists, anthropologists, educational sociology and literary rhetorical traditions. It has been influential, beyond all other linguistic paradigms, in and as pedagogy, in the United Kingdom and in Australia. It is something feminist theory and feminist pedagogy should therefore concern itself with; particularly, it seems to me, in contexts where more Cultural Studies- and Women's Studies-oriented English curricula are being pressured, as they should be, to rethink their positions on language and rhetoric. A feminist pedagogy and a feminist poetics, it seems to me, might very well not wish to adopt all of the currently institutionalised forms of that linguistics, but it will not and cannot know that without addressing the question of linguistics itself.

In the Australian context there has been a great deal of poststructuralist and feminist interest in Hallidayan linguistics. Much of that interest concerned itself with the usefulness of the functional grammar and the lack of an adequate social theory (Kress and Threadgold 1988; Lee 1993) or of a theory of language and gender (Poynton 1985, 1993) to support the grammatical theory. In Chapter 5 I have suggested that Halliday's metafunctional hypothesis (that each function of language is linked to an element of social structure) has actually contributed to the tendency to read contexts off from texts in mechanical and unhelpful ways. In Chapter 6 I have used Habermas as an example of a worse case scenario, where the social world is also confined to a number of limited spheres of action, and I have read it through feminist critique, pointing to the patriarchal limitations of these kinds of modernist readings of the social and cultural space. My conclusion has been that the kinds of social and cultural theory I have explored in Chapters 2 to 4 offer a significantly more useful bag of tools for a feminist intent on textual and cultural analysis, but that the idea of the language as a semiotic that functions in three ways simultaneously remains useful. It is useful so long as the questions of contextualisation and framing remain always at issue, always to be negotiated again in every case, always acknowledged as at best partial and interested accounts. In Chapter 6, then, I have concentrated on the kinds of contextual and textual networks, the kinds of legal and theatrical apparatuses, which might frame and make some sense of the functions and the intertextual histories of the two texts I have looked at. In both cases the readings are feminist readings, as in the reading of Habermas.

In Chapters 7 and 8, I have tackled the problem of how to take the tools and ideas developed in the earlier chapters of the book and make them work together on a very large and various set of textual questions. With only three exceptions, the narratives that transmit the stories I have of the Governor murders are written by men, and – despite the differences in genre, media, history and place – certain aspects of the discourses of class, race and gender remain constant throughout all the public versions of the story. I was concerned, among other things, about how to think the intersections of literature, law, media and everyday life. I also wanted to focus on the traces of corporeality in the texts, on the consistency of white masculine public voices across a century, on the way these voices silence other voices and on the difference and ambivalence of Aboriginal and private/popular voices when they are available to be heard. In these chapters I have also wanted to question the tidy separation of public and private, high and popular.

I wanted to show that a textual analysis, using a functional grammar, only has any meaning when it is contextualised and framed in this way by some of the huge stabilities and the less well-recorded fractures in them that constitute a culture. But I also wanted to show that there are things the metalanguage of linguistics will allow you to say about such processes, about the relations between the micro-processes of texts and the macro-processes of cultural and social difference – that the other feminist and post-structuralist discourses cannot address. My reading of these texts, and of these masculine processes of sexual and racial othering, is a specifically feminist reading, the performance of a feminist poetics.

I prefer for all kinds of reasons not to have to define *the* meaning of 'feminist'. In Chapter 5, in the context of linguistics, I have rehearsed Elizabeth Grosz's attempt (1995b) to define what 'feminist' might mean in this context. Suffice it to say here that I agree with her that the status of a particular text as patriarchal or as feminist is at best provisional. There is no need to privilege particular modes of engagement or to privilege particular discourses or knowledges as the subject-matter or content of a feminist text. This book deals with a number of male theorists. I hope that it does so in ways which question the patriarchal contexts in which it works, ways which problematise the standard modes of enunciation in those places, the position of 'the one who knows', and in ways which open up new discursive spaces for feminist work. Whether it does so or not will depend on as-yet non-existent negotiations with so far only textually and semiotically projected readers. The writing carries the histories and memories of many readings, many writings, and many lived and embodied negotiations with others and their texts. I hope it anticipates many more.

The poetics of rewriting
Poiesis, transmission, discipleship?

Galileo interpreted observations on the pendulum, . . .
But that interpretive enterprise – . . . can only articulate a paradigm, not correct it. Paradigms are not corrigible by normal science at all. Instead, as we have already seen, normal science ultimately leads only to the recognition of anomalies and crises . . . Scientists often speak of 'the scales falling from their eyes' or of the 'lightning flash' that 'inundates' a previously obscure puzzle . . . No ordinary sense of the term 'interpretation' fits these flashes of intuition through which a new paradigm is born.

(Kuhn 1962/1974: 122–3)

It may seem a trifle idiosyncratic to begin an account of the poetics (or the *poiesis*) of feminist rewritings with a long quotation from a male scientist whose work is no longer in the forefront of currently productive theory. However, I think there are good reasons for looking again at Kuhn's ideas on paradigm shifts in 'normal' science at a time when, for some time, feminisms of various political and theoretical persuasions (e.g. Pateman and Gross 1986; Pateman 1988; Caine et al. 1988; Irigaray 1974/1985, 1977/1985a) have been arguing that it should be possible to effect paradigm shifts of a major kind by rewriting the theories, narratives and stories of patriarchy to reveal their gaps and fissures and the binary logic which structures them. This argument depends on the prior argument that all texts – whether theories or the semiotic system of patriarchy itself – are constructions, stories told (or lived) from someone's interested perspective. If science, theory, is narrative, story, fiction, it can be rewritten, made differently, in order to reveal, as Kuhn's scientific revolutions do, 'new and different things when looking with familiar instruments in places we have looked before'. By the end of this chapter, it will have been important to have explored some of the possible meanings of 'rewriting'. It will also have been vital to have reconstructed some of its histories, in order to contextualise feminist practices of rewriting which have been conceived more as the hard work of rereading and working to create new realities than as the 'lightning flash' that might change the interpretation of 'data' (a world of already given reality), and which have found 'the familiar instruments' already in need of reconstruction.

KUHN AND PARADIGM CHANGE

Elsewhere Kuhn speaks of the 'network of regularities' (1962/1974: 125) which produce new ideas and then constrain or convert communities of scientists to accept them. Thus, to make the transition from Newtonian physics to Einstein's universe, 'the whole conceptual web whose strands are space, time, matter, force, and so on, had to be shifted and laid down again' (1962/1974: 149), but at the same time these shifts are never complete. The paradigm provides scientists with an inextricable mixture of theory, methods, tools, problems and solutions, a kind of map, a guide to map-making in the scientific community. But there are always contesting paradigms involving 'questions and answers' (1962/1974: 140), dialogue between competing paradigms, so that the paradigms 'inevitably talk through one another'. Kuhn's examples are instructive. When the Copernicans argued that the sun was not a 'planet', they were not only learning what 'planet' or 'sun' meant, they were also changing the meaning of 'planet' so that it could continue to be used in a world where all celestial bodies, including the sun, were now seen differently from the way they had been before (1962/1974: 128–9). There is continuity as well as change; but above all there is recontextualisation, resignification.

Kuhn conducts a similar discussion of the relative meaninglessness of the term 'element' as usually attributed to Boyle in science textbooks, an attribution, he argues, that ignores history (the term can be traced back to Aristotle and forward through Lavoisier into modern texts) and is decontextualised. The term 'element', says Kuhn, is in no sense a 'full logical specification of meaning' (1962/1974: 142), but, rather, a 'pedagogic aid' and only meaningful when fully textualised and contextualised in relation to a particular set of 'scientific concepts, manipulative procedures, and to paradigm applications' (1962/1974: 142). Kuhn's sense of the relativity of meanings and of their histories within the complexities of scientific communities is associated with his early deconstruction (not a term he would use) of the tendency of what he refers to as the normalising genres of science (the philosophical paradigm derived from Descartes and Newtonian dynamics) to represent 'revolution', or sudden change, as cumulative 'addition', steady progress (1962/1974: 136–7). Revolution, as Kuhn uses it here, clearly signifies a paradigm shift, a radical rewriting or remaking (*poiesis*) of the observed world, a rewriting which is discontinuous with the 'normal' paradigm. But when Kuhn actually uses the term 'rewriting', it is not in a revolutionary sense:

> Textbooks, however, being pedagogic tools for the perpetuation of normal science, have to be *rewritten* in whole or in part whenever the language, problem-structure, or standards of normal science change. In short they have to be *rewritten* in the aftermath of each scientific

revolution, and, once *rewritten*, they inevitably disguise not only the role but the very existence of the revolutions that produced them.

(Kuhn 1962/1974: 137; my italics)

This rewriting conceals revolutions, denies histories, and is instrumental in the construction of the scientific fictions of fact, of objectivity and of linear, cumulative progress. These fictions, Kuhn argues, are constitutional both in the construction of science itself and also in the research histories of individual members of the scientific community. He comments on Dalton, who apparently omits all account, in his documentation of his own research, of 'the revolutionary effects of applying to chemistry a set of questions and concepts previously restricted to physics and meteorology' (Kuhn 1962/1974: 139). Dalton's research, it seems, is the result of becoming 'undisciplined' or of making surprised discoveries in interdisciplinary spaces (my explanation, not Kuhn's). What this kind of rewriting seems to accomplish is the erasure of the intertextual histories of scientific texts, the loss of the trace of the previous paradigm, the silencing of the dialogue between paradigms.

NEWTON AND RHETORIC: THE SOCIAL CONSTRUCTION OF GENRE AND SCIENCE

Charles Bazerman (1988) is concerned precisely with these histories and with the processes that the book or text, as product, fails to record. His account of the histories and intertextualities of Newton's research, and of his writing of the *Opticks*, carefully retraces the complex interrelationships between Newton's notebooks, his Cambridge lectures, his early journal publications and the rewriting/remaking of Newton's research in response to the opposition and debate his articles provoked in the scientific community of the day. Bazerman argues that the construction of the style and writing strategy (the genre) that would dominate eighteenth-century science, and indeed provide the *literary* basis (a way of 'making' scientific facts) for the development of the scientific research article, in both the human and social sciences, is dependent on the complex textual and interpersonal negotiations which he documents. Newton, it seems, never ceased to believe in the facts and rightness of his own research, research first documented in the 'discovery narrative' of the articles. To deal with opposition and control debate, however, he had to develop an authorial voice and rhetorical modes of positioning the reader which would construct his discoveries indeed as facts, not personal discoveries, and which would, more importantly, persuade the rest of the scientific community to see the same world he saw. The story of Newton's *Opticks*, then, is also a story or a history of 'rewriting', but one which opens out to scrutiny the enormous complexities of any such enterprise, and points to the dialogic and heteroglossic aspects of the things Kuhn calls, somewhat monologically, 'community' and 'paradigm shift':

As the evidence reviewed in this chapter indicates, the book [the *Opticks*] is far from the spontaneous workings of the creative mind. The book is a hard-won literary achievement forged through some hardwon literary wars. The texts that are closer to the spontaneous outpourings of Newton's mind, such as his student notebook, have hardly the compelling presence.

The compelling effect of Book 1 of the *Opticks* is rather evidence of how well, totally, and precisely Newton has gained control of the reader's reasoning and perception, so that he can make the reader go through turn by turn exactly as he wishes.

(Bazerman 1988: 124)

This is a complex history which provides the intertextual history for the *Opticks* as book, and ultimately for the development of the typical research article now – but again not in any clear-cut or linear way. As Bazerman (1988: 126) points out, while it took Newton about a decade to develop the sophisticated form of scientific argument that is evident in the *Opticks*, it took the rest of the scientific community over a century to reach the same point. Those learning processes, moreover, not only 'incorporated' Newton's rhetoric but learned how to move beyond it. Newton had perceived the necessity for a coherent system to provide a powerful account of phenomena, and he had learned how to make it in his struggles with writing, but its very coherence created difficulties for integrating 'viewpoints, discoveries and claims from outside the system' (1988: 126).

Bazerman argues that, in time, the scientific community developed a communally constructed framework that allowed for this integration. This involved the invention of a number of other textual and generic strategies – the modern apparatus for the embedding and citation of others' ideas, new forms of theoretical argument, new synthetic genres that would allow argument and negotiation over and around codified beliefs (the review article, the conference forum, and so on) – but these did not develop until the nineteenth and twentieth centuries. When they did, this integrative technology of writing, produced in countless rewritings, made the communal system much more flexible, 'allowing for changes in argument without stepping outside or causing breakdowns in the system' (Bazerman 1988: 127). Rewriting here then, although it derives from a significant paradigm shift (Newton's science), results, in Bazerman's narrative, in technologies of 'rewriting' (citation, quotation and controlled argument and negotiation) which precisely do not cause revolution, but allow the system and the community to adapt and adjust to change and to go on evolving – one supposes cumulatively, even if heteroglossically. What matters in the end – in the case of Newton himself, and of science in general – is control, consensus and the values of community.

The clear succession of stages in Kuhn by which normal science adapts to change or 'paradigm shift' and moves on – renormalises itself (a representation of events that parallels structuralist accounts of literary evolution) – have been blurred in Bazerman in the writings and presence of Newton, a rhetorical presence which is all-pervasive long after the man himself existed to control and constrain his reader. In both Bazerman and Kuhn, the person of the scientist hovers like a ghostly presence, whose bequest to the present is the consequence of sudden intuitions and rhetorical strategies and activities that (in Bazerman) go on working long after the event and in discontinuous and unpredictable ways. What was a revolution becomes a part of an integrated system for the incorporation of change. This, of course, is a potential nightmare for a feminist seeking 'regeneration, not rebirth' and longing for a 'cyborg politics' which would be 'the struggle for language and the struggle against perfect communication, against the one code that translates all meaning perfectly, the central dogma of phallogocentrism' (Haraway 1991a: 176). Kuhn's and Bazerman's accounts, important contributions to the understanding of the 'made', constructed, nature of scientific registers and genres and of the conservative and productive possibilities of this process I am calling 'rewriting', stand as some indication of the potential difficulties that may have to be encountered in the business of feminist rewriting. What is at stake here is the process that Joan Scott (1988) has characterised as 'restoration', the tendencies of systems to appropriate and incorporate that which is 'other', heterogeneous, heteroglossic, the reason why in the face of feminist rewritings, feminist struggles for meanings, 'the conditions of women's inequality are constantly restored' (Cornell et al. 1992: 68).

SCIENTIFIC FICTIONS: MAKING NEWTON DIFFERENTLY

Markley (1991), in a review of the Bazerman book, argues that, despite this fascinating work on the development of scientific rhetoric, Bazerman remains constrained by the very disciplinary structures his work begins to deconstruct. In Bazerman's story, Markley argues, it is the great scientist, his modes of enunciation, and his conscious, controlled interactions with other scientists that in the end are 'influential', not the complex of discursive networks which that generic rhetoric tries to control. Moving beyond Bazerman to an attempt to produce an interdisciplinary (rather than a disciplined) Newton, Markley attempts to locate Newton's unpublished manuscripts and the work on optics within a complex network of contemporary discourses, including those of alchemy, mathematics, theology, history and mythography. He finds these discourses in other texts, in the work of other scholars (Dobbs 1975; Manuel 1974; Knoespel 1989). This enables him to demonstrate Bazerman's disciplinary bias in that Bazerman had concentrated on the 'closed' controlled nature of Book 1 of the *Opticks* as the source of later scientific rhetoric, relegating the other two books to the sphere of the speculative, the unscientific, and thus re-establishing the oppositions his work on Newton's rhetoric tends to deconstruct – science vs literature, order vs chaos, and closed vs open. From Markley's point of view, these second and third books of the *Opticks* locate Newton's work in a wider discursive context, showing him struggling with the concept of material complexity and theological voluntarism. In this view it is possible to demonstrate the way these other discourses intertextually traverse both Newton and his texts, the way the master of the scientific genre is discursively and socially constructed in 'unscientific' ways (Markley 1991: 431–2). Markley's poststructuralism is a less relentlessly progressivist narrative than Bazerman's, in which there are spaces for possibly different outcomes, and genuinely different histories.

PERFORMING THE SCIENTIFIC BODY

There is more than one way in which the philosophical paradigm derived from Descartes and Newtonian dynamics continue to inhabit and to inflect the realities produced in rewritings of science. One of the most interesting elements of these accounts is the gradual disappearance of the embodied masculine subject of science from the scene of his scientific activities – something that happens in the gradual change from the *performance* of science, indeed before an audience at the Royal Society, to written reports of it, which begin to circulate in different institutional spaces (journals, the publishing industry) in an economy of symbolic and cultural as well as epistemological and economic capital. The function of the audience of witnesses was to verify what they had seen as part of a process of transforming claims and speculations into matters of fact and generally accepted knowledge (Swales 1990: 111).

The generic organisation of the scientific article and the business of citation now functions, disembodied and desexed, in a similar way. Every scientific text, every scientific genre, every scientific discourse – with its mixture of the visual, the corporeal, the technological and the verbal – is a performance still of those pressures. Knorr-Cetina's (1981) account of the contemporary production of scientific reports for publication under the constraints of governmental, institutional, organisational, managerial and political pressures confirms that this is no merely historical phenomenon. At the same time stories like Bazerman's – interdisciplinary even if still disciplined – have, according to Markley, 'revolutionised' the way in which the relations between rhetoric and science, the literary and science, are now studied (Paulson 1988; Hayles 1989; Spariosu 1989). The performance or making of science, even in written forms, is understood as a processual phenomenon, like the making or performing of the literary, or the theatrical performance, or the legal judgement or affidavit or statute. It is a profoundly embodied and disciplined process, subject to all kinds of policy, institutional, private and power relationships, and it is always narrative, dialogic and rhetorical. There is an interesting recursivity in these processes of rewriting around Newton – writing the body and the social out, writing the body and the social back in – but there is also a constant dialogism between texts and their writers, a desire to effect change, a will to power and to knowledge.

FOUCAULT REWRITING THE DISCIPLINES

Foucault's (1970/1971) inaugural lecture at the Collège de France actually marks the performance of something like a paradigm shift, offering an absolutely other way of seeing and reading the disciplined communities of Kuhn's and Bazerman's accounts. It does not, of course, emerge fully formed from nowhere, and neither is it actually 'sudden' or apocalyptic. He had been working hard at it (like Newton) for some years by this stage and in the final section of the lecture in its printed form Foucault acknowledges his intellectual debt to Dumèzil, Canguilhem, Hyppolite, and ultimately to Hegel (1970/71: 235). There is an interesting absence of Althusser, who was his teacher, and a fascinating representation of his own practice of rewriting as an 'escape' from Hegel and a coming to understand 'the price we pay to detach ourselves from him' (1970/1971: 235). This is a very brief, but important, illusion to the process of discipleship, the question of a reading formation, which systematically structures even a paradigm shift.

Foucault's lecture shares something, too, of Haraway's recognition of the need for 'the struggle for language and the struggle against perfect communication'. Like Haraway, Foucault makes an immediate and explicit link between discourse, power and desire: 'discourse is the power which is to be seized' (1970/1971: 221). The genre of the scientific research article, the product of Newton's rewriting, can be reread (or rewritten) in Foucault's terms as 'true discourse', part of 'a system of exclusion in the process of development' (1970/1971: 218), 'true discourse' which, 'liberated by the nature of its form from power and desire, is incapable of recognising the will to truth which pervades it' (1970/1971: 219).

In Foucault's account, the order of discourse, the social organisation of the disciplines, is controlled and delimited by procedures of exclusion. Certain things cannot be said (are not able and not permitted to be said). Institutional or disciplinary divisions or categorisations construct some discourses as inaudible, 'outside' reason, outside disciplinary knowledges (e.g. the discourse of the madman). The will to truth (the will to knowledge, the desire to know and be 'in the true') excludes from discourse both the acknowledgement of the power and desire within it and that which in the terms of the discourse is false, that which true discourse refuses to recognise as truth (which is, of course, why Newton had to write so hard to construct his version of things as truth). Discourse is also bounded, delimited, by procedures internal to itself which function to control events and chance. The first of these is commentary, a ceaseless recitation of the same ('a meaning to be rediscovered, an identity to be reiterated' [1970/1971: 223]). In Foucault's argument, it is this which performs the relationship between primary and secondary texts (including the relationship between 'data' and 'theory' or 'observation/interpretation') as well as the relationship between all those undisciplined or extradisciplinary rewritings of narrative which mark the connection between the disciplined and the popular. Authorship and its various historical and authenticating forms also works to control chance, as do the disciplines themselves, despite the fact that Foucault argues that disciplines are set up in opposition to the principles of commentary and authorship. Discipline is unauthored, anonymous. It is not owned by those it disciplines, and it remains a discipline only as long as it can continue to produce – 'ad infinitum – fresh propositions' (1970/1971: 223). One might remember here the need to escape Hegel and to move beyond Hyppolite (not to speak of forgetting Althusser). Even this radical discourse is not immune from the desire and the need for the new.

In Foucault's work, all of these various delimitations on discourse function within specific historical and institutional sites (the asylum, the clinic, the school, the university or the human sciences) and they function without the violence of coercive power. Subjects (disciplinary knowledges *and* speaking subjects) are positioned within them, position themselves within them, in much the same way as Althusser, attempting to explain the role of the body and consciousness in the reproduction of the conditions of production, describes subjects as being 'interpellated' into (and by) what he called the ideological state apparatuses – religion, education, the family, the law, politics, trade unions, communications (the media), the cultural (literature, the arts, sports, etc.) (1971/1977: 136–7). It is important to recognise the textual traces of Althusser in Foucault and to note that 'discourse', in its positioning and disciplining functions in Foucault's early writing, comes very close to constituting what Althusser called ideology when he put forward the thesis that 'ideology has a material existence' (1971/1977: 51). Althusser's argument was that 'the "ideas" of a human subject exist in his actions', that actions are inserted into *practices*, that these practices are governed by the *rituals* in which these practices are inscribed, and that the rituals are a small part of *an ideological apparatus* (1971/77: 158). Althusser is also remarkably explicit about the process of his rewriting of the Marxist concept of ideology as material, as practice not consciousness/idea. The rewriting is 'indebted' to Pascal, to 'the wonderful formula which will enable us to invert the order of the notional schema of ideology' (1971/1977: 158), the formula which said, 'Kneel down, move your lips in prayer and you will believe' (1971/1977: 158):

> Ideas have disappeared as such (insofar as they are endowed with an ideal or spiritual existence), to the precise extent that it has emerged that their

existence is inscribed in the actions of practices governed by rituals defined in the last instance by an ideological apparatus. It therefore appears that the subject acts insofar as he is acted by the following system (set out in the order of its real determination): ideology existing in a material ideological apparatus, prescribing material practices governed by a material ritual, which practices exist in the material actions of a subject acting in all consciousness according to belief.

But this very representation reveals that we have retained the following notions: subject, consciousness, belief, actions. From this series I shall immediately extract the decisive central term on which everything else depends: the notion of the *subject* . . .

I say: the category of the subject is constitutive of all ideology, but at the same time and immediately I add that the *category of the subject is only constitutive of all ideology insofar as all ideology has the function (which defines it) of 'constituting' concrete individuals as subjects.*

(1971/1977: 159, 160)

It was Althusser, then, who rewrote ideology (false consciousness) as material practice and who provided a way of conceptualising the non-coercive, non-violent power relations which structure Foucault's arguments. It was also Althusser who identified the subject as the 'central term' in understanding how discursive practices function. These were crucial moves in a paradigm shift (change in the order of discourse and change in a way of seeing) that, after Foucault's work, flattened out the Marxist base–superstructure hierarchy, rewriting it as networks, multiple nodes in social space. This was the beginning of what would become poststructuralist and postmodernist constructions of subjectivity and of the emergence of a new set of spatial metaphors. The 'social order' would be flattened out, discourses and bodies would begin to 'circulate' in space, rather than be 'constrained' from above or below. Foucault's work on discipline and discourse was fundamental to this change, a change which in the long term will have come to constitute the difference between a modernist view of the social and a postmodernist one.

There are various ways in which these Foucauldian ideas provide a commentary upon the positions I have explored above and contribute more complexities to an understanding of what 'rewriting' might mean. The structured regularities of discourse are related to the subject through desire, desire in the form of the power of knowing, and the will to know, the will to truth. Of the will to truth Foucault has this to say:

There is doubtless a will to truth in the nineteenth century that differs from the will to know characteristic of Classical Culture in the forms it deploys, in the domains of objects to which it addresses itself, and in the techniques on which it is based. To go back a little further: at the turn of the sixteenth century (and particularly in England), there appeared a will to know which, anticipating its actual contents, sketched out schemas of possible, observable, measurable, classifiable objects; a will to know which imposed on the knowing subject, and in some sense prior to all experience, a certain position, a certain gaze and a certain function (to see rather than to read, to verify rather than make commentaries on): a will to know which was prescribed (but in a more general manner than by any specific instrument) by the technical level where knowledges had to be invested in order to be verifiable and useful.

(1970/1971: 216)

In this context, Bazerman's Newton – Newton's will to truth/to know – is seen to be as much a product of the available scientific technologies, objects, practices and discourses as he is a maker of them. Even his position as controlling, knowing author, the rhetorical development which I have discussed above, is produced by and within this will to know, 'in the true' of a very specific and emerging discipline. In the process, his discourse – his genre of scientific argument – comes to produce the objects of which it speaks, the knowing subject, the facts, evidence and observations, the modes of experiment and argumentation, the cohesive and integrated system.

Commentary and discipline (in Foucault's sense) are both hard at work here, citing, making new, but also remaking the same. Foucault's examples of commentary include religious or juridical texts, literary texts and scientific texts. Commentary is clearly, even at this very early stage in his work, perceived to be *both* constraining, repetitive *and* innovative, giving rise to many different types of discourse. Thus *The Odyssey* produces translations and Joyce's *Ulysses*, remakings or rewritings which come close to the intertextuality that is explored in contemporary cultural studies. Commentary also includes both institutionalised discourses: 'those discourses which, over and above their formulation, are said indefinitely, remain said, and are to be said again' (1970/1971: 226), and 'those which are said in the ordinary course of days and exchanges, and which vanish as soon as they have been pronounced' (1970/1971: 225): those, in other words, which are non-discursive, outside disciplinary structures but also – and therefore not 'within the true' – inaudible, not heard. Discipline and discourse then both position and 'produce' the subject, investing the subject with a desire for power, a will to know and a practised body that remembers and forgets, escapes and returns to, the practices that form it. There are other spaces, other practices, but this body, Foucault's textual body, which has escaped the panopticism of discipline but remains *interdisciplinary*, is deaf to those.

DE CERTEAU READING FOUCAULT REWRITING

It was de Certeau who developed the implicit resistance in Foucault's concept of discipline. De Certeau rewrote the Foucauldian story and the story of change in ways that would focus on the 'undisciplined' subject, on 'tactics' that were outside the range of the panoptic gaze of the disciplines, that did not have the 'proper' place of the disciplined 'strategy'. He located the process of change in difference, in the instability of systems and in the relation to the other and the self:

> It is in fact difference which carves the isolating gaps into the homogeneity of language and which, conversely, opens in each system the paths to another. There is both continuity *and* discontinuity, and both are deceptive, because each epistemological age, with its own 'mode of being in order', carries *within itself* an alterity every representation attempts to absorb by objectifying . . .
>
> Alterity always reappears, and in a fundamental way, in the very nature of language. A truth is spoken by the organisation of a culture, but it escapes its own collaborators. Certain relations predetermine subjects and cause them to signify something other than what they think they say or can say.
>
> (de Certeau 1986: 181)

What I want to try to explore here is the question of Foucault's 'otherness' to the disciplines which never really contain him – history, philosophy, literary criticism. Is Foucault the expression of the alterity in the system of which de Certeau speaks? How is his alterity formed by, and in, the very system it contests? If Foucault's writings mark in some sense a 'paradigm shift', then why is it that he is not 'disciplined'? How does he escape the system he describes for us? This question of escaping systems we have constructed will have been seen to be important by the end of this chapter. It would probably be truer to Foucault's agendas to try to think just what it was, in the 1960s, that made a whole way of knowing apparently transform itself into something other; what it was that allowed that transformation to speak Foucault, Althusser and others like them. Here I will reread Foucault through the rewriting of (commentary on) his work by Michel de Certeau.

Trying to work out what it is that Foucault says and how it is possible for him to say it, de Certeau begins with *Discipline and Punish*, the book which examines the organisation of medical, academic and penal 'surveillance' at the beginning of the nineteenth century (de Certeau 1986: 185). What Foucault describes is a new organisation of space, the development of various forms of a cellular grid (for prisoners, soldiers, students, workers or the ill), which allows space to be transformed into a technology of discipline, an apparatus for the control of populations. It is here that Foucault makes the distinction between ideology and technology (or practice) which allows him to show how a political technology of the body succeeded in triumphing over an elaborated system of doctrine. A 'minor instrumentality', the penal grid, a 'panoptical' machinery, a particular stratum of non-verbal practices – developed in the army, the school, the prison – came to prevail over the complex judicial apparatus of the eighteenth-century

Enlightenment. This 'microphysics of power' which functioned by naming and classifying, distributing and positioning, belonged to no individual but located everyone. Foucault sought to map these non-verbal practices and to show how they had subsequently been articulated through the discourses of the contemporary social sciences.

What this foregrounded was the decisive role of technological procedures and apparatuses in the organisation of a society (not ideas, not consciousness, not ideology but practices), and the question of why it should have been the one particular category of the panoptical which should have dominated. Attempting to answer this question (that of the conditions of possibility of a discourse), de Certeau recalls that optical epistemology (panopticism) had been fundamental since the sixteenth century in the development of the modern sciences, arts and philosophy. In this sense the panoptic is both the product of these knowledges and that which continues to produce new versions of itself. But that iterability, that repeatability, realised in the existence of normative institutions in a society, can never be the whole story. There always exist, side by side with these institutions, innumerable other practices which have failed to give rise either to a discursive configuration or to a technological system. They remain 'minor', preserving the elements of difference from one society to another. They bear some relationship to what Raymond Williams has called 'residual' and 'emergent' forms of cultural production (1980: 43).

They are the forms which de Certeau suspects exist behind the 'monotheism' of the dominant panoptical procedures, a 'polytheism' of 'concealed or *disseminated practices*' dominated but not silenced by the dominant forms (1986: 188). They are the forms, in this analysis, which provide the possibility for change – 'infinitesimal procedures that have remained underprivileged by history, yet which continue to flourish in the interstices of the institutional technologies' (1986: 189). It is these procedures which do not have a proper place, which are outside the panopticon, which have the potential to function as rhetorical 'tactics' and to subvert the dominant discourse and procedures. De Certeau's argument, then, is that Foucault is to be explained as a 'tactician', working within a panoptic discourse to subvert it by indeed making its operations *visible* (1986: 189). He is a tactician not a strategist, because he refuses the tools of commentary, the hierarchical relationship between a metalanguage and an object language, theory and data, text and criticism, and so on. His rewriting is a reformulation of the whole question of how one might make theories differently.

According to de Certeau, what Foucault does is to isolate a 'foreign body' of procedures, an alterity within the dominant system, and to foreground it, to make it the dominant. His theory is itself a network of micro-procedures. It obeys rules analogous to the panoptic procedures themselves. Foucault's text (de Certeau is speaking of *Discipline and Punish*) only pretends to show, and not to explain, how the machinery of panopticism worked, constructing a calculated alternation between three different types of *exhibition* – case-study narratives (representational tableaux), theoretical distinctions (analytical tableaux) and past images (figurative tableaux, engravings and photographs). This alternation produces an effect of the self-evident even as it systematically displaces, 'rewrites', the fields into which it intrudes and intervenes. It uses *clarity/visibility* to introduce 'otherness' into an order of discourse, reorganising the panoptical space of current scientific language by telling stories, making extraordinary quotations, juxtaposing old texts and contemporary formations, seducing and convincing its audience. Just as Bazerman was to say of Newton, de Certeau says of Foucault: 'His rhetorical art . . . is the literary gesture of a certain way of acting' (1986: 191). It is worth recalling here the performance skills of the scientists in the theatre of the Royal Society, for it was they who constructed these orders of discourse which Foucault's tactics are colonising.

What is most remarkable about de Certeau's reading of Foucault is that he is very clear that 'exhibition', 'showing', 'making visible' is actually a form of analysis and of theory-making; that it is not, in the end, any more than Newton's fictions, actually or merely a literary gesture. It intervenes, it changes things, it contributes to one of those major changes in the order of discourse in the humanities and social sciences which Foucault originally sought to understand. It is clearly a very systematic and structured, if different, mode of writing; but, while that structure may be non-hierarchical, its effects are not. Foucault as textual subject is still the subject who knows, who tells, who shows, and his rhetorical tactics do not protect him from the silencing and excluding tendencies he began by making visible. The disciplined body is a very forgetful body. It forgets gender, class, colour, while at the same time providing invaluable technologies for remembering them.

Foucault is a reader who 'poaches', who gathers up bits of other texts, other histories, other voices, and makes them into a theory, a convincing system:

> Hunting through the forests of history and through our present plains, Foucault traps strange things which he discovers in a past literature and uses these for disturbing our present securities. He has an almost magic power for pointing at surprising confessions in historical documents as well as contemporary ones, for gathering both these past and present curiosities into a system, and for transforming these revelations of non-verbal practices determining our political and epistemological institutions into convincing evidence.
>
> (de Certeau 1986: 191)

Foucault's theory-making, then, depends upon reading 'improperly', outside the proper place, and in ways not permitted by the 'proper' of discipline. His texts on panopticism are 'the literary gesture of those procedures themselves' (de Certeau 1986: 192); that is, they are themselves an instance of panopticism, the making (*poiesis*) of theory, but in literary ways. Foucault tells stories, stories which clarify the relationship between theory and the procedures which produce it, deconstructing the binary opposition between theory and narrative, theory and practice, in the process. Story works through a logic of displacement, a logic of metonymy, to subvert the panoptical procedures and discourses it appears to represent. For Foucault, stories were always a way of contemplating 'how and to what extent it would be possible to think otherwise'. The stories he poached were for him the 'citations of an unthought', something that 'exceeds the thinkable', something that could help him 'recount how new problematics appear and become established'. He was interested in the surprise of what history made visible, in 'exhuming the implications of aleatory events, . . . the forgotten systems of reason, the chance encounters, the things that events show us without our knowing it' (de Certeau 1986: 194–7).

His was an interdisciplinary endeavour, one that connected explicitly the business of reading, reading as poaching, with the business of rewriting as subversion, rewriting for social and ethical change. What he refused, above all, was the positioning within a discipline which his theoretical writings articulated so clearly as the position for the rest of us. His was not that process he called commentary in others, and nor was it designed to allow business as usual. It seems to me to be critical to see that Foucault made visible the panoptic in order to disrupt it, to understand that while he recognised the productivity of discipline and governmentality he actually always positioned himself outside it.

If Foucault's rewriting is different from those kinds we have explored above, it is because it is a politics of rewriting that is at stake, an ethical rewriting which defines a distance between what is and what ought to be. It is not a dogmatism which imposes laws on the basis of a single reality which it claims to represent. It is a refusal of the hierarchies and the continuities of commentary. It is a rewriting which revalidates the 'narrative of discovery' which, you will remember, was written out of scientific activity in the adversarial exchange of meanings surrounding the making of Newton's *Opticks*. It is a rewriting which attempts to reconstitute the subject that Newton was before his scientific persona, his textual voice, was constituted, a rewriting which attempts to understand the disciplining of that subject in the material practices of institutions. It is a rewriting that Roland Barthes (1953/1968) prefigured in his structuralist and semiotic analyses of a certain kind of textual realism, a certain understanding of the production and reception of texts, analyses that are in some ways among the conditions of possibility for Foucault's textual productions.

ROLAND BARTHES AND THE SUBJECT OF READING AND WRITING

I want to refer here briefly to just two of Barthes' later short essays: one called 'To Write: An Intransitive Verb?' (1986a) and the other 'Writing Reading' (1986b). In the first Barthes is concerned with writing his reading of Benveniste and Jakobson on the question of linguistic shifters, the deictic pronouns and adverbs which constantly shift in reference according to the context of utterance and reading. He is concerned, in particular, with the difference between discourse and history (*discours* and *histoire*) and with the subject in language, the subject who writes (the 'I' of discourse) and the subject who is written (the 'he'/'she' of history and narrative). These relationships centre for him around the question of time – the relationship of the 'I' who speaks to the moment of utterance and the shifts in reference that must occur when the utterance is reread in a different context: the 'now' of my utterance 'now' cannot be the 'now' of your reading 'now'. Likewise there is a problematic relationship between the 'I' who speaks and the history/narrative she/he recounts. Third person narration is always the mark of the absence of the 'I' who speaks, who tells: every third person narrative is told of a non-person, a 'she/he' who is told by an absent 'I'. The non-person cannot enter into the relation between the 'I' and the 'not I' (thou/you) that is discourse. 'She'/'he' is constructed by that 'I', projected by 'I' as history. But nor can the 'I' who writes ever be the same as the 'I' who is told, the 'I' who is read by 'thou'. 'I' can no longer be the place 'where a previously stored-up person is innocently restored' (Barthes 1986a: 17), which is why, of course, neither Newton nor Barthes is available for comment.

The verb 'to write', then, is a problematic verb, a verb whose subjects and objects are of uncertain status as linguistic shifters, both of them made in language. It becomes even more problematic for Barthes when he observes that we now tend to use the verb apparently intransitively – 'he's writing', despite the fact that one always writes *something* (1986a: 18). Barthes' argument is that this is not a case of intransitivity (the lack of an object), but an example of the use of the middle voice, the voice where the subject neither simply acts externally on some goal (active), nor is the goal of someone else's action (passive), but the voice where 'the subject affects himself in acting; he always remains inside the action even if an object is involved' (1986a: 18). Whenever the subject writes, the subject *is written*, even when the apparent object of the writing (*histoire*/history) bears no signs of the writing 'I'. Speech (understood as discourse, text in its relation to context) is always somehow implicated in writing. The writer is always written, made in language. There is no fixed reality (referent) to which the one who writes can refer.

In 'Writing Reading' (1986b), Barthes explains the 'new reading' he had tried to describe in *S/Z*. He explains that what he tried to do was to ' "film" the reading of Sarrasine in slow motion', to record *S/Z* as 'that text which we write in our head *when we look up from reading*', because of the associations the book has provoked (1986b: 29–30). This 'text-as-reading', he says, is rarely discussed, because for centuries we have concerned ourselves more with what *authors meant* than with *what the reader understands*. There is, he argues, a clear distinction between the rules of composition and the logic of reading. The logic of reading is associative. Other ideas, other significations, other texts are associated with the text as we read. It is a corporeal process and a game:

> [T]o read is to make our *body* work (psychoanalysis has taught us that this body greatly exceeds our memory and our consciousness) at the invitation of the text's signs, of all the languages which traverse it and form something like the shimmering depth of the sentence.
>
> (Barthes 1986b: 31)

There is a different discourse here; one that is not found in Foucault, although it contributed to Althusser's work and to his understandings of the interpellated subject. It is the discourse of psychoanalysis, a discourse of memory and consciousness, of a body traversed by signs, a body that works. It is not the disciplined body of Foucault, but this collusion around bodies, around subjectivities, has its discursive effects. In Barthes, as in Foucault, we have a subversion of the accepted wisdom of the disciplines, a questioning of the objectivity of the third person realist or scientific text. We also have a cry to tell the story of the self as split, shifting, made in language, a self with an unconscious that associates, a body that reads. There is a narrativity here, too, and a different story (psychoanalysis), but there is also a textual play with metalanguage, using the metalanguage of linguistics to subvert the discourses of the literary.

The stories Althusser, Barthes, Foucault and de Certeau tell about the subject differ and they appropriate different aspects of the stories of Marxism, structuralism, psychoanalysis, linguistics and history and philosophy. They are constructed intertextually, not according to the rules of composition of rhetoric or genre (although rhetorical and generic they still are), or the field of a single discipline. Their conditions of possibility are intertextual, but they are also explicitly inter*disciplinary*, and that is the mark of their difference from the extraordinary account of the creation of God and the angels told to the Inquisition by the miller Menocchio, as recorded by Ginzburg and rewritten by Tony Bennett in his 'Texts, Readers, Reading Formations' (1983/1993).

READING FORMATIONS AND THE OUTSIDE OF DISCIPLINE

Barthes' concern is with the subject who reads and writes, Foucault's with the subject who is discursively produced. Bennett's is rather different. He is concerned with 'untutored reading', undisciplined reading, outside rather than inside or straddling the disciplines, outside rather than inside the academy. He uses the term 'untutored' strategically, preferring 'popular' because of its more positive connotations. What is clear is that the story – the reading (like Foucault's inaugural lecture), for which Menocchio was twice hauled before the Inquisition – does not come from nowhere. It is the product of a 'reading formation' which the academy in the form of the Inquisition is hard-pressed to comprehend. Menocchio, like Barthes, has been looking up from the text, his body and memory working to produce the opinions which, when asked, he said, 'came out of my head' (Bennett 1983/1993: 207).

Menocchio's story went like this: God and the angels were created from worms that emerged from a vast primordial cheese before the elements had separated (Bennett 1983/1993: 207). Ginzburg's aim, as reported by Bennett, was to establish how that story got into Menocchio's head, and he did that by looking at the social context which produced him and the books he had been reading. He found the clues to these things in the transcripts of Menocchio's trials – his reading of Genesis, 'lives of the saints and the virgin Mary, medieval chronicles, the *Travels* of Mandeville, Boccaccio's *Decameron*, and perhaps the Koran in Italian translation' (Bennett 1983/1993: 208). Menocchio 'produced' his reading of the Bible at the intersections of Renaissance humanism, biblical culture and the oral culture of the peasantry, socially positioned as a miller to have dealings with both the feudal nobility and the peasantry (1983/1993: 209). This is the reading formation that in this case regulates the 'encounter between texts and readers' (1983/1993: 211). Bennett argues from this, following Ginzburg, that 'only knowledge of the historical and social variability of the person of the reader' (1983/1993: 211) will enable an understanding of those encounters. And he is insistent that the 'popular' reader is engaged in a legitimate encounter which cannot be judged from a 'disciplined' or 'tutored' position to be a misreading or an improper use of the text. In fact he is insistent that such popular reading formations are not 'dominated' by 'intellectual humanism', but are actually independent modes of knowing (1983/1993: 210). In this, his work is considerably influenced by Bakhtin's *Rabelais and His World*, which Ginzburg had used to argue that the 'traffic between the official (high) culture and the popular culture' is not all one way (1983/1993: 209). Readers do not encounter 'the same text'. The encounter is already 'overcoded' and productively reactivated within the complex social, historical, institutional and material relationships that constitute a particular reading formation. It is therefore impossible to read off from the textual analysis of cultural products their possible reception and uses in 'popular' contexts. This was why Barthes said that 'only the text' does not exist (1986b: 31); that is, that the text can never be extricated from the complexities of these contextual encounters with socially and historically produced readers.

POIESIS AND DISCIPLESHIP

This, of course, applies to theories as to any other texts. Rewriting, then, may vacillate between citation, reproduction, system-integrated innovation (what Kuhn calls the normal paradigm at work) and the production of something not entirely new, but 'undisciplined', derived from somewhere else, which effects 'revolution' or radical change of a kind that cannot be easily contained within the existing structures of the integrated system.

Rewriting may be transmission or transformation. More often than not, as Kuhn said, new and old paradigms, and new and old discursive and reading formations, 'speak through one another', so that the process of change or transformation is uneven, heteroglossic and therefore inevitably both slow and unpredictable or nicely accommodating change – depending on your point of view. What Kuhn describes in this way seems to me to be close to what Fairclough has more recently characterised as the 'hybridisation' of orders of discourse (1992a: 222), or, with less happy connotations, the 'colonisation' of an order of discourse by another. It is arguable that the particular rewritings I have rewritten above have themselves all participated in a colonisation of the discourses and disciplines of the humanities which has displaced or recontextualised other discourses such as structuralism and semiotics. These terms, of course, imply an agency. I suggested above that this was an agency for social and disciplinary change, but there is more to be said than that.

What none of the male writers discussed so far have addressed is the issue of gendered subjectivity. Nor have any of them actually addressed the issue of discipline and discipleship, or the different teaching and learning stories that might be consequent upon the colonisation/hybridisation of the disciplinary discourses of the humanities and social sciences by the kinds of interdisciplinary subversions I have discussed. Both Kuhn's and Bazerman's story assume a transmission model, the work of the great man passed on, or the sudden apocalyptic insight and paradigm shift which then settles back into a transmission model. Foucault unsettles that, not always in the stories he tells but in the way he tells them and in his understanding of the productivity as well as the constraints of discourse and discipline. Barthes and Bennett recover from the murmur of Foucauldian discourse a socially and historically produced subject who acts and produces meanings and readings, who writes (and is written) in a structured but not necessarily disciplinary space. The question of how the interactions of men and women produce the disciplines, of what desires for knowledge and power (and, indeed, for one another) motivate those relationships, is not addressed, except in the work of Bazerman, which suggests something of the power of a homosocial audience, the need to perform one's knowledge, and the constraints imposed on *poiesis* by interpersonal as well as institutional, political and disciplinary structures.

Jane Gallop (1995) has begun to theorise these questions in a more contemporary feminist context, finding her 'tactics' in psychoanalysis. Others have questioned the tactical nature of that discourse, suggesting that it focuses too narrowly on white, middle-class Western women (Pheng 1994). What it raises, nevertheless, is a set of issues that are central to this book: the question of a different model of the mother and of mother–daughter relationships, of different kinds of performances of the relations of ruling among women in the academy:

> What if your mother refuses her gaze, turns her attention elsewhere? Does not serve as your mirror, your nurturance, your ground of continuity of being or of the semiotic, fertile source of aesthetic meaning ungoverned by the Father's Law? If she is no longer outside, but inside, power? If she wields power not as care, nurturance, preservative love, but as assertion, need, desire of her own? Or if she is off playing, with other women or men? Or in her own head? Can daughters stand to be cut off, outside the dyadic circuit?
>
> (Flax 1993: 67)

These are interesting (if unresolved) questions, which have to be a part of what rewriting is understood to be and of how it is understood to be motivated, to succeed or to fail. Rewriting is always a dialogue with significant others who claim, or have claimed, to know. The issue becomes immediately more relevant in the present context when one understands that Foucault was a student of Althusser, and Derrida of Foucault. It is a crucial matter for feminist rewriting when the normative heterosexual cultures that shape sexual difference operate within and through the knowledge structures that make that rewriting possible.

There are many feminist scholars whose work would have served in this context to illustrate both the particular difficulties and successes of feminist rewriting, and the questions raised by the issues of the 'hybridisation' and 'colonisation' of orders of discourse by others (among which would have to be questions of the ethics of discourse). Teresa de Lauretis is important to this book for two main reasons: because of the variety of rewriting strategies she has adopted, both narrative and analytical/metalinguistic; and because of her dialogues with women (Mulvey and Kristeva) and her continuing dialogues with Umberto Eco and psychoanalysis – dialogues which raise issues of *poiesis* and discipleship that are explicitly gendered, which do not fit at all into accounts of simple 'doctrinal transmission'.

Chapter 3

Teresa de Lauretis

Sexing the subject of semiosis

Writing in 1987 of the habits of male philosophers, Teresa de Lauretis spoke of their constant denial of sexual specificity in favour of metaphors and textual play, a tendency which she suggested was producing a subject who was not only decentred but also desexualised, a tendency which, moreover, reappropriated femininity for itself. Few of the current masters of philosophy and critical theory escaped her critique:

> So it is that, by displacing the question of gender onto an ahistorical, purely textual figure of femininity (Derrida); or by shifting the sexual basis of gender quite beyond sexual difference, onto a body of diffuse pleasures (Foucault) and libidinally invested surfaces (Lyotard), or a body-site of undifferentiated affectivity, and hence a subject freed from (self-)representation and the constraints of identity (Deleuze); and finally by displacing the ideology, but also the reality – the historicity – of gender onto this diffuse, decentered, deconstructed (but certainly not female) subject – so it is that, paradoxically again, these theories make their appeal to women, naming the process of such displacing with the term *becoming woman* (*devenir femme*).
>
> (de Lauretis 1987: 24)

She comments, in the same way that Meaghan Morris will do later (1988), and that Spivak (1983, 1989) and Braidotti (1990) have also done, that these habits are older than the Cartesian subject and actually harder to break. She suggests that they account for the disregard by male intellectuals of feminist theorising and for their refusal, in fact, to read it. This should not, and does not, she says, 'prevent feminist theorists from reading, rereading and rewriting their (i.e. male intellectuals') works' (1987: 24).

Her use of the term 'rewriting', the implication in that of rereading, and the actual practice of rewriting – feminist rewriting – which she has refined over the past twenty years, suggest in themselves some of the achievements and difficulties of this enterprise. They also raise some crucial questions: How do women read? When is rewriting feminist? When is feminist rewriting theory? Why does feminist rewriting seem always to operate within the gaps and interstices, or as a supplement to, *his* stories? And what might detailed semiotic and textual analyses have to do with this enterprise? What is the difference between the female subject of representation and the female subject who might herself represent (make) or receive (interpret) representations? De Lauretis has differed from many feminist writers in the American tradition in her continued materialist-semiotic interests, as well as her post-structuralist and psychoanalytic ones. She has been one of the few feminist theorists in that context who has continued to dialogue with structuralism, in its linguistic/semiotic (as well as its psychoanalytic and anthropological) forms, to recognise, to use, and to go on contesting, its continued operation in and through the discourses of so-called poststructuralism.

Her first book, *Alice Doesn't* (1984), attempted a number of things at once and much of it operated in constant dialogue with Umberto Eco, reformulating his questions and answering in ways which redefined the field of semiotics. This dialogue, among other dialogues with male theorists in that book, articulates very clearly what de Lauretis calls the 'contradiction of feminist theory itself', the fact that it is always both excluded from discourse and imprisoned within it so that the only way to begin to challenge it is from within, by in fact 'displacing oneself within it', and rewriting the voice of the master from somewhere else – a different text, a contradictory position. Her metaphorical/literary explanation of this is very powerful. She quotes from Italo Calvino's *Invisible Cities*, the vignette of the city of Zobeide, using this as a metaphor for the production of woman as text in male theory:

> Zobeide, a city built from a dream of woman, must be constantly rebuilt to keep woman captive . . . The city is a text which tells the story of male desire by performing the absence of woman and by producing woman as text, as pure representation.
>
> (quoted in de Lauretis 1984: 12–13)

The city is a metaphor for the sedimented history of meaning-making, the stratified intertextual history, the modes of enunciation and address, and the irreducible contradictions of the structures of theory and knowledge which must always be the site of that feminine displacement – the devious answer, the reformulated questions, the quoting against the grain – which constitutes feminist theory (de Lauretis 1987: 7). As Meaghan Morris pointed out some time ago, this work is therefore all too likely to position the feminist writer 'in a speech genre all too familiar in daily life . . . the woman's complaint or *nagging*. One of the defining generic rules of "nagging" is unsuccessful repetition of the same statements' (1988: 15). It is typical of most male theory that it puts the woman who wants to argue with it, to theorise herself, in that position. This is why the issue of speaking position and the strategies associated with it are so critical in feminist theory. It is why a constant theme in de Lauretis's work is the difference between the woman represented and the 'real' woman who is not yet there in those representations but still contained within them, the woman whose material existence outside those discursive formations is in fact the condition of feminist theory. One of de Lauretis's theoretical tasks, then, was to find a way of theorising that excluded feminine experience, of semioticising it, so that it had to be recognisable, readable, within the frameworks which excluded it.

De Lauretis began with 'the unholy alliance of feminism, semiotics and film' (1984: 4), showing how in the 1960s and 1970s feminist film criticism had first used the Marxian critique of ideology to explain how the dominant traditions of narrative cinema operated to keep woman in her place. It had then appropriated the semiotic notion that language and other systems of signification (visual or iconic systems) work through coded systems of signs, to theorise the way that image of 'woman in place' was constructed through the codes of filmic representation. Psychoanalysis had also become a dominant discourse in cinema studies (Metz 1981). De Lauretis was concerned to debate what she saw as the subordination of cinema to language in the use of discourses such as semiotics and psychoanalysis (which were dependent on language) to theorise cinema. This agenda explains how, in her work with Stephen Heath, there is a more materialist and Foucauldian inflection (she points out that their work in cinema studies was developing contemporaneously with, but not dependent on, Foucault's work [1987: 13]) so that the cinematic apparatus came to be understood in both its historical and ideological forms as a relation of the technical and the social, an apparatus that spanned the industrial, the economic, and a range of technologies, all of which were machines of the visible (de Lauretis and Heath 1985), and none of which was separate from the making of meaning or from ideology.

For de Lauretis, questions of how men and women are addressed by cinema and film, of whether they are addressed differently, of how perception and vision might be connected, and of how the perception of signs as visual images might be related to the construction of gendered subjectivity: all were central for a materialist, semiotic theory of culture to address:

> The social subject is constructed day by day as the point of articulation of ideological formations, an always provisional encounter of subject and codes at the historical (therefore changing) intersection of social formations and her or his personal history. While codes and social formations define positions of meaning, the individual reworks these positions into a personal, subjective construction. A social technology – cinema, for example – is the semiotic apparatus in which the encounter takes place and the individual is addressed as subject.
>
> (1984: 14–15)

Neither the structuralist linguistic model, on which classical semiology is based (a model which excludes any consideration of address altogether), nor the psychoanalytic model (which does allow a subjectivity constructed in language, but explains that subject in terms of processes dependent on the instance of castration, and thus predicated on what can only be a male subject), were adequate to answer these questions. They were inadequate primarily because they, like the whole 'historical materialist theory of cinema' (1987: 14), were founded on unacknowledged premises of sexual difference. Her rereadings of Lévi-Strauss, Lacanian psychoanalysis and semiotics were designed to demonstrate this fact and to point to their inextricable implication in one another's theoretical fictions.

TELLING (HIS)TORIES

De Lauretis begins her rewriting by telling stories, quoting the semiologist (who has to be Eco) against himself (de Lauretis 1984: 18ff.). The reasonable, ironic voice, which points narratively in these pages to the absurd oversights and assumptions of men who theorise, works most effectively because it is precisely 'the oversight' who speaks. She returns to Calvino's city, suggesting that the semiotician, in making his theory, is interested only in how the stones are put together, not why they are put together that way or for whom. When he is asked about woman (yes, he knows about her) – when he is not making his theories – she is a human being like man, and her function is reproduction and social cohesion. Sexual difference is merely a division of labour and, as de Lauretis points out, that is 'fully explicit in Lévi-Strauss's theory of kinship' (de Lauretis 1984: 18) which, along with de Saussure's linguistics, forms the theoretical basis for semiotics. It is certainly the explicit beginning point for Eco's theory of semiotics (1979: 24–6).

De Lauretis's semiotician has heard that the incest prohibition is an 'historical event' which constituted culture, and he understands that this event requires that women be possessed and exchanged among men to ensure the social order. He also knows that kinship structures are really quite like linguistic structures and that marriage relations and kinship systems can be *treated as a kind of language* (de Lauretis 1984: 18). Because he knows that, he also understands that women are not just objects of exchange among men but also signs or messages that circulate to ensure social communication. Like Irigaray (1977/1985b), Derrida (1978) and Butler (1990), among others, de Lauretis smells a rat at this point (Irigaray's, Derrida's and Butler's rats are slightly different, but rats nonetheless), finding it remarkable that, although both women and words are objects of exchange, words in becoming signs have lost the value that women as signs still have, a value that explains the richness of relations between the sexes which it seems once characterised the whole universe of human communications (Lévi-Strauss 1969: 496, as told in de Lauretis 1984: 19). Lévi-Strauss is nothing if not a romantic. His rosy view of the relations between the sexes extends, as Judith Butler has pointed out, to a denial of the actual historical existence of incest:

Presuming the heterosexual masculinity of the subject of desire, Lévi-Strauss maintains that: 'the desire for the mother or the sister, the murder of the father and the sons' repentance undoubtedly do not correspond to any fact or group of facts occupying a given place in history. But perhaps they symbolically express an ancient and lasting dream'.

(Lévi-Strauss 1969: 491, quoted in Butler 1990: 42)

More problematic still is the fact that in this theory, which explains the ultimate separation of nature and culture, emergence of culture from nature, women appear to be both nature *and* culture, and, as Derrida (1978: 283) has pointed out, and Lévi-Strauss knew was a *scandal*, incest itself is *both* nature (universal) and culture (prohibited). The act of exchange which is supposed to found culture is based upon a fundamental contradiction (or two). The exchange of women, women's economic value, must in fact be predicated upon an existing symbolisation of sexual difference. At the very moment of the institution of culture (which is supposed to give women value and institute that difference), it is discovered that the items of exchange are already subject to culture, to the symbolic function, already constituted in a hierarchy of value. 'How', asks de Lauretis, with supreme irony, 'can such an oversight have occurred?'

De Lauretis puts it down to a discursive contradiction between the Marxian and Saussurean notions of value – woman as bearer of economic, positive value and as bearer of semiotic, negative lack (1984: 19). In 1977 (1977/1985a: 196) Irigaray, also speaking of Lévi-Strauss's amazing narrative, had asked: 'But what if these "commodities" refused to go to "market"? What if they maintained another kind of "commerce", among themselves?' De Lauretis's irreverent story and this feminist dialogism in and around the text of Lévi-Strauss is one answer to that question. The dialogue also demonstrates de Lauretis's point that sexual difference is the founding premise of the semiotics which denies it and of the psychoanalysis which still does not get it right.

But her story continues. The semiotician has forgotten Lévi-Strauss and has been reading Lacan. The metaphor of the city continues. Passing through the city becomes a metaphor for Lacanian suture, the moments when the subject-in-process is momentarily fixed, located, before it moves on again. The semiologist, who has become a 'she', wants to know if there is some way that the 'blatantly oppressive aspects' of the city can be changed, but finds that the city is ruled by the name of the father which 'determines in advance all urban planning' (de Lauretis 1984: 21). It is at this point that the semiotician rereads Lévi-Strauss only to discover that he is also implicated in Lacanian psychoanalysis. The Lacanian symbolic is related to Lévi-Strauss's formulation of the unconscious 'as the organ of the symbolic' (de Lauretis 1984: 22–3). The Lévi-Straussian unconscious was the structuring condition for all signification just as the symbolic will be in Lacan. Lacan changes the focus to the subject, but the subject becomes a subject only by acceding to the law of the symbolic. All the trappings of Lévi-Strauss's structuralism – the incest prohibition, the structure of exchange and the name of the father – are maintained: and the process of becoming subject is now essentially phallic. The same contradiction – between sexual difference as a meaning-effect in representation, and as 'the very support of representation' – is present again (1984: 24).

FEMINIST FILM THEORY

There are problems, then, in basing a theory of cinema, which clearly addresses both men and women, on either of these theoretical models. Neither can explain the gap which linguistics leaves between discourse and reality. That, she says, is what semiotics must do. It must explain 'how the physical properties of bodies are socially assumed as signs, as vehicles for social meaning, and how these signs are culturally generated by codes and subject to historical modes of sign production' (1984: 25). And it will not do to explain this in the terms of a psychoanalytic view of film, which is doomed from the start to see woman as only the support for a masculine subject's projection and identification, the object of a male gaze (Mulvey 1989b).

Mulvey's work on 'Visual Pleasure and Narrative Cinema' (first published in 1975) had set out to use psychoanalysis as a political weapon, to use the tools of patriarchal society against itself, to show how 'the unconscious of patriarchal society had structured film form' (1989b: 14). It was an assumption of this work that Hollywood cinema of the 1930s, 1940s and 1950s derived its 'magic' from the manipulation of visual pleasure, and that that pleasure was related to the unconscious fears and desires of the viewing subject. The first pleasure cinema offered was scopophilia (pleasure in looking), defined by Freud as 'subjecting others to a controlling and curious gaze' (Mulvey 1989b: 16), usually involving the surreptitious watching of an unwilling or unknowing subject. Mulvey's argument was that the conditions of film screening, in a dark auditorium, replicate this illusion of voyeuristic separation, and give the spectator an illusion of looking into a private world. The second source of pleasure in Mulvey's argument comes from identification with the image seen, an identification developed through narcissism and the development of the ego (Lacan's mirror-stage).

Mainstream Hollywood film 'neatly combines spectacle and narrative' and thus supports both kinds of pleasure (Mulvey 1989b: 19). Traditionally, Mulvey argues, woman has been the spectacle, functioning on two levels: as erotic object for the characters on screen, and as erotic object for the spectator. This same active/passive division of labour characterises the structure of narrative, the hero always being the one to advance the story, the one controlling the film fantasy. The male viewer, then, identifies with the hero as a more powerful ideal ego, takes scopophilic pleasure in the female form displayed for his enjoyment, and through identification with the hero gains control and possession of the woman within the narrative. Narrative and visual pleasure constantly interact.

There is, however, a problem with the woman. She is also a sign, the visual evidence of the reality of the castration complex. The male unconscious, according to Mulvey, has only two alternatives, to punish, devalue (*film noir*) or fetishise (the female star). The problem with narrative is associated with the look. There are three looks: that of the camera, that of the audience and that of the characters as they look at each other on screen. The conventions of narrative cinema work to deny the first two, naturalising the fictional reality of the image as 'real'. The fetishistic look also 'fixates the spectator and prevents him from achieving any distance from the image in front of him' (1989b: 26). Mulvey's solution, and that of many feminist and alternative film-makers after her, was to destroy the visual pleasure by attacking and changing 'the monolithic accumulation of traditional film conventions' (1989b: 26). This has been a familiar strategy in many fields. Feminist literature, narrative, drama, performance, art and theory have all at various points attempted this kind of revolution – what Julia Kristeva called, in another very masculine context, 'revolution in poetic language' (1974/1984).

This, then, was the position de Lauretis was contesting in *Alice Doesn't*. It explains her desire to demonstrate again the basis of psychoanalysis in sexual difference, the ethics of this discourse which positions and locates Mulvey's account, its inadequacy as a theoretical tool to deal with the very complex issues Mulvey's paper had raised. It also explains de Lauretis's need to demonstrate that meaning was nowhere near as fixed, positions of enunciation (the telling) and announced (the told) not so binary, the cinematic apparatus and narrative not so monologic, and the question of visual pleasure not so clear-cut (not so inevitably masculine and based in biology) as the psychoanalytic story would have it. She was, in fact, forced to argue yet again as the 'oversight' in this story, to start again with her explanations that, yes, she was here, and no, she was not like that, and nor was her sense of the pleasure she (as a female subject) took in cinema like that either. This time she was arguing with a feminist writer whose own narrative and speaking position are very much inflected by Lacan's psychoanalytic stories, a situation which explains de Lauretis's urgent felt need at the beginning of her book to think about where her theories come from, to remember their structuralist grandfathers and the basis of their theoretical stories in gender difference. Hence, too, her important advice, quoted from Kaja Silverman, that only ' "an extreme immersion in discourse" can alter the female subject's relationship to the current monopoly held by the male "discursive fellowships" and make her participate in the production of meaning' (1984: 55–6). It is that question of the books one reads again, of the need to belong to and to exceed a reading formation. It should be recorded here that Mulvey later, in a paper first delivered in 1983 (1989a), considerably rewrote the position de Lauretis was contesting here.

IMAGING: THE PERCEPTION/SIGNIFICATION NEXUS

To begin to displace the psychoanalytic feminist view, then, and in a sense to speak from 'outside' it, from an immersion in a different discourse, de Lauretis moves to Eco's (1979) theory of sign-production, finding it useful to appropriate his rewriting of the classical system-based and static code of classical semiology, an account which had already been soundly critiqued in work on film. In Eco's work, that code became one of many, and it was an active, dynamic set of rules which might make, as well as fix, meaning-relations. After Eco, whose work depended on that of Hjelmslev (1943/1961) and Peirce (1931–58), the sign was a sign-function, a transient and processual correlation of expression-form and content-form. The content was a culturally pertinent semantic unit. This made it possible to think of semantic fields of systems of cultural units to some extent independently of the systemic organisation of sign-vehicles or expression forms. Culture as semantic system could then be conceived not as a single system, but as a 'hypercode, a complex system of subcodes' involving many codes or networks of correlations across the planes of content and expression (Eco 1979: 125). Most importantly, and after Peirce and Hjelmslev, it was possible for a sign to become the expression form for another content, an interpretant in a process of what Eco would call 'unlimited semiosis' (1979: 71). The move from sign to sign, through a series of interpretants, allowed exchanges of meaning between the verbal, the visual, the corporeal and so on. Eco records Peirce's definition of the interpretant as 'that which the sign produces in the quasi-mind of the interpreter' (1979: 67), but Eco, doubtful about minds, prefers to conceive of the *'interpretant as another representation which is referred to the same object'* (1979: 68; Eco's italics).

For de Lauretis,

> The theoretical hypothesis of semantic fields makes it possible to envisage a non-linear semantic space constructed not by one system – language – but by the multilevel interaction of many heterogeneous sign vehicles and cultural units . . . In other words, signification involves several systems or discourses intersecting, superimposed, juxtaposed to one another, with the codes mapping out paths and positions in a virtual semantic space which is discursively, textually, and contextually constituted in each signifying act.
>
> (de Lauretis 1984: 35)

This was the kind of complex model of semiosis, of meaning-making, which she needed to contest Mulvey's story, but there were still elements missing.

For Eco, the correlations between these planes and the possibility of their transformation were located in the 'subject of semiosis' who laboured to produce signs. If anything, this was a Marxist subject. There are certainly traces of Rossi-Landi (1977:31) in Eco's insistence on the relations between labour and language. However, there is still no sign of a gendered subject of semiosis, and that is where de Lauretis will need to rewrite Eco.

She turns first to the question of perception, to the ways in which cinema binds fantasy to images and 'institutes for the spectator[,] forms which are unequivocally social', wanting to explore the 'current notion of spectator-ship as a site of productive relations, of the engagement of subjectivity in meaning, values, and imaging' (1984: 51). At the end of a lengthy discussion on the inadequacy of using theories of semiosis modelled on the verbal to account for the meaning and functioning of cinema, de Lauretis produces Pasolini, arguing that his 'heretical' pronouncements on the semiosis of cin-ema (Pasolini 1991) anticipated in prophetic ways the work of Eco in semi-otics. What was crucial about Pasolini for de Lauretis was that he had argued that 'cinema's writing, its representation of human action, institutes a "cultural consciousness" of that encounter with reality' (quoted in de Lauretis 1984: 51). He had also seen that the context which makes certain 'features' pertinent, to use Eco's terminology, was not just a textual co-text, but the context of social practice (1984: 52). And he had written of the rela-tion between language and image in cinema as being both *in* the film and *before* the film, arguing that the relation had to be sought in 'a complex nexus of *significant images . . .* which *prefigures* cinematic communication and *acts as its instrumental foundation*' (quoted in de Lauretis 1984: 50). For de Lauretis, this raised the question of what she referred to as 'inner speech', 'forms of "imagistic, sensual, prelogical thinking" already suggested by Eikhenbaum and Eisenstein in the twenties' (1984: 50), and seen then as cen-tral to understanding the relationship between language and sensory percep-tion, including filmic, iconic and verbal signification.

De Lauretis drew on the physiologist Colin Blakemore and again on Eco, using the concept of mapping which is common to them both, to reframe, in non-psychoanalytic terms, the notion of visual pleasure. According to Blakemore (1973), the human perceptual apparatus does not copy reality but symbolises it, effecting 'a mapping of visual space on to the substance of the brain' (quoted in de Lauretis 1984: 52). What is more, perception appears to be coded and therefore 'predictive'. The same concept, mapping, is used by Eco to theorise the way the process of semiosis operates in what he calls 'invention', the making of new meanings, mapping pertinent fea-tures from one material continuum to another. For Eco, this process is always a mapping from a perceptual model to a semantic model to a unit of expression (Eco 1979: 250–6), so that, for example, a death mask is a kind of sign-function where points on the surface of the expression token corre-spond to selected points on the space of '*toposensitive perceptive or semantic models'* which produced it (Eco 1979: 257). There are strong rules of similitude at work and one must, in fact, learn how to recognise this kind of image: but the explanation works two ways. It explains how one might project the image of the death mask in the first place, and how one makes meaning with the mask once it is made. It was the latter aspect, the working of perception/signification, which interested de Lauretis in her development of a theory of the spectator.

For Eco, inventions are important and different modes of sign-production, because they are capable of making new codes and of transforming both the representation and the perception of reality. The Blakemore model is an adaptive model which, de Lauretis argues, is a model of production, articulating the constant activity of feeling, memory and cognition involved in 'survival, pleasure and self-maintenance' that is perception:

> The notion of mapping common to these models implies that perception and signification are neither direct or simple reproduction (copy, mimesis, reflection) nor inevitably predetermined by biology, anatomy or destiny; though they are socially determined and overdetermined. Put another way, what is called reproduction – as women well know – is never simply natural or simply technical, never spontaneous, automatic, without labor, without pain, without desire, without the engagement of subjectivity.
>
> (de Lauretis 1984: 55)

There are two parts to her argument here. First, Mulvey's psychoanalytic arguments that 'seeing', perception, is based on biology, cannot be maintained. Second, since every (re)production is still embedded in a speech act, it can never be separate from a process of enunciation that involves the whole history of the speaking subject – memory, desire, pain, expectations, and so on. Thus, just as there is no semiosis without subjectivity, there is no subjectivity or perception without semiosis, and the semiosis at work in sensory perception is corporeal, inscribed in 'the human body and the film body' (1984: 56). This extremely complex process which she has constructed – making meaning, not transmitting it – she calls 'imaging'. It can be reduced to neither the linguistic nor the iconic. It involves different codes and modalities of sign-production and includes the production of difference through the interaction of the social and these complex perceptive/signifying mechanisms.

This is a position that is certainly indebted to Eco's (1979) critique of iconicity, and to his rewriting of the Peircean concept of the interpretant as perception. But, again, by moving outside Eco and back to Pasolini and Blakemore, de Lauretis has produced a very much more 'embodied', desiring, feeling subject of semiosis than he had. Her next step, which is complex and lengthy, is to offer a critique of Mulvey's description of the cinematic apparatus:

'*Cinematic codes* create a *gaze*, a *world*, and an *object*, thereby producing an *illusion* cut to the measure of desire'. It is an amazingly concise and precise description of cinema, not only as a social technology, a working of the codes (a machine, an institution, apparatus producing images and meanings for, and together with a subject's vision); but also as a signifying practice, a work of semiosis which engages desire and positions the subject in the very processes of vision, looking and seeing.

(de Lauretis 1984: 59)

De Lauretis is here quoting Mulvey against herself, using what was for Mulvey a definition of the realist and narrative evils of Hollywood cinema as a definition of cinema *tout court*. For de Lauretis, then, in absolute contradiction to Mulvey, narrativity and scopophilia, visual pleasure, are the essential ingredients of cinema, the measure of desire for women and for men. Given the complexity of the codes involved, and their fluidity, the message of realism is no more problematic or definitive than any other message, and visual pleasure is not biologically based. It is not the apparatus which is the problem, but the fact that it has been produced, used and defined within patriarchal ideological and social formations. The project of feminist cinema, then, is not to destroy narrative coherence, to block the process of identification which produces visual pleasure. Dominant codes do not own narrative and visual pleasure. Understanding how to rewrite 'the monolithic accumulation of traditional film conventions' (Mulvey 1989b) requires a much more complex understanding of the semiotics of 'imaging' than Freud's story of scopophilia and an Oedipal understanding of narrative structure can provide.

There are messages here for many different kinds of feminist enterprise. Rewriting is always a complex and unpredictable business, and it cannot be done without detailed and careful understandings of the gendered, discursive, linguistic, semiotic and social and historical contexts in which it takes place.

NARRATIVE AND DESIRE

De Lauretis is not, however, unconvinced by Mulvey's story of the Oedipal agenda of narrative. Chapter 5 in *Alice Doesn't* is concerned with a detailed account of various moments in narrative and narrative theory, from Propp (1928/1968) and the early Barthes (1979), to Lotman (1979) and Freud, moments which demonstrate the workings of male desire in narrative, validating Barthes' early hunch that a connection exists between language, narrative and Oedipal desire. De Lauretis quotes Scholes as the *reductio ad absurdum* of this position – 'the archetype of all fiction is the sexual act . . . For what connects fiction – and music – with sex is the fundamental orgastic rhythm of tumescence and detumescence, of tension and resolution, of intensification to the point of climax and consummation' (Scholes

1979: 26) – commenting that those of us who do not feel incipient tumescence in reading may be denied the pleasures of the 'full fictional act' Scholes envisages. It is this which prompts her to explore further Mulvey's connections between sadism and story, and to explore that history precisely in the works of theory – structuralist narrative theory and Freudian psychoanalysis. Again, her argument is that none of these narratives as theories theorises the female reader; the materially, historically and experientially constituted subject, the subject who is engendered in and through the various narrative genres.

Her historical work here functions to make visible the basis of sexual difference on which narrative and narrative theory is also founded (that is, as well as structuralism and semiotics and psychoanalysis). However narrative is produced – in fictional genres, in rituals, in film, in knowledges (and it has complex relations with genre and epistemology) – the movement always seems to be that of a passage, an obstacle to be overcome, a situation to be transformed, all predicated upon the figure of a male hero, a mythical subject. It is the Oedipal story which links myth and narrative, whatever their historical or cultural provenance. Her reading of Lotman's derivation of fictional narratives from myth and oral story (the plot-text) also links the literary fiction to narrative and myth.

De Lauretis's arguments here are that these stories (theories) cannot be simply dismissed; Propp's, because he emphasises the interdependence of material social relations and the cultural production of narrative; and Freud's, because he emphasises the way in which those material social and narrative relations are inscribed in a theory of subjectivity (de Lauretis 1984: 121). If narrative is endlessly about the way in which the human person 'creates and recreates himself out of an abstract or purely symbolic other – the womb, the earth, the grave, the woman; all of which, Lotman thinks, can be interpreted as mere spaces and thought of as "mutually identical"', this must have consequences for female subjectivity (de Lauretis 1984: 121). De Lauretis's analyses, at this point, of the parallels between shamanistic practices and psychoanalysis (pointed to by Lévi-Strauss), and the narrative of 'the long journey' of the sperm to the ovum in a medical textbook (1984: 122–3), make the point very powerfully. Lévi-Strauss reads the shaman's narrative, which uses myth to explain her labour pains to a labouring woman, as a process of 'giving her a language' to understand that process (hence the comparison with psychoanalysis). De Lauretis's reading is rather different. The shaman's narrative, she says, has the performative effect of a somatic transformation in its addressee, of bringing about a transformation of her body, enabling the active expelling of the foetus. You would think, she says, that the myth to be used for this purpose might have a feminine hero, but not so. The hero of the myth is engaged in a struggle with the villain, a *female* deity (de Lauretis's italics), who has taken possession of the woman's body. He is personified by the shaman and his helpers. The incantation or narrative, as de Lauretis points out, is aimed at 'detaching the woman's identification or perception of self from her own body; it seeks to sever her identification with a body which she must come to perceive precisely as a space, the territory in which the battle is raged' (1984: 123).

The medical narrative is remarkably similar, representing biological difference in mythical terms, in fact constructing the narrative of biology itself as a myth. Her conclusions point to the complex web of intersections that implicate ethnography and psychoanalysis, in the figure of Lévi-Strauss, in the mythical-narrative order, and thus explain (for the moment) the influence of Freud. For de Lauretis at this time, Freud was the only theorist who 'tried to imagine woman as a subject in culture' (1984: 125). She recognises that, once again, *her* story turned out to be *his* story, but suggests that this was the work of Lotman's (1979) 'text-generating mechanism', the mechanism of patriarchal culture which is still at work 'in contemporary epistemologies and social technologies' (1984: 125). Freud is written by the cultural discourses which contain and limit his perceptions, traversing his generic constructions of what it might be that woman is or wants.

Rewriting that deeply entrenched cultural story will be no easy matter, but for de Lauretis that process will have to involve interrupting the triple track by which narrative, meaning and pleasure are constructed from *his* point of view. It will not be enough to simply disrupt narrative structure, or even to change the plot. Narrativity, in its process and its meaning effects on subjectivity, works on many levels simultaneously. The question of the position of enunciation is again foregrounded here, and the issue of address. How to address a different reader? How to perform female desire within his story? De Lauretis again suggests that what is needed is a very detailed understanding of the codes of narrative, of the complexity of the technologies and contexts in which narrative is produced. These involve a multiplicity of speaking positions and modes of address, many of them related to the connections between narrative and genres, narrative and knowledges, narrative and the technologies of production. The use of the camera does not have to be complicit with the narratives of voyeurism or of Renaissance perspective. The Oedipal nature of narrative needs to be made visible, not destroyed, if it is to be changed and a new and different social subject made visible. And, by way of concluding this section of her argument, she suggests several entertainingly different versions of the Oedipus story, turning again from metalanguage to (his)tories.

SEXING THE SUBJECT OF SEMIOSIS

How does semiosis become experience and experience become semiosis? What 'engenders the subject as female'? (de Lauretis 1984: 159).

In *Alice Doesn't*, it was a rereading of Eco against Peirce (although there are traces of many other texts circulating in this discussion) that provided the answer. There are traces in that discussion of Althusser, but they are more explicit in an essay published in 1987. What de Lauretis was trying to theorise was made explicit in *Alice Doesn't* as what Virginia Woolf had called 'instinct' in her description of her response to the beadle as she walked on the turf at Oxford – the 'instinct' that she was both a woman and out of place, a learned habitual mode of behaving and understanding, 'a kind of knowledge internalised from daily, secular repetition of actions, impressions and meanings, whose cause-and-effect or otherwise binding relation has been accepted as certain and even necessary' (1984: 158). Subjectivity, de Lauretis argued, is produced 'by one's personal, subjective, engagement in the practices, discourses and institutions that lend significance (value, meaning and affect) to the events of the world' (1984: 159). It is the introduction of 'value, meaning and affect' which makes this a different formulation to a Foucauldian or Althusserian position on the subject.

In 1987 she makes more explicit than she does here the connection between the ideas she is developing and Althusser's (1971) concept of interpellation (1987: 12), arguing that, when Althusser described ideology as 'the imaginary relations of individuals to the real relations in which they "live" and which govern their existence', he was in fact describing very effectively the functioning of gender as a technology for making subject/s (1987: 6). She is careful to point out that ideology cannot be equated with gender and that Althusser certainly does not so equate it in his Marxist theory, since ideology belongs to the properly public sphere of the superstructures, while gender belongs in the private sphere of reproduction and the family. But she goes on to suggest (1987: 6) the following substitution of *gender* for *ideology* in the Althusserian dictum: '*Ideology* [substitute gender] *has the function (which defines it) of "constituting" concrete individuals as subjects* [read: gendered subjects]' (1987: 6).

She points out that the statement still works, and, in working, demonstrates the distance between the discourses of philosophy and political theory and 'reality' – the other (place and person) that they never talk about – a distance which actually constitutes these discourses themselves as powerful technologies of gender. Here, she also makes the very important point that, as a consequence, there is for the subject of feminism not even the 'outside of ideology' – science or knowledge – that exists for the Marxist intellectual. Even 'in' knowledge the feminist subject cannot be 'outside' ideology. The only place that is 'outside' for feminism is the place of the other that is disempowered by not being 'within' knowledge: a state of affairs that explains the particular need for the genre of feminist rewriting and its sometimes impossible positions of enunciation.

For de Lauretis, it was Foucault's *History of Sexuality* (1976/1980), and his earlier work on discipline, the body and discourse, which explained what Althusser's (1971) account of the interpellation of the subject into ideology had not – how the representation in which the subject was positioned by ideology was made and how it was then 'accepted and absorbed'. But it was specifically the understanding of cinema as a social technology which had helped to show how gender was the product of both representation and self-representation (de Lauretis 1987), something Foucault's work did not quite say. There are some amazing discontinuities in these very productive arguments, which succeed in weaving a new theoretical position from what were certainly at the time apparently incompatible positions: Foucault, like Eco, had left 'consciousness' behind and 'ideology' was not to be confused with 'discourse', nor the intersecting surfaces of the social space with meanings. Yet the insistent female/feminist subject of semiosis had a way of bringing all these ideas back together again in the embodied experience they all denied.

MEANING, HABIT AND SOCIAL CHANGE

In *Alice Doesn't*, embodied experience was theorised at the intersection of Lacanian psychoanalysis, which focused on the subject as the effect of the signifier, and Eco's semiotics, which stressed the social aspect of signification and construed meaning as a social production based on shared codes. It was indeed a semiotics of experience that de Lauretis was constructing, and for that a way of theorising meaning and consciousness was essential, even if both worked through the body. What she sought to do here was to contest the feminist position which would see feminist experience as an untheorised 'nearness to nature, the body, or the unconscious' (1984: 186) – a formulation in which there may well be a refusal of the work of Julia Kristeva in particular – and to contest Eco's (1979) refusal to consider either consciousness or the embodied and gendered nature of the subject of semiosis in his theory of semiotics.

As Peirce formulated it, the process of unlimited semiosis involved the object–sign–meaning nexus – the relation between Dynamic Objects (states of the outer world), Signs (representations) and Immediate Objects (meanings) – in a constant series of mediations between the 'outer world' and the 'inner world' of mental representations. The interpretant is what supports this series of mediations (de Lauretis 1984: 173). 'If the chain of meaning comes to a halt, however temporarily, it is by anchoring itself to somebody, some body, an individual subject. As we use or receive signs we produce interpretants' (de Lauretis 1984: 178). In Peirce, 'habit-change' is a very specific concept. 'Meaning' is only to be understood by studying the interpretants or 'proper significate effects' of signs. These are (like most things in Peirce) of three kinds: the *emotional* interpretant (e.g. the effect of a piece of music), which may be the only effect produced by a sign; the *energetic* interpretant, which is produced through the effect of the first and involves 'effort', muscular exertion or mental effort; and '*habit-change*', which is produced through the first two and 'modifies a person's tendencies towards action'. This last is the *logical* interpretant because 'its real and living logical conclusion is that habit' (quoted in de Lauretis 1984: 173–4). This semiotic production of habit is 'the result and the condition of the social production of meaning' (1984: 179).

De Lauretis traces the process by which Eco, in his dialogue with Kristeva and psychoanalysis, and his rewriting of Peirce for his own semiotics, excises this connection with the body and with consciousness. In a chapter called 'The Subject of Semiosis' at the end of *A Theory of Semiotics* (1979), Eco quotes at length from Kristeva's challenge to the semiotics which 'runs from Saussure and Peirce to the Prague School and structuralism', a challenge which argued that a critique of this school must begin from 'a theory of the speaking subject'. She outlined two possible directions for semiotics: to continue with the semiotics of systems, conceiving meaning 'as the act of a transcendental ego, cut off from its body, its unconscious and also its history':

> [O]r else . . . it will attune itself to the theory of the speaking subject as a divided subject (conscious/unconscious) and go on to attempt to specify the types of operations characteristic of the two sides of this split: thereby exposing them . . . on the one hand, to bio-physiological processes (themselves already an inescapable part of signifying processes; what Freud labelled 'drives'), and, on the other hand, to social constraints (family structures, modes of production, etc.).
>
> (Kristeva 1973: 1249)

Eco's response was to insist that 'semiotics can define the subject of every semiotic act only by semiotic categories' (1979: 315), and later in *The Role of the Reader* (1981), speaking of Peirce's understanding of the interpretant as including mental events, he said:

> I am only suggesting that from the point of view of the theory of signification, *we should perform a sort of surgical operation* and retain only a precise aspect of this category (the interpretant). Interpretants are the testable and describable correspondents associated by public agreement to another sign. In this way the analysis of content becomes a cultural operation which works only on physically testable cultural products, that is, other signs and their reciprocal relations.
>
> (Eco 1981: 198; the italics are quoted from de Lauretis)

Testable cultural products, in the materialist tradition within which Eco is working, include the traces of 'real' subjects in texts but do not include embodied consciousness or sexually differentiated bodies. Similarly, while Eco discovers in Peirce (or in Rossi-Landi) that human action is the missing link between semiosis and reality, for Eco that human action '*must be excised* . . . of its psychological, psychic and subjective component' (de Lauretis 1984: 176; my italics).

Her strategy of rewriting here, then, has been to put back in what Eco took out. But there is more at stake here than Eco. Elsewhere de Lauretis has commented briefly that she does not find Kristeva's theory of the speaking subject helpful (1984), and indeed Kristeva's work has been found problematic by many feminists (Threadgold 1988; Grosz 1989; Butler 1990). It is important here to consider why, because this also in part explains de Lauretis's very different agenda.

Butler (1990) reads Kristeva as challenging the Lacanian narrative which assumes that cultural meaning depends on the repression of the primary relationship to the maternal body. In Lacan, language, the symbolic, structures culture by suppressing the libidinal multiplicity which characterised the relation to the maternal body. Kristeva's 'semiotic' preserves that multiplicity and relationship to the body, and is expressed in language, in the symbolic, through the multiple meanings of poetic language. There are two problems here. First, the semiotic is always relegated to the position of subverting or displacing a paternal law which remains dominant, indeed has to be maintained for the theoretical fiction of the semiotic to be possible at all. Second, the semiotic may make its appearance in language from time to time, but it is theorised as actually having an ontological status prior to language as a site of cultural subversion, but apparently a dangerous one, since it cannot be sustained in language without leading to psychosis or cultural breakdown. In many ways, then, the law of the father is still the constitutive element of culture in this story.

The link between the semiotic and the maternal body is also problematic, since it clearly defines maternity as an 'essentially precultural reality' and 'thus precludes an analysis of its cultural construction and variability' (Butler 1990: 80). Thus Kristeva accepts Lévi-Strauss's story of the exchange of women, seeing it as 'the cultural moment in which the maternal body is repressed, rather than a mechanism for the compulsory cultural construction of the female body *as* a maternal body' (and a heterosexual one) (Butler 1990: 90). For Butler, beginning to elaborate a theory of the lesbian body, this maternal body, conceived as a principle of pure generativity, is based on a univocal conception of the female sex, a 'natural' maternity which is pure *poiesis*, the act of making 'upheld in Plato's *Symposium* as an act of birth and poetic conception all at once' (1990: 91). Butler rereads the maternal body through Foucault's *History of Sexuality*, declaring that 'the maternal libidinal economy' is in fact 'a product of an historically specific organisation of sexuality' (1990: 92). Femaleness cannot be external to the cultural norms by which it is repressed and, for Butler, this time following Foucault's repressive hypothesis, 'repression may be understood to produce the object that it comes to deny'. There is no true, female body 'beyond the law' (1990: 93), as imagined in Kristeva's semiotic.

The strand of Kristeva's thesis that Butler does not unwind (thereby proving de Lauretis's point about the cultural and individual pertinence of perception) is the construction of 'poetic language' as the place for subversion *par excellence*. This is the link between Kristeva and Eco, for whom the invention of codes is also primarily associated with 'productivity', the creative labour of making art (again, *poiesis* in both senses). In Eco (1979) there is also the Marxist inflection of the value of labour, the creative work requiring new and greater labour than the reproduction or replica. In both Kristeva and Eco there is the continued productivity of Jakobson's (1958/1981) structuralist poetics, with its focus on the aesthetic as the site for radical change and multiple meanings in language, the site for the poetic uses of language which 'exceed' the system constructed by de Saussure. This is a model of violent revolution if ever there was one, and actually not so dissimilar to Butler's Foucauldian concept of the generative function of repression.

HIGH AND POPULAR CULTURE

This albeit sketchy intertextual history explains the move de Lauretis makes to connect discussions of production and consumption (or the absence of such discussions) to a high/popular culture opposition in the work of Eco and others (1984: 178). Her argument is complex but important, and it works on several fronts at once. First, she contests the typical representation of the consumer as 'passive', arguing that the interpreter or 'user' of signs is also the producer of meaning because she is the 'body in whom the significate effect takes hold' (1984: 179). Here she is careful not to conflate the reader and writer (as Barthes had effectively done in 1979), pointing to the critical differences between enunciation and reception and all the issues of address and power surrounding the question of 'who speaks to whom and why' (1984: 179). She then compares the Lacanian concept of the subject constructed in language – the subject who is always divided from itself at the moment of utterance, split between the enunciation and the enounced (whom Benveniste, Jakobson and Barthes also described) – to the Peircean subject who is also divided from itself by means of its relation to a chain of interpretants. 'As each interpretant results in habit or habit-change, the process of semiosis comes to a halt, fixing itself provisionally to a subject who is but *temporarily* there' (1984: 180). This fixing she sees as related to Lacanian suture, but she notes that suture is 'bad' both in Lacanian psychoanalysis and in Althusser's theory of ideology, whereas the process that joins the subject to the social in Peirce is neither good nor bad. 'Suture' carries connotations of delusion, imaginary closure, false consciousness. What de Lauretis asks us to consider is whether consciousness has always already to be false consciousness, whether the opposition in Lacan between the truth of the unconscious and the deception of the conscious might not be the discursive product of a 'cold war'. That 'cold war', she suggests, is a discursively produced inheritance, in which Eco's contrary refusal to countenance the 'subjective' (the unconscious) in the social also participates.

She has accomplished two things here. She has insisted on the consumer's right to a socially and historically located position in social space, and she has made that consumer an active maker of meaning who need not always be seen as duped, deceived, the subject of ideology. She has reasserted the consumer's right to an embodied consciousness which can change as well as reproduce meanings and codes. The next step is to revalue the social spaces of everyday life as sites for the production and changing of meaning: 'such practices – political or more often micropolitical: consciousness raising groups, alternative forms of labor organisation, familial and interpersonal relations . . . effectively intervene upon the codes, codes of perception as well as ideological codes' (1984: 178). The gendering of the bodies who participate in these everyday activities involves the solidarity of habit and belief which is consequent upon a body which is physically implicated in the production of meaning. Habit is the crystallised form of past muscular and mental effort, but the overdetermination of meaning, perception and experience which folds the subject and reality into one another also potentially involves a continual modification of consciousness and thus the possibility of social change (de Lauretis 1984: 184). De Lauretis gives an example from the work of Kaja Silverman (1983) of how the complexity of these overdeterminations works. In Silverman's textual example, the whipping of a heroine by her master prompts her to remember a picture of a woman about to be beaten by a man, and to remember all the connotations of guilt and subjugation that the image has for her. Silverman's argument is that although the 'memory' of the picture, the representation, postdates the event of the whipping, it nonetheless structures and gives meaning to that event:

> The nexus sign–meaning, in other words, is not only significant for a subject, the heroine in whose body the muscular/mental effort produces the 'logical' significate event (her identification with the 'guilty woman'), the memory and the habit (women's subjection and masochistic pleasure). But the significance of the sign could not take effect, that is to say, the sign would not be a sign, without the existence or the subject's experience of *a social practice* in which the subject is physically involved; in this case, the use of corporal punishment to chastise and to educate, or rather, chastise and educate to give pleasure.
>
> (1984: 183)

The importance of this example, and the theorising of it, is to emphasise the 'practice' in the commonly used term 'signifying practice' to contest the dominance of the linguistic in theories of the subject (e.g. 'the discursively produced subject', 'the subject produced in language'), and to reject the notion of a 'signifying practice' (the term is Kristeva's), or a labour of semiosis (Eco) which looks only at verbal or textual practices (a charge of which, of course, both Eco and Kristeva are guilty).

It is hard to read this work without seeing the similarities with Bourdieu's notion of the habitus (1980/1990: 71–2), which is also constructed on the basis of the solidarity between bodily habit and belief, and which recognises the sexual principles at work in that solidarity:

> Every social order systematically takes advantage of the disposition of the body and language to function as depositories of deferred thoughts that can be triggered off at a distance in space and time by the simple effect of re-placing the body in an overall posture which recalls the associated thoughts and feelings, in one of the inductive states of the body which, as actors know, gives rise to states of the mind . . . Symbolic power works partly through the control of other people's bodies and belief that is given by the collectively recognised capacity to act in various ways on deep-rooted linguistic and muscular patterns of behaviour, either by neutralising them or by reactivating them to function mimetically.
>
> (Bourdieu 1980/1990: 69)

The difference is Bourdieu's emphasis on the body and *language*, not image or cinematic apparatus, but if one were to substitute 'semiotic systems' – visual, filmic, spatial, architectural – for 'language', the argument would work just as well. And de Lauretis has much to say about just how those behaviours and muscular patterns are produced in the micropolitics of social practice and through the technology of gender that is 'imaging'.

Where she perhaps overstates her case is with respect to Eco's (1981: 14) model reader, whom she rightly points out is a somewhat contradictory construction, presumed to be unproblematically there before he reads and simultaneously constructed in his reading, an artefact of the text, certainly not a presence whose body is any part of these processes. But he does have a certain 'logical' understanding about things to do with texts – and some of those things – even if they are also text structures: discursive structures, narrative structures, actantial structures, ideological structures, experience of the 'world' (for which might be substituted 'practices'), and 'inferential walks' – are no doubt part of the accumulated practical belief ('belief is a state of the body not of the mind') that Bourdieu (1980/1990) calls 'habitus' and de Lauretis calls 'being subject/ed to semiosis'. In Wonderland you might even begin to see a relationship between this inferential walker and de Certeau's (1984/1988) walker in the city, the nomadic, poaching reader – but we are not in Wonderland yet and, anyway, Alice doesn't.

WHOSE FEMINIST POETICS NOW?

The two future paths of semiotics which de Lauretis signals in her discussion of Eco's refusal of Kristeva's 'subject in process' have by now well and truly eventuated. Semiotics itself has in many places become transformed into cultural studies as a result, a cultural studies which is as sceptical now of linguistic and literary analyses of signifying practices as she was in 1983. Her work on cinema and her championing of the popular may even have contributed to that tendency, despite the richness of its semiotic analysis, and her profound understandings of the inheritance of structuralisms in the theories that purport to have moved beyond them. Her work was the forerunner of new theories of the female subject and the feminist intellectual (e.g. Butler 1993; Probyn 1993), and heralded new work on the reception and the audiences of texts (Radway 1984; Pribram 1988; Ang 1991, 1996). It is in some ways ironic that, in her most recent book (1994), although she republishes the chapter that was called 'The Semiotics of Experience' in *Alice Doesn't* with the new title 'Sexual Structuring and Habit-Change', the female subject has become a lesbian subject and the theory that dominates the book is psychoanalysis not semiotics.

It seems relevant, after analysing in such detail the successful strategies of rewriting and theory-making that constituted the earlier book, to point to the limits of continued psychoanalytic feminist rewritings of patriarchal texts by quoting from Elizabeth Grosz's (1995b) review of *The Practice of Love*. While Grosz finds this book important, she questions de Lauretis's 'revisionist' readings of Freud (1995b: 169), finding the book 'a last-ditch effort to preserve psychoanalytic theory' (1995b: 166), asking, in the light of the book: What is feminist theory? Is it a reading practice that demonstrates that every text (however patriarchal) can be read otherwise? Or is it an attempt to produce new knowledges which might attempt to deal with the emerging issues of difference which unsettle its very foundations – the neocolonial subject, the working-class women, the man and woman of colour, the fact that the feminist theorist is coloured white? Can feminist interests really be equated with lesbian interests? And:

> Why do we need psychoanalysis to think lesbian desire? What are the limits of its explanatory power regarding subjectivity and desire, the points beyond which it risks incoherence and contradiction? . . . What is at stake in trying to include what was previously excluded . . . Does de Lauretis function to provide a political rationale and credibility for psychoanalysis as it lies dying?
>
> (1995b: 158–9)

In some ways *The Practice of Love* (de Lauretis 1994) marks another forking of the way (although it is certainly not the first such work to do so), the development of a new interdisciplinary formation of queer theory and gay and lesbian studies out of the cultural studies that was semiotics. It marks another division between *those* areas and postcolonial and neocolonial studies, both of which have raised issues that this feminism cannot any longer pretend to speak for. Anna Yeatman said in 1993:

In the contemporary era of multiply contested oppressions feminism has been forced to lose its innocence. It has had to discover that it is predicated upon the assumption that gender is the most salient basis of oppression, and this assumption is always going to be most compelling for those women who do not experience ethnicity, race and class as additional bases of oppression.

(Yeatman 1993: 228)

And Ien Ang added to that in 1995:

In short because all female persons 'do not inhabit the same sociohistorical spaces' [Chow 1991: 93], (white Western) feminism's assumption of a ' "master discourse" position' [Chow 1991: 98] can only be interpreted as an act of symbolic violence which disguises the fundamental structural divisions created by historical processes such as colonialism, imperialism and nationalism.

(Ang 1995: 73)

These are salient issues which have emerged for feminisms and for feminist pedagogies since de Lauretis did her ground-breaking work in writing into existence the female subject of semiosis. What should not be forgotten is that that subject is potentially rewritable, and that, without it, some of these other issues might never have been speakable.

And all the while the semiotics of language, the ethics of discourse, critical discourse analysis, the kinds of work that might put back on the agenda the crucial point that Grosz makes at the end of her review, seem further and further away from these interests. Grosz's final point is this: that to put lesbian desire under the microscope of intellectual and discursive investigation may result in another form of normalisation. Whether it does or not, she says, 'depends to a large extent on the status and effects of the discourses one uses. Perhaps now is the time to rethink what those discourses should be' (Grosz 1995b: 171).

This is a timely reminder of the fact that one cannot in fact write at all without rewriting; without, as Barthes said, 'being also written', or, as Bakhtin might have put it, engaging with the heteroglossia of where the word (or the text, or the body) has been before. Derrida called this 'this citationality, this duplication of duplicity, this iterability of the mark' (1988: 12). If we want to 'rewrite' in a different sense, not transmission but transformation (and this will not always be appropriate), it seems to me that there has to be a very thorough understanding of the contexts, both material and discursive, in which we write, and a very detailed understanding of the materiality of texts (the resistances they offer to the meanings we want to make), as well as a sense of the new discursive spaces, the unthought, the unspoken, that we are trying to make visible and audible in our writing. We also need to be constantly aware of who the 'I' is who writes.

Perhaps it is also time to reconsider the need for some other theoretical frameworks – theories of language, discourse, discursive change and discursive communities – which might help us to make decisions about the 'ethics' of the discourses we use to make theories with. This might also help us to remain perhaps more conscious than we are of the 'depositories of deferred thoughts' (Bourdieu 1980/1990: 69), 'the historical tenacity and material longevity of oppressive orders and structures, such as these entailing sedimented consequences of white/Western hegemony' (Ang 1995: 67), which are the things that Rossi-Landi (1973) argued a long time ago stood between us and our understanding of our own positioning in discourse and language.

Chapter 4

Discourse, expressibility and things to do with Foucault

'Discourse' is a term with a complex and heterogeneous history within semiotics and cultural theory. It is currently used in a variety of disciplines and interdisciplines to serve a number of disparate functions. In linguistics, and elsewhere, at a very general level, it means 'language in use' (*parole*), but there remains a large gulf between poststructuralist and linguistic modes of discourse analysis. The analyses of the particular instance of a linguistic or semiotic kind, which might establish the limits and interrelations between the enunciative and the discursive, have not been occurring in the poststructuralist work. And the kind of radical rethinking that this work has been doing has not, as Fairclough (1992a) shows, been generally taken up in the linguistic forms of discourse analysis. A recent editorial by Teun van Dijk in the journal *Discourse and Society* (van Dijk 1995), suggesting that poststructuralist forms of discourse analysis have no place in the journal, and the heated responses to it in a later issue, offer some indication that the divisions between these knowledges are still closely guarded in some quarters.

FOUCAULT AND DISCOURSE

The term 'discourse' has come to carry a very different set of connotations and determinations since the work of Michel Foucault. That work, while it had a great deal to do with cultural and social formations, was in some senses specifically and intentionally not linguistic or semiotic. What Foucault's work did was to insist on the controlling, positioning and productive capacities of signifying practices, denying in the process the primacy of signification itself and radically unsettling common theoretical assumptions about the ways in which signifying practices operated. His work also explicitly connected the discipline of the body, the production of knowledges and the making of subjectivity.

In this context, the term *discourse* has come to mean something that was precisely not limited to, or by, the categories of linguistics or semiotics. A discourse is a way of categorising and limiting, but also producing, the objects of which it speaks: for example, the discourse of childhood, the discourse of gender, and so on. In this very broad definition of 'discourse', a discourse might be said to consist of all the statements – visual, verbal, bodily – that might be made about childhood, for example.

In Foucault's early work (1966/1973), the term *episteme* had been used to characterise the discursive regularities, the 'rules of formation', of the discourses of the emerging disciplines of biology, economics and grammar (linguistics). That term was later replaced by the more fluid term *archive*, which Foucault defined as follows:

> The archive is first the law of what can be said, the system that governs the appearance of statements as unique events. But the archive is also that which determines that all these things said do not accumulate endlessly in an amorphous mass, nor are they inscribed in an unbroken linearity, nor do they disappear at the mercy of chance external accidents; but they are grouped together in distinct figures, composed together in accordance with multiple relations, maintained or blurred in accordance with specific regularities; . . . it is that which, at the very root of the statement-event, and in that which embodies it, defines at the outset *the system of its enunciability*.
>
> (1969/1972: 129)

In this and earlier work (1970/1971), the systems of enunciability of statements (the conditions of their possibility) which grouped them together in distinct figures had been clearly associated with the disciplines, with specific bounded kinds of knowledges. This work had made it clear that, for Foucault, the power invested in knowledge, in the will to truth, meant that discipline as institution was a mode of constraining and producing both knowledge and the subjects (people) positioned by and within the enunciative modalities of the knowledges of the disciplines. This is the source of contemporary definitions of discourse like the following:

> Discourses are systematically organised sets of statements which give expression to the meanings and values of an institution . . . A discourse colonises the social world imperialistically from the point of view of an institution . . . Discourses do not exist in isolation but within a large system of sometimes opposing, contradictory, contending or merely different discourses.
>
> (Kress 1985: 6–7)

and:

> Social structures and processes are organised through institutions and practices such as the law, the political system, the church, the family, the education system and the media, each of which is located in and structured by a particular discursive field . . . The concept of a discursive field was produced by Foucault, as part of an attempt to understand the

relationship between language, social institutions, subjectivity and power. Discursive fields consist of competing ways of giving meaning to the world and of organising social institutions and processes.

(Weedon 1987: 35)

Neither definition takes full account of the radical difference of Foucault's work, but both are typical of the generalising tendencies in the appropriation of his work in the humanities and social sciences in the last twenty-five years. In particular, both reduce Foucault's 'discourse' to language, to the verbal, although both do allow that the space of language, of discourse, is the site for struggle and contestation, and involves subjectivity, power and institution. Weedon's is typical of a poststructuralist feminist position which has effectively substituted the term 'discourse' for 'language', so that work on the relationship between subjectivity and language becomes almost entirely conceived in relation to 'discourse' as defined above.

In his early work, Foucault maintained an opposition between what he called the discursive and the non-discursive. For him, as Deleuze (1986/1988) has shown, this distinction was set up as a first step in rethinking some of the more traditional binarisms of linguistics (and semiotics): form/content, expression/referent, and text/context. His desire to rethink these issues emerged from a questioning of concepts like

1   the traditional unities of the book and the *oeuvre*
2   the speaking subject as defined by psychology and humanism
3   context as a simple experience-based explanation of what that intending/knowing subject does
4   the notion that what such a subject does is to construct unified discourse according to laws, and
5   the a priori authority of knowledge.

His ultimate rewriting of the linguistic/semiotic binaries was a consequence of his perception that they participated in the construction of 1–5. His agenda was arguably one which emerged from the early structuralist arguments that cultural products were the result of social, not individual, labour or creativity, and indeed were constructions of meaning, not the sources of them. It was thus not anti-linguistic *per se*, but certainly opposed to the dominant forms of Chomskyan linguistics at the time of writing.

What he calls the discursive (the verbal) here is what linguistics and semiotics see as representing or containing the non-discursive (the non-verbal). He also saw a homology between this and the tendency in traditional social theory to differentiate, to keep separate, the discursive, the languages of institutions, and the 'institutional milieu', the 'context', of those languages – the non-discursive formations of institutions (their architecture, spaces, technologies), political events, economic practices and processes, and so on. This separation he saw as allowing 'power' to be located in these 'non-discursive' areas (e.g. the state, the economy, the law). There is, then, a tendency to establish a vertical causality whereby events and institutions (the non-discursive/the context) are seen as determining the discursive so that the power is elsewhere, not in discourse itself. This is what Deleuze (1986/1988: 27) identified as the 'pyramidal Marxist image' of the social space. The Habermasian separation of socially integrated (depending on intersubjective consensus) and system-integrated (driven by the media of money and power) action contexts is a case in point (Fraser 1995: 25). The alternative metaphor to this is the Hegelian one of the dialectic where the two separate spheres are resynthesised in a process of mutual constitution. The difficulty with this is the isomorphism that then seems to characterise the relationship, as if there were a one-to-one correspondence between the discursive and the non-discursive.

According to Deleuze, it was to recover the specificity and difference of these two spheres, then – to dislocate their apparently self-evident opposition, to break the homologising tendencies of any easy dialectic between them – that Foucault first separated them (1969/1972). This explains his initial concentration on the discursive and the institutional. Here he was interested, above all, in the discontinuities and the transformations that occurred within what he came to call discursive formations – clusters of institutionally located discourses which he defined, among other things, as spaces 'of positions and of differentiated functions for subjects' (1978: 13). These positions were themselves discontinuous and even contradictory, contributing to the dispersion or fragmentation of the subject across these sites. Thus a member of the medical profession or the teaching profession is actually constituted through a whole configuration of enunciative modalities, each offering a speaking position, and all of them held in place by the rules of the medical discourse or discipline. Enunciative modalities are activities which may form parts of ensembles of other activities – practices such as hypothesising, making regulations, forming descriptions, making observations, asking questions, performing examinations (touching as well as seeing, in the medical case), or 'teaching' which is part of a whole discursive formation of pedagogy. This was the beginning of the poststructuralist concept of the discursively produced subject, the subject positioned in discourse. For Foucault, discourse (here roughly equivalent to the practices, behaviours and languaging within a discipline) was a 'curious entity', and not something to be taken for granted. What could be more enigmatic, he asked, than speaking of *psychiatry, grammar* or *medicine*? (1978: 8).

In trying to answer that question he sought to define the play of dependencies that effected transformations in discourses and discursive formations. Among these he included: *intradiscursive* dependencies (between the objects, the operations and the concepts of a single formation), *interdiscursive* dependencies (between different discursive formations such as history, economics, grammar and the theory of representation [1966/1973]), and *extradiscursive* dependencies (between discursive formations and others not produced in discourse, e.g. the correlation between medical discourse and economic, political and social changes in *Madness and Civilisation* and *The Birth of the Clinic*). The crucial point to note here is that already the 'discursive' begins to include behaviours, events, practices, technologies and procedures as well as the linguistically or verbally discursive. Discourse is already not only language, and nor is the verbal aspect of it homologous with language (either as system or as use).

This agenda explains the non-semiotic or anti-interpretative move in this early work:

> I do not question the discourses for their silent meanings but on the fact and the conditions of their manifest appearance; not on the contents which they may conceal, but on the transformations which they have effectuated; not on the meaning that is maintained in them like a perpetual origin, but on the field where they co-exist, remain and disappear. It is a question of an analysis of the discourses in their exterior dimensions.
>
> (1978: 15)

His focus was on surfaces and intersections. Hence the definition (1978: 14–15) of what he was doing as not exegesis but archaeology, and of the archive not as an accumulation of texts, but as the rules which for a given society defined the limits and forms of

- *expressibility* (what is it possible to say in what domain?)
- *conservation* (what statements disappear, what survive and where and why?)
- *memory* (what are the terms everyone remembers, what are the relations between the present and past systems of statements?)
- *reactivation* (what is valued, reconstituted, of the discourses of past epochs and how?), and
- *appropriation* (who has access to what discourse and how is that relationship institutionalised?).

FOUCAULT, LINGUISTICS AND THE VISIBLE (NON-DISCURSIVE)

Central to this process was the argument that language was also the realisation of something that the structural categories of linguistic analysis (propositions, speech acts, etc.) have always failed to identify, what he called the *statements* that constitute a discourse. These statements are not themselves words and objects, but they lead to the formation of words and objects (all the statements about madness or sexuality which produce these 'objects'), and they provide ways of positioning speaking subjects which have little to do with the intentional 'I' of the linguistic utterance. A set of statements, articulating the same rules of formation, the same conditions of possibility, might include a graph, the paradigm of a verb in traditional grammar, or a mathematical equation. The statement is not limited by, or co-extensive with, such categories as the speech act although it does occur *as* language:

> The enunciative analysis does not lay down for linguistic or logical analyses the limit beyond which they must renounce their power and recognise their powerlessness; . . . it is deployed in another direction which intersects them.
>
> (Foucault 1969/1972: 113)

It is also crucial to note that the *enunciative* analysis is one that derives from an earlier binary opposition worked through by linguists and semioticians such as Benveniste (1966) and Jakobson (1957/1971a), and later reworked by Barthes (1986a; see Chapter 2 above) and Kristeva (1973). Foucault's term 'enunciative' blurs these two categories of subject, apparently referring to what in these other contexts was called the subject of the *enounced*, but using the term *enunciation*, which referred there to the moment of utterance. This blurring actually also elides an important difference between the positioning of the subject in the 'anonymous' statements of a discourse/discipline and positioning of a subject in the generic utterances which may inflect or change those statements. Fairclough comments in passing that, whereas the discursive formations of the early work are characterised in terms of disciplines and disciplinary formations (Foucault 1969/1972), the salient discourse categories of the later Foucault (1975/1982, 1976/1980) 'are of a more "generic" character (e.g. interview and counselling, as discursive processes associated respectively with what Foucault calls "examination" and "confession")' (Fairclough 1992a: 51).

Foucault knew that 'the subject of the statement should not be regarded as identical with the author of the formulation – either in substance or in function' (1969/1972: 95), but he never considered in any consistently theorised way the constant and necessary interaction of the two in all forms of social interaction in which discourse might actually be instantiated in practice. His subject of discourse is actually much more like Althusser's interpellated subject of ideology (1971) than Kristeva's 'subject in process' (1974/1984) or de Lauretis's active subject of semiosis.

Foucault was very clear that the analysis of statements and their realisations is not an exhaustive description of language (*langage*), that it does not replace other methods of linguistic analysis: 'it is another way of attacking verbal performances, of dissociating their complexity, of isolating the terms that are entangled in its web, and of locating the various regularities that they obey' (1969/1972: 108). Statements produce their own correlative objects (knowledges) and the points where they occur (repeat themselves) can be mapped or diagrammed, but a statement is not a proposition (or a sign) designating a state of things or a visible object. This suggests that the kind of linguistics Foucault was opposing was a specifically logical semantic or logical/philosophical tradition concerned with the formal definition of the proposition, the sentence and the speech act.

On the other hand, his arguments that statements offer (specifically in their repeatability across a range of historically formed discursive practices and different social technologies) a range of positions for speaking and acting subjects – a range of modes of production of subjectivity – has to be read in a different structuralist linguistic context. Discourses are constructed from statements that are 'functions that operate vertically' in relation to 'the various units of linguistic analysis' (Foucault 1969/1972: 87). It is important to recognise the ghost in the machine here, the indeed exterior and surface relationship of this 'vertical function' – the 'system of its [the statement's] enunciability' – with accounts of the system of *langue* and paradigmatic textual repetition. In structuralist accounts of text, paradigms are sets of repeated forms that vertically transgress the linearity of the syntagm (Jakobson 1958/1981). The difference is that, in Foucault, the elements of the paradigm are not linguistic categories; nor can the text contain them. They link it to a wider context of other discursive domains.

Eco has already commented on this 'linguistic-ness' of Foucault, pointing to the parallels between the way power and discourse constitute one another in Foucault and the idea of the system, *la langue* in linguistics:

> The given language (*la langue*) is true, coercive (it forbids me to say 'I are him' under pain of being incomprehensible), but its coercion doesn't derive from an individual decision, or from some centre that sends out rules in all directions: it is a social product, it originates as a constrictive product precisely through general assent . . . I'm not sure we can say that a given language is a device of power, . . . but it is surely a model of power.
>
> (1967/1986: 244)

The implications of Foucault's work which are less often discussed and which do contest the linguistic/semiotic are that the discursive is now seen not to refer directly, or to 'have' a meaning that is located in, the non-discursive as content. The relations between the two can only be mapped across the whole adjacent field of other concepts, objects and subjects, all of which are statements that constitute a system of values which characterise 'their place, their capacity for circulation and exchange, their possibility of transformation' (Foucault 1969/1972: 120). Again, the parallels with the linguistic system and the concept of value in de Saussure, as well as the linguistic and structuralist economic metaphors of circulation and exchange (Rossi-Landi 1973), are very clear here, but they are not precisely what Foucault was about.

To understand the complexities of this particular attempt to rewrite the relations between content and expression, I think we need to see a series of aspects of the relations between the visible and the articulable (Deleuze's rewriting of the terms 'discursive', 'non-discursive') as co-extensive. The two forms are heterogeneous, anisomorphic; but they exist in mutual pre-supposition. Their relationship is characterised by what Foucault calls 'a whole series of criss-crossings', a mutual grappling and capture in which discourse 'cuts into the form of things' (Deleuze 1986/1988: 68). Deleuze's use of contemporary film to illustrate this complexity is worth quoting in full:

> In Marguerite Duras' *India Song*, voices evoke or revive a ball in the past which will never be shown, while the visual image shows another ball, in silence, without any flashback making any visible link or any voice-off a sound link; while, even earlier, *La Femme du Gange* was made up of two films, 'the film of the image and the film of the voices', a void being the only 'linking factor', one that simultaneously acts as a hinge and a crack. Between the two there is a perpetual irrational break. And yet they are not any old voices on top of any old images. Of course, there is no link that could move from the visible to the statement, or from the statement to the visible. But there is a continual relinking which takes place over the irrational break or crack.
>
> (1986/1988: 65)

In *Discipline and Punish*, the non-discursive and the discursive take the forms of the visibilities of the prison (its architecture and allocation of space) and the statements of penal law, both of them realisations of optical and panoptical procedures, but also quite different, and not homologous formations. Deleuze provided a very useful, although still linguistic/semiotic, way of thinking the originality of what Foucault was saying here. He argued that Foucault specified knowledges as strata, historical formations, 'sedimentary beds' that are made up of various combinations of the visible and the articulable, things and words, seeing and speaking, the visible and the sayable, bands of visibility and fields of readability, contents and expressions (1986/1988: 47). Deleuze borrowed the last two terms from Hjelmslev but applied them to Foucault in an entirely different way.

For Hjelmslev (1943/1961), both the expression (the signifier) and the content (the signified) had a form and a substance. What Deleuze sees Foucault doing is refusing the signifier/signified relation, but using the concepts of content and expression, form and substance. Thus, penal law as a form of expression defines a field of sayability (the statements of delinquency); the form is penal law and the substance is 'delinquency', which is the object of statements. Similarly, prison is a form of content which defines a place of visibility ('panopticism', a place where at any time one can see everything without being seen); its form is the prison and its substance the prisoners (these arguments are rearranged but derived from Deleuze 1986/1988: 47). The 'encounters' between the expression and the content, the fact that they may appear to co-adapt, are a function of the multiple 'dependencies' that may exist within a discursive field.

It hardly needs to be pointed out that this Hjelmslevian reading of Foucault bears no small resemblance to Eco's (1979) rewriting of Hjelmslev with the latter's much more Marxist focus on the labouring subject of sign-production. This subject only processually and transiently manages to realign expression and content to produce not a cartography, but a meaning; one that might transform the universe of codes. At the same time, it would have to be said that Deleuze's reading of Foucault here intersected with his own thinking on the relations between the articulable and the visible in cinema in ways which bear little relationship to Eco.

INTERTEXTUALITY AND INTERDISCURSIVITY

Foucault himself was no more specific about what he meant by discourse than he was about enunciability:

> Instead of gradually reducing the rather fluctuating meaning of the word 'discourse', I believe that I have in fact added to its meanings: treating it sometimes as the general domain of all statements, sometimes as an individualizable group of statements, and sometimes as a regulated practice that accounts for a certain number of statements; and I have not allowed this same word 'discourse', which should have served as a boundary around the word 'statement', to vary as I shifted my analysis or its point of application, as the statement itself faded from view.
>
> (1969/1972: 80)

The statement may have faded from view for him, but it has remained foregrounded for those who have tried to use his work, providing a means for actually tracing the material repetitions of the elements of a discourse across a discursive formation. For example, Pêcheux's use of the term 'interdiscourse' describes the material traces in a text of its wider discursive context.

The statements of a discourse, along with the variety of dependencies recognised by Foucault within and between discourses and the non-discursive, are among the various discursive and textual relations which are regularly identified as 'intertextuality' or 'interdiscursivity' today. This is a usage which often conflates and confuses Foucault's agenda with that of the notions of heteroglossia and dialogism, citation and iterability, which are derived variously from Bakhtin (1981) via Kristeva (1970) and Barthes (1953/1968), or from Derrida (1988). Kristeva's usage is actually most precisely different from Foucault's when she describes intertextuality as the transposition of one or more systems of signs into another *with always a consequent difference in enunciative and denotative positionality*. Her examples are of the transposition of the sign systems of carnival, courtly poetry and scholastic discourse into the novel (Kristeva 1970). This definition emerges from her uses of Bakhtin in her own work on the novel, where her discourse analysis involved locating the transformations of the sign systems listed above within the text of a single novel (Kristeva 1970). Her aim was to explore a genre which was the hybridisation or mixing of several earlier genres or modes of utterance.

The Bakhtinian terms which are important here are 'heteroglossia' and 'dialogism'. The first ensures the primacy of context over text, in that every word, every utterance, brings (noisily) to the present context the history of where it has been before. Dialogism is 'the characteristic epistemological mode of a world dominated by heteroglossia' (Bakhtin 1981: 426–9). That is, the meanings of textual elements are always part of a much greater system than the word or the text. There is a constant interaction between meanings, all of which have the potential to recontextualise and resignify others. A word is dialogised when it becomes relativised in this way. It is important to understand that what is translated here as 'word' could also mean a 'method of using words' (i.e. discourse). There is no way that any word/discourse can be rearticulated or transposed to another context without the moment of utterance reshaping it. Since that always involves what Bakhtin (1986) would later call 'speech genres' the genre itself always dialogues with the discourses it embeds (dialogisation), involving new and complex kinds of interactions between voices and positions. This is what, it seems to me, is lost when you separate, or conflate, as Foucault does, the moment of utterance from that which is uttered, the *enunciation* from the *enounced*.

THE MICROPHYSICS OF POWER AND THE ETHICS OF THE SELF

Foucault's critical story of modernity is the story of the restructuring of power and knowledge, the making of new kinds of subjects, in the course of the late eighteenth and early nineteenth centuries in the capitalist societies of Western Europe. He argued that the rise of parliamentary institutions and of new conceptions of political liberty were accompanied by a profound and pervasive transformation in the functioning of power. The total power of the absolute monarch is replaced by an unprecedented discipline of the body, a 'microphysics' of power which fragments and partitions the body's time, its space and its movements (Foucault 1982: 28), and is realised but unremarked in the smallest gestures and postures of everyday life. The seat of this capillary effect of power is a new 'technology', a mode of making visible, the move (*le geste*) of gridding (*quadriller*) a visible space in such a way as to make its occupants observable, which operates through a constellation of institutions, all of which resonate the structure and effects of Jeremy Bentham's panopticon. They include the school, the prison, the police force, the army and the factory. Their disciplinary techniques (of regulated isolation and surveillance) train, position and produce a hierarchy of social subjects, subjected and practised bodies, 'docile bodies' (1982: 138). The state of permanent and conscious visibility produced by these 'disciplines' assures the automatic functioning of power as each inmate becomes his own gaoler (1982: 228) and the heightened self-awareness and perpetual self-surveillance which results produces the 'individualism' of modernity.

At the same time, these increasingly invasive apparatuses of power and surveillance require and generate a new kind of knowledge of the very subjects and behaviours which they themselves produce: the disciplines of modern psychology (Henriques et al. 1984) and sociology (Smith 1987), and the discourses of the social sciences. These new knowledges, then, produce new effects of power which operate through new technologies of behaviour – the microtechniques of the interview, the medical examination, the social survey and the questionnaire. What is different about this story is the way in which panoptic and instrumental reason becomes flesh, investing and traversing, specifying and differentiating, taking hold of the body (not just the mind) of the social subject. What is the same is that the social body, like the social mind, is desexed, universalised, masculine and white, as if the lived bodily experiences of men and women (Bartky 1988: 64), of men and women of colour, and of different social classes, were the same, as if the disciplining of those bodies and their characteristic relations to the institutions of modern life were not everywhere marked by specificity and difference.

Foucault called this kind of power (which he argued had emerged since the seventeenth century) 'bio-power' which 'brought life and its mechanisms into the realm of explicit calculation and made knowledge/power an agent of transformation in human life' (1976/1980: 143). This is why, in his later work, Foucault concentrates on the analysis of the micro-level, the local instance, the specific scene. The great discursive and non-discursive formations which traverse and construct institutions and knowledges, the representational fields which constitute culture, are made/produced in, and diffused through, the microphysics of power in local and interpersonal interactions under the very specific generic constraints of the rhetorical modes (my terminology not his) available within a social field:

> Power is everywhere; not because it embraces everything but because it comes from everywhere . . . Power comes from below; there is no binary and all-encompassing opposition between ruler and ruled at the root of power relations, and serving as a general matrix – no such duality extending from the top down and reacting on more and more limited groups to the depths of the social body. One must suppose rather that the manifold relations of force that take shape and come into play in the machinery of production, in families, limited groups and institutions, are the basis for wide-ranging effects of cleavage that run through the social body as a whole.
>
> (Foucault 1982: 93–4)

For Deleuze, 'the diffuse centres of power do not exist without points of resistance that are in some way primary; and . . . power does not take life as its objective without revealing or giving life to a life that resists power' (1986/1988: 94). This kind of reading of Foucault's work, together with readings of his latest work on the history of the construction of sexuality which concluded with the development of an ethics of the self, tend to produce very contradictory understandings of Foucault's position on power. Indeed, this is because there are contradictions in Foucault himself.

I feel that it is important to challenge the entirely productive view of power which emerges in readings like that of Deleuze, and later in Hunter (1988, 1994) and, in different ways, in Butler (1990, 1993). This is the view that power *necessarily* produces its own resistances or that it produces knowledges and discourses that are themselves *invariably* productive. Bartkowski (1988) argued that Foucault's work still participated in the dominant modernist stories, still depended on the identification of the social with the institutional, still excluded the voices of resistance to the dominant stories, and thus 'reproduces and produces as history the dominant patriarchal history of sexuality' (Bartkowski 1988: 47). Hers is a challenge to the repressive hypothesis of volume 1 of *The History of Sexuality*, the argument that what produced sexuality in its current forms was not repression, but discourse:

> More important was the multiplication of discourses concerning sex in the field of the exercise of power itself: an institutional incitement to speak about it, and to do so more and more; a determination on the part of the agencies of power to hear it spoken about, and to cause *it* to speak through explicit articulation and endlessly accumulated detail.
>
> (Foucault 1976/1980: 18)

Bartkowski's response is that this prioritising of the speaking of sexuality – from the confessional to the psychoanalyst's couch – ignores precisely the specificity and localisation of sexual discourse in a place where it can only be spoken of in certain kinds of ways and by certain people.

What must be spoken must also remain secret. It is to remain restricted to the closed space of the confessional discourse (presided over by the institutions of the church or psychoanalysis or the heterosexual bedroom), constrained by its articulation in (and through) the relations of power which constitute the privileged and coupled space of the inquisitor/victim, confessor/confessant, analyst/analysand and master/slave. This is the sanctioned place, the space, of sex and confession, a private, specifically not-public space. Here the desires, the body and words of women (and, indeed, of those of other races and classes) are appropriated through socially ratified voyeurism and eavesdropping, produced and possessed as knowledge, made the property of the hegemonic and masculinist discourses of power and sexuality. They are incorporated into the social by way of the public, rationalised, repressive and institutionalised discourses of patriarchal power.

The voices of those who speak in this place, the voices of resistance, are never heard. We hear only the voices of the men who listen (but clearly do not hear), the men who translate the voices of resistance (in different periods and contexts) into witchcraft, and later as the institutions of medicine take over the functions of the church, into hysteria or nagging – the men who speak the appropriated voices and desires of the other as knowledge. Bartkowski's view, then, is that Foucault's work, despite its interest in the marginal, actually tells another story. This story recounts how the 'nature' of sexuality has been framed/classified/categorised by (and for) the voices, eyes and ears of those in the place of power, the eavesdroppers in the confessional and behind the analyst's couch. In this feminist story the confessional actually silences, rather than gives voice to, resistance (Bartkowski 1988: 45–50).

Deleuze, on the other hand, argues that the book *The Use of Pleasure* (1984/1985) marks a clear difference in Foucault's work, treating a much longer span of history than the earlier books, and discovering a relation to oneself that cannot in fact be reduced to the power relations and the understandings of discursive and disciplinary power of the earlier books. The crucial question Foucault asked in *The Use of Pleasure* was whether the relation to oneself had an elective relation to sexuality. In Deleuze's words,

> The reply is a vigorous one: just as power relations can be affirmed only by being carried out, so the relation to oneself, which bends these power relations, can be established only by being carried out. And it is in sexuality that it is established or carried out.
>
> (1986/1988: 102)

What Foucault seemed to be moving towards in this book, as in the earlier *History of Sexuality*, was a dimension of subjectivity derived from power and knowledge, but not dependent on them:

> Finally, I have sought to study – it is my current work – the way a human being turns him- or herself into a subject. For example, I have chosen the domain of sexuality – how men have learned to recognise themselves as subjects of 'sexuality'.
>
> (1982: 208)

It is important not to conflate this move in Foucault with a return to free individuality. The argument is that there is always a relation to oneself that resists codes and powers. It may even, as Deleuze argues, 'be one of the origins of those points of resistance which we have already discussed' (1986/1988: 103). Foucault's later work has been problematic for many readers, including Macdonell (1986):

> But his model disengages discourse from history, and idealises discourse and its effects . . . In the event, by looking only at the free-born and rul-

ing point of view of male dominance in antiquity, Foucault provides an analysis which takes the standard notion of the 'subject' at face value. Through his genealogy, the 'subject' appears too simply as an individual who is active in relation to others who are the passive, subordinated objects of his desire.

(Macdonell 1986: 127–8)

For others, particularly in the development of queer theory and gay and lesbian studies, it has often been a crucial point of departure (for example, Halperin 1995). It has not, however, been taken up in work in critical-linguistics-based discourse analysis, which has tended to stay with the versions of power and subjectivity that characterised the earlier work.

Thus Fairclough (1989, 1992a) has worked extensively on the discursive analysis of the construction of social relations in the kinds of genres of social interaction singled out by Foucault's work, looking at the construction of social relations and of the self in the medical interview, or the conversational anecdote, exploring the construction of reality in various regimes of power and discourse, such as the literature on antenatal care and the discourses of enterprise culture. In these contexts, he has begun to address some of the specific questions of differences in power that were Bartkowski's concern. It is the earlier work, too, which produces Fairclough's interest in 'the investigation of historical transformations in the discursive practices of the orders of discourse, and their relationship to wider processes of social change' (1992a: 54). This work takes heed of the anxiety about objectifying science which is articulated in Foucault's early work, an anxiety that is further fuelled by the discursive strategies Foucault himself adopted in *I, Pierre Rivière . . .* (1973/1975). Here he attempted to show rather than 'analyse' how the operations of power worked discursively to criminalise. Here critique involved the tactic of ceasing to critique. And yet this ceasing is not typical of Foucault, and even in this case it is more an appearance than a reality. The book is edited, the primary texts are accompanied by a commentary (including Foucault's own), and the whole is, after all, published under the editorial name of Foucault. This is not a discourse that is indifferent to the workings of power.

THE OUTSIDE OF KNOWLEDGE

It was Michel de Certeau (1984/1988) whose work made clear the need to think about both the way disciplinary knowledges work to conceal the positions and interests of those who enunciate them and the way conceiving knowledge as discourse excludes an account of the power of enunciation to subvert or change it. His work is a direct response to the Foucauldian concept of discipline, resignifying and rewriting much of the Foucauldian metalanguage of surveillance, panopticism and technology, in an attempt to account for the ways in which populations succeed in resisting disciplinary mechanisms. He rewrote the term 'non-discursive' to mean that which remained outside discourse or knowledge. He used the linguistic metaphor of enunciation – the creative and dialogic uses and appropriations of the language system by its speakers – to articulate what he conceived as a rhetoric of practices which manipulates, subverts and infiltrates the panoptic technologies of the body politic, the body of the State and the disciplining networks of the city or the factory.

At another level, de Certeau's work was also an attempt to account for the 'popular' culture which is not contained or accounted for by theories of institutionalised knowledge as discourse. Like de Lauretis (1984), he sought to rewrite the 'consumer' of knowledge and of culture as user, not used. His is a theory of practice as *poiesis*, as a making, a production which is a way of using imposed systems, of working in ways that are always hidden beneath their surface. The central metaphor is the distinction between strategies and tactics. Strategies are the 'calculus of force-relationships' which are proper (*propre*) to political, economic and scientific rationality. They involve a subject of will and power (a proprietor, a city, a scientific institution) located in a 'proper' place (which it owns), distancing itself from what it regards as exterior to itself (clients, adversaries or the 'objects' of research) so that it can control or 'know' them. Tactics, on the other hand, are like a kind of guerrilla warfare, a logic of momentary occupation without ownership, a calculus which 'cannot count on a "proper" (a spatial or institutional localisation)' (1984/1988: xix). He is interested in the ways tactics make use of strategies which they cannot control and cannot escape, but he refuses (or tries to) the calculus of force-relationships which would position him as the distanced, knowing analyst of practices as artefacts or texts:

> The act of walking is to the urban system what the speech act is to language or to the statements uttered . . .
> The village, the neighbourhood, the block are moreover not the only things that make the fragments of heterogeneous strata function together. The smallest sentence in common language works (*marche*) in the same way. Its semantic unity plays on compensatory equilibria that are just as subtle, on which semantic or lexical analysis imposes a superficial framework, that of an 'elite' that takes its models for reality.
>
> (de Certeau 1984/1988: 97, 201)

He wants to explore practices as processes, to try to understand and to represent the fact that the omitted 'bits' of the strategist's story, the bits that deny the reality of his models, were never 'nowhere'. They were always 'somewhere'. That is, their representations, their discourses, their stories, myths and metaphors always circulated alongside, simultaneously with and in opposition to, imbricated in, and in subversion and maintenance of, the stories told from the proper place of power.

The question of practice is what prompts de Certeau's critique of Foucault and Bourdieu. It is, he says, in the use of an 'old recipe' that the question of place arises, specifically the place of the 'other', the 'other' of scientific and written discourse – practice, the everyday (de Certeau 1984/1988: 63). According to de Certeau, Foucault and Bourdieu use an 'old recipe', which can already be found in Durkheim, Freud and Marx, to deal with these questions (1984/1988: 64). The problem arises, he argues, when theory has to explore an area where there are no longer any discourses (disciplinary knowledges 'articulate a discourse on non-discursive practices' (de Certeau 1984/1988: 61)). He shows how 'discourse' is then identified with 'verbal language' (the proper place of the theorist becomes language, all there is) so that the problem is that of a terrain which, for the theorist, is 'the ground on which verbal language begins to fail' – that of the immense ' "remainder" constituted by the part of human experience that has not been tamed and symbolized in language'. This is a remainder, he says, that theory has been trying to deal with at least since Kant. De Certeau's contrary argument is that the only place non-discursive practices do not exist, where they have not been 'symbolized', is precisely in 'discourse' (theory, knowledge), which is therefore the place with the lack, the absence, and not the non-discursive (which is, despite its name, abundantly discursive). The non-discursive is not a ' "know-how" without a discourse, essentially without writing' (de Certeau 1984/1988: 65). It is a 'know-how' which has been systematically excluded from – or 'translated' as meaning 'other than what it says' in – certain theoretical discourses and certain kinds of disciplinary writing (de Certeau 1984/1988: 67).

It is this problem of exclusion and translation that de Certeau locates in Bourdieu and Foucault, in their apparently very different 'ways of making' a theory of practices. Both, he argues, 'cut out' certain practices from the social whole, treat them as being a 'coherent' whole, but as being 'foreign' to the place where the theory is produced. In Foucault's case, it is 'panoptic' procedures (a genre), in Bourdieu's the 'strategies' of the inhabitants of Bearn or Kabylia (a place), which are cut out and then metonymically construed as a figure for the totality of practices. The second move involves 'turning over' what has been 'cut out' as obscure, remote and silent, and making it the element that 'illuminates theory and sustains discourse'. Hidden panoptic procedures become the key to understanding the human sciences, and allow Foucault's discourse to see everything. In the same way the strategies exteriorised in the habitus, which do not know what they know, enable Bourdieu to recognise the same order everywhere, and to explain everything (de Certeau 1984/1988: 61–3). 'The principle of an ethnological operation on practices is thus formulated: their social isolation calls for a sort of "education" which, through linguistic inversion, introduces them into the field of scientific written language' (de Certeau 1984/1988: 67). This is exactly the procedure of a Marx, a Durkheim and a Freud, to situate practices in primitive and closed spaces, ethnological with respect to 'enlightened' society, and then to civilise them in theory. It is a recipe, according to de Certeau, which remains a 'figure of modernity' (1984/1988: 64), and, one might add, of postmodernity and neocolonialism.

In all of these theoretical enterprises, what keeps returning is the repressed of place and of what is 'proper' (appropriate and one's own) in certain places. Nearly all attempts to subvert the tradition of the strategist remain (partially at least) dogged by the stability of the topographical metaphor, and by its connections with the idea of a 'proper place' and that of a coherent but unconscious system which constitutes one level and explains (actually re-inserting the person of the theorist, the ethnographer, as 'the one who knows' [de Certeau 1984/1988: 56]) how a society can be a system without knowing it. Such topographies, the synoptic metalanguages and models (e.g. the maps of the city viewed from above, from outside) which purport to explain the rationale of everyday life in the social world, continue to conceal or elide or transform what de Certeau has called the 'tactics' of everyday life and practice, the enormous potential for resistance and play within the system (the walking in the streets of the city).

These practices of resistance themselves do not observe the logic of that topographical metaphor, nor of modernity's understandings of what it is to be creative or resistant:

> Imbricated within the strategies of modernity (which identify creation with the invention of a personal language, whether cultural or scientific), the procedures of contemporary consumption appear to constitute a subtle art of 'renters' who know how to insinuate their countless differences into the dominant text.
>
> (de Certeau 1984/1988: xxii)

> More generally a way of using imposed systems constitutes the resistance to the historical law of a state of affairs and its dogmatic legitimations . . . That is where the opacity of a 'popular culture' could be said to manifest itself – a dark rock that resists all assimilation . . . Innumerable ways of playing and foiling the other's game [jouer/déjouer le jeu de l'autre], that is, the space instituted by others, characterize the subtle, stubborn, resistant activity of groups which, since they lack their own space, have to get along in a network of already established forces and representations.
>
> (de Certeau 1984/1988: 18)

Seeking, then, a different way of representing this kind of practice, he finds it in the metaphors associated with the 'problematics of the enunciation' (de Certeau 1984/1988: 19). What is at issue is the fact that Foucault's 'discourse' or Lévi-Strauss's myth has to be 'cut out' from its context, removed from everyday linguistic practices and the spaces of their tactics, in order to be 'treated': '[o]nly what can be transported can be treated' (1984/1988: 20).

The speech act, on the other hand, cannot be parted from the circumstances of its enunciation. De Certeau finds the basis for these arguments in Austin's analysis of performative utterances, Greimas's semiotics of manipulation, and the semiology of the Prague School (1984/1988: 19). He appropriates their concern with the speech act through which a speaker actualises and appropriates his mother tongue in a particular situation of exchange of meanings. De Certeau also uses it as a metaphor for the culture as a whole, where enunciative procedures 'which articulate actions in both the field of language and the network of social practices' (1984/1988: 19) are what makes it possible to remain 'undisciplined' within the structures of panopticism, but also to remain 'outside the disciplines' in the sense of not being reduced to the knowledge of the strategist.

His view of language is ultimately quite romantic and totally contradictory. On the one hand, for the popular subject, the tactician, the contextualised position of enunciation establishes a present relative to time and place, and a contract with the other (the interlocutor) in a network of places and relations. It also provides an agency (consumerism rewritten as *poaching*, renting) which consists in *poiesis*, the act of making, 'the use made by the common people' of the culture disseminated by the 'elites' (1984/1988: xiii). But this use, if 'undisciplined', is not unsystematic. Derived from the speech act theory of Austin and the Prague School, it hardly could be. It obeys the rules of the 'discipline of rhetoric', 'the science of the ways of speaking' and the 'formal rules of action' that constitute language games in a more Wittgensteinian transformation – 'morphology of use', 'pragmatic rules' (1984/1988: 12). It is well and truly circumscribed, as a form of resistance, within the theoretical discourses that de Certeau has been reading, and within a contextualised and specific problematic *for him* – the fact that philosophy (or Chomsky) has no way of dealing with 'ordinary language'. Thus it is that de Certeau unashamedly articulates his theory of practice, 'the microbe-like, singular and plural practices which an urbanistic system was supposed to administer and suppress' (1984/1988: 98), as a structuralist linguistic and semiotic metaphor: the city as metalanguage and practice as 'pedestrian speech-acts' (1984/1988: 97):

> I would add that the geometrical space of urbanists and architects seems to have the status of the 'proper meaning' constructed by grammarians and linguists in order to have a normal and normative level to which they can compare the drifting of 'figurative' language. In reality this faceless 'proper' meaning [*ce 'propre' sans figure*] cannot be found in current use, whether verbal or pedestrian; it is merely the fiction produced by a use that is particular, the metalinguistic use of science that distinguishes itself by that very distinction . . .

The act of walking is to the urban system what the speech act is to language or to the statements uttered.

(de Certeau 1984/1988: 97, 100)

Walking, as speech act, has a semantics, a syntax, a rhetoric, and out of
these are constituted the myths, the metaphors and the stories that 'organize
the topoi of a discourse on/of the city' at the everyday level (1984/1988:
105). Together, these seem to constitute de Certeau's semiotics of 'tactics'.
They circulate within and across, and thus transgress and make fictive, the
rational theoretical organisation of the city as metalanguage, as map (produced in another place), as master-discourse. The conflict between the
ordering discourse and the multiple resistances of the 'other' spatial world
of the city and its pedestrians is 'read' metaphorically as a process akin to
signifying practices in language, as a text. This strategy of apparently 'reading' and 'writing' metaphors allows de Certeau to construct a very different
kind of metalanguage to 'write' the 'non-discursive' of everyday practice.
The semioticisation of practice *and* its urban environment reads both as
text, as signifying practice, as itself *poiesis*. In this construal, resistance is a
metaphor – the emergence of rhetoric, the figurative, the poetic, the mythic
– within the master-text. The creative aesthetic moment of revolution and
change is relocated not in the nowhere of the other place (utopia [Ricoeur
1986]), but as part of everyday practice and within the dominant discourses,
which then have to relocate themselves in relation to it (de Certeau 1986:
Ch. 12).

Such is the metaphor and the fiction with which de Certeau attempts to
remake his theoretical discourse from within, to make it *perform* its reading
and not to objectify and analyse. The problem is that the citation of authors
from many different fields, and from classical rhetoric, ordinary language
philosophy and Prague School linguistics (and semiotics, in particular) – and
the need for de Certeau to make his intervention and his metaphor of practice from within an existing set of disciplinary and interdisciplinary dialogues, narratives and discourses about the practice of language – means
that his intervention can never indeed be more than that, a metaphor, and
that it cannot avoid again controlling, containing, translating the discourse
of practice from the place of power and of knowledge. His discourse
remains a metalanguage which enables one semiotic process (or a multiplicity of them) to be read, indeed to be constructed in terms of another. The
practices de Certeau describes are transient and not available to 'treatment'.
They cannot be 'cut out' because he refuses that option. They therefore have
to be made in language, as metaphors; and they are therefore, once again,
contained in the theorist's fictions.

There is, in the metaphor of textuality outlined above, an explicitly
acknowledged notion of bricolage in Lévi-Strauss's sense (de Certeau
1984/1988: xviii), a reminiscence of a Bakhtinian heteroglossic or dialogic

text (there are no references to Bakhtin in de Certeau's work, although there are to the Tartu School of semiotics [1984/1988: Ch. 9, n. 6]). The metaphor also recalls Kristeva's theory of intertextuality and later of the semiotic and the symbolic. Speaking of citation, of the 'sounds of the body' which are 'the reminiscences of bodies lodged in ordinary language and marking its path', de Certeau unwittingly provides a metaphor for the position of the 'popular' in his own writing:

> In scholarly writing, it is nothing other than the return of the voices through which the social 'body' speaks in quotations, sentence fragments, the tonalities of 'words', the sounds things make . . . This glossolalia disseminated in vocal fragments includes words that become sounds again: . . . or noises that become words, . . . or rhymes, counting jingles, . . .
> Through the legends and phantoms whose audible citations continue to haunt everyday life, one can maintain a tradition of the body, which is heard but not seen.
> These are the reminiscences of bodies lodged in ordinary language and marking its path, like white pebbles dropped through the forest of signs. An amorous experience, ultimately . . . They are the linguistic analogues of an erection, or of a nameless pain, of tears.
>
> (1984/1988: 163)

I will not remind you of the habits of philosophers (see Chapter 3 above). John Frow's (1995a) recent critique of de Certeau is worth quoting in this context:

> There is a politically fraught substitution of the voice of a middle-class intellectual for that of the subject of popular or indigenous culture; and it is characteristically in the space of this substitution that the categories of the popular and the indigenous are constructed.
>
> (Frow 1995a: 59)

The parallelism between de Certeau, Lévi-Strauss, Kristeva and Bakhtin is not surprising, given the Freudian intertexts which are common to all of them. For de Certeau the significance of Freud's work is his reversal of positivism's rejection of the discourse of subjectivity as non-scientific, and his rewriting of analytic discourse as 'literature' (that is, as a discourse where the speaker's affectivity is made audible). The recovery of affect involves relearning a language ' "forgotten" by scientific rationality and repressed by social norms. Rooted in sexual differences and in early childhood stages, this language still circulates, disguised in dreams, in legends and in myths' (1986: 27), hence the metaphor of the narrativity of everyday life. Freud's 'stylistics', then, founds a 'linguistics of speech', which concerns itself with the enunciation, or the 'elocution', of ancient rhetoric, and provides an analysis of the 'modalization of utterance by speech acts' – that is, a theory of 'affects and their representations', a modern equivalent to the ancient theory of the passions (1986: 27).

This Freudian moment in de Certeau is accompanied by the reading of Benveniste and Barthes, and of three other areas of investigation where 'the logic of unselfconscious thought has been taken seriously' – the work of sociologists, anthropologists and historians (from Goffman to Bourdieu, from Mauss to Détienne and Vernant), of ethnomethodology and sociolinguistics (Fishman, Garfinkel, Labov, for example), and the work on the extension of formal logics in analytical philosophy to the domains of action, time and modalisation (e.g. von Wright, Prior, Hughes and Cresswell) (de Certeau 1984/1988: xvi). But the dialogic and intertextual making of a poetics of practice is only completed, it seems, with the linguistics of the speech act. De Certeau privileges the act of speaking, the enunciation (that is, *parole*, not *langue*), as have many critical linguists and discourse analysts (Halliday 1985a), but he does this without any reference to the actualities of speech acts 'in context'. Nor does he allude to the sedimented histories, the institutional and generic practices or the habituated bodies which Bourdieu and Foucault did recognise as offering other kinds of resistance to a theory of practice in de Certeau's sense, and which only contextualised and intertextualised discourse analysis will probably ever begin to understand.

'Linguistics', of course, even in the mythologised and homogenised disguises it wears in a good deal of recent philosophical and theoretical work, has looked at such questions. It will have been interesting to pause for a minute over the metaphors and the representations of the 'non-standard' languages, the dialects and the registers, the speech genres and the anti-languages, which have been the 'objects' of linguistic research and which hover in the margins and the interstices of de Certeau's story. If we start from the point of theoretical resistance to the linguistic construction of a standard language – one of those partial realities which consigns its others to the nowhere of the non-discursive with which we began this section – we will find both Deleuze and Guattari and Bourdieu hard at work making metaphors and stories to contest what Bourdieu called 'the illusion of linguistic communism which haunts all linguistic theory' (1991: 43), here articulated in the form of Chomsky's 'competence' and de Saussure's *langue*:

> To speak of *the* language, without further specification, as linguists do, is tacitly to accept the *official* definition of the *official* language of a political unit. This language is the one which, within the territorial limits of that unit, imposes itself on the whole population as the only legitimate language.
>
> (Bourdieu 1991: 45)

> The linguistic tree on the Chomsky model still begins at point S and proceeds by dichotomy . . . Our criticism of these linguistic models is not

that they are too abstract, but on the contrary that they are not abstract enough, that they do not reach the abstract machine that connects a language to the semantic and pragmatic contexts of statements, to collective assemblages of enunciation, to a whole micropolitics of the social field. A rhizome ceaselessly establishes connections . . . There is no mother tongue, only a power takeover by a dominant language within a political multiplicity.

(Deleuze and Guattari 1980/1987: 7)

It is perhaps not necessary to point out here that what Bourdieu and Deleuze and Guattari are about is the same 'cut out' and 'turn over' technique that de Certeau has described in other major theorists of the social, the linguistic and the political. Chomsky and de Saussure are 'cut out' and 'turned over' to become the whole of 'linguistics'. While this may have some truth, it remains at best a partial vision. It is interesting to compare this position with Deborah Cameron's much less metaphoric and more pragmatic account which sees this as a social problem, not a problem with linguists:

In theory, 'prescriptivism' could refer to any form of linguistic regulation, but in practice it is strongly associated with those forms that are most conservative, elitist and authoritarian. Attempts to promote an elite standard variety, to retard linguistic change . . . are the instances most readily evoked.

Yet it is crucial to see that this narrowly conceived 'prescriptivism' – elitist, conservative and purist – is only one kind of verbal hygiene among many, only one manifestation of the much more general impulse to regulate language, control it, make it 'better' . . . for example, campaigning for the use of plain language on official forms; belonging to a spelling reform society, a dialect preservation society . . . going for elocution lessons, . . . editing prose to conform to house style; producing guidelines on non-sexist language, or opposing such guidelines . . . the group of schoolchildren mimicking a classmate's 'posh' accent are also practising verbal hygiene.

(Cameron 1995: 9)

Cameron actually produces a much less romanticised view of what the 'other' of the standard language, the realities it cannot encompass, might look like. Importantly, they are not just realities that 'resist', they are realities which also seek to regulate and control, which are classist and racist and also not those things. And, unlike the practices in de Certeau's account, they name themselves, they are not metaphorised. They are realities which are more like some of the linguistic accounts of language difference and change which none of Deleuze and Guattari, Bourdieu or de Certeau refers to.

I want here to turn briefly to Michael Halliday's (1978) account of language in the city (an account which could have been supplemented by any

number of others, notably Labov [1972]) in order to consider to what extent
the monologic view of 'linguistics' articulated in current social and critical
theory can actually be substantiated. It is important to realise that the *system* of language (the semantics, the lexicogrammar and the phonology) and
the *institution* of language (dialect and register) were already differentiated
in Halliday, the salient feature of the latter being its variability (1978: 183).
In this scheme of things, dialect (regional and urban) variation reflected the
hierarchy of social structure and register reflected the social order in the
sense of the 'diversity of social processes' (Halliday 1978: 185); language in
use in context. Moreover, and *contra* the theorists quoted above for this linguist, '[t]here is no evidence that the man in the city street has some overall
integrated speech system lurking somewhere at the back of his mind' (1978:
155). Linguistic variation has indeed been for some time a regular focus of
sociolinguistic work. Labov (1972) showed that the attitude of people
towards variation in the speech of others was remarkably uniform and that
that uniformity of attitude, the belief that 'non-standard' or regional forms
of variation were inferior, contributed to the maintenance of a hierarchical
social structure. Those continuing attitudes, and their power to inflect and
mediate social change and stasis, are in part the subject of Deborah
Cameron's much more recent book (1995). Labov, in his work on the language of black inner-city populations, was in fact so intent on arguing that it
was not the black children and families who had the deficit, but the educational psychologists and the educational system who were categorising them
in this way (1972: 202), that he insisted on the value and logic of the 'nonstandard' or 'urban ghetto' form of speech, characterising the narratives
produced in these contexts as 'the vehicle of communication used by some
of the most talented and effective speakers of the English language' (1972:
396).

He was trying to change attitudes, deeply entrenched attitudes (engaging
in verbal hygiene). But what, of course, he could not do was to *give* those
narratives the cultural value that he saw in them. His revaluation could not
change the hierarchy of social structure, although by now, in the 1990s, one
would have to say that his work contributed to the shifting of those attitudes. It is here, it seems to me, in understanding the tenacity of the structures Labov fought against, that Bourdieu's (1991) work on linguistic capital
comes into its own. His understanding of the development of modern societies was strongly influenced by the work of Max Weber. Bourdieu saw the
modern social order as differentiated into distinct spheres or fields of practice, each involving specific institutions and specific forms and combinations
of capital and value. It was in this context that he spoke of the structures of
the linguistic market 'which impose themselves as a system of specific sanctions and censorships' (Bourdieu 1991: 38), articulating very clearly the role
of the education system and of everyday practice in assisting with that
imposition (1991: 49). It is the fact that these positions of compliance, the

attitudes which Labov made visible, become embodied practice and do not pass through 'language or consciousness' in the making or the transmitting, that makes the arguments so persuasive:

> The power of suggestion which is exerted through things and persons and which, instead of telling the child what he must do, tells him what he is, and thus leads him to become durably what he has to be, is the condition for the effectiveness of all kinds of symbolic power that will subsequently be able to operate on a habitus predisposed to respond to them.
>
> (Bourdieu 1991: 52)

Halliday's (1978: 163) story of the city is a story of social and cultural change through conflict and interaction which has also focused on the need to 'make visible' through pedagogy the unconscious modes of meaning and being that are lived in and through language. This story recognises the sedimented structures of social hierarchy, but it also recognises the regularity and unpredictability of social change – its only ever probabilistic nature. It is certainly not a hegemonic or a monologic story, and, unlike de Certeau's story, it does not leave conflict or resistance always beneath the surface, waiting to insert itself into the structures of power where it has no place and cannot win:

> But a city is an environment in which meanings are exchanged. In this process conflicts arise, symbolic conflicts which are no less real than conflicts over economic interest; and these conflicts contain the mechanism of change . . . they contain some of the mechanisms of linguistic change . . . but they are also the source of new insights into the nature of cultural change, changes in the nature of the reality that each one of us constructs for himself in the course of interaction with others. The city dweller's picture of the universe is not . . . one of order and constancy.
>
> (Halliday 1978: 163)

Halliday also recognises that the normal linguist's distinction between standard and non-standard forms exists on a cline with the anti-language, which 'is a desperate attempt to rescue and reintegrate the self in the face of the cumulative oppression which threatens to disintegrate it' (Podgórecki 1973: 24, quoted in Halliday 1978: 168).

De Certeau has constructed a stylistics, a poetics, on the basis of an observation of the everyday, out of an appropriation of Freudian, linguistic, rhetorical and other discourses. This allows him to construct a narrative, a set of metaphors, about reading, writing and textuality. He then enacts the narrative and the metaphors *as* his own resistance to theory and *in* his construal of popular culture as resistance. Ricoeur's understanding of the relationship between narrative and metaphor is helpful here:

> It is this synthesis of the heterogeneous that brings narrative close to

metaphor. In both cases the new thing – the as yet unsaid, the unwritten – springs up in language.

As a result whether it is a question of metaphor or of plot, to explain more is to understand better . . . I risked speaking not just of a metaphorical sense but also of a metaphorical reference in talking about this power of the metaphorical utterance to describe a reality inaccessible to direct description.

(Ricoeur 1986: ix–xi)

Metaphor is a way of saying the unsaid just as narrative is a way of telling different stories or of telling stories differently. De Certeau's use of metaphor *as* metalanguage makes important statements about the narrativity, corporeality and subjectivity of science and theory, of reading and writing and of the popular, but it remains a *meta*language, a language about language. If the terms of metaphor are inevitably part of 'a schematisation that is their signifying matrix' (Ricoeur 1986: ix), that schematisation also has a discursive history in which the terms are inextricably involved. That is why there is no way that narrative and metaphor *per se* can somehow escape the objectifying and alienating tendencies of the metalanguages from which they derive and which they continue to enact.

BUTLER AND DISCOURSE AS PERFORMATIVITY

Judith Butler has read Foucault rather differently in her feminist arguments about the productivity of power always to construct what it appears to exclude. Her arguments about the potential power of the excluded 'other' derive from her feminist deconstructions and rewritings of Lévi-Strauss on kinship and of the Oedipal story in Freud. She combines Foucault's arguments about the productivity of power with Austin's notion of performativity (a performative utterance which effects what it utters rhetorically, e.g. 'I name this ship . . . ') and Derrida's (1988) rewriting of performativity (in his debate with Searle), as iterability (repetition that involves constant recontextualisation and thus change), to produce the following argument:

> The question for rethinking discourse and power in terms of the future has several paths to follow: how to think power as resignification together with power as the convergence or interarticulation of relations of regulation, domination, constitution? How to know what might qualify as an affirmative resignification – with all the weight and difficulty of that labor –
>
> Performativity describes this relation of being implicated in that which one opposes . . .
>
> The effects of performatives, understood as discursive production, do not conclude at the terminus of a given statement or utterance, the passing of legislation, the announcement of a birth. The reach of their signifi-

ability cannot be controlled by the one who utters or writes, since such productions are not owned by the one who utters them. They continue to signify in spite of their authors, and sometimes against their authors' most precious intentions.

(Butler 1993: 240–1)

Her desire is to 'resignify' gender, to see compulsory heterosexuality as the product of a law which must also be productive of other excluded performances. Of that law she asks: 'What is its ontological status – is it juridical, oppressive and reductive in its workings, or does it inadvertently create the possibility of its own cultural displacement?' (Butler 1990: 38). This feminist work moves a long way from power as envisaged in the earlier Foucault, and much closer to the question of the elective nature of sexuality in the later books. It shares many intertexts with de Certeau and it is also metatheoretical, failing to engage with the specificities of genres, contexts, semiotic labours and material practices that might actually be involved in 'power as resignification' or in the pragmatics of performatives at the moment of utterance. As such, it is similar to much psychoanalytic feminism, which, in attempting to reverse or subvert the Cartesian dualism of mind and body, has in fact converted a politics of language into a political poetics of the body; never, however, without language effects. This move is accomplished through Lacan, who provided the concept of the imaginary body constructed in language – a body which is basically, therefore, fictional and can be rewritten, reinscribed. What is more, it can perhaps be recovered from the moment before the violence of the institution of cultural form, the Oedipal moment of the entry into the symbolic. Pheng (1994: 137), speaking of Jane Gallop's work, has argued that this move constitutes the 'violence' of academic feminism, since it accomplishes the relegation of 'the other woman' to a nowhere that is not even the pre-symbolic which, in this move, is thus coloured white (and probably middle-class and intellectual).

Butler's work is more sophisticated than this. She does not accept that there is a body before the law, and she has tried very hard to rewrite the narratives of psychoanalysis so that the law which produces heterosexual difference would also produce racial difference (Butler 1993: 182). Her metaphor/narrative of performing gender is seductive and productive in her writing, but the gendered body which performs does so in fictions, again in a place apart from the material and institutional constraints on real bodies. Pheng, echoing some of the sentiments of Ien Ang quoted at the end of Chapter 3, therefore questions the political sense of the metaphor of inscription, and rewriting which is very close in fact to the metaphor of performativity – asking whether it constitutes an adequate model of agency in a neocolonialist space, whether that space may not be one in which even the *nature*, the materiality of bodies, is constructed against their will:

But if we cross to decolonised space, inscription will unfortunately exceed the undoubtedly important horizons of sexual preference and the choice to cross-dress or engage in sado-masochistic sex. Because we would here have to consider embodiment at the mundane level of food production, consumption and super-exploitation outside wage-labour, the concept-metaphor of inscription will have to be rethought as habitation. This might suggest that oppression occurs not at the level of the affective experience of our bodies but in the very crafting of the materiality of our bodies . . . Materiality . . . bears the instituted trace of the spacing and timing of imperialism.

(Pheng 1994: 138–9)

Butler argues that woman is an ongoing discursive practice which cannot be said to begin or end, and is therefore open to intervention and resignification (1990: 32). She does appear to be conscious of the difficulties of knowing what might consititute 'an affirmative resignification' (1993: 240). However, the politics of the performative speech act, its iterability, its unforeseen effects, its productivity, cannot be substituted for social and political theory, for textual analysis, for understandings of the materiality of corporeal alienation. The kind of crafting of the materiality of the body of which Pheng Cheah speaks cannot be so easily made to signify differently. There is, in fact, a whole set of questions about habituation, about musculature, about branding, about the training and disciplining (also in the sense of punishing) of bodies which I do not believe Butler's theory really manages to address. Actual performance and rehearsal in the theatre would belie any simple theory of the transformation of the body of the actor into another differently lived or crafted body. And there are social sites – the domestic space where a 'battered woman' kills her battering spouse, for example – where a theory of the performative speech act is hardly adequate to describe either the pain which precedes, or the institutionalised battering which follows – an act which may or may not be characterised as an act of resistance. What I am suggesting here is that it may be unwise and perhaps dangerous to accept these metaphors as empirical tools. The material realities are more complex and it may well be that it is only those with a certain level of cultural and economic capital and the right colour skin whose lives as discursive practices are really open to any intervention or resignification of this theoretical kind.

Chapter 5

Rewriting linguistic poetics
The trace of the corporeal

I argued in the first chapter of this book that there had been a gradual shift in the course of this century from a focus on the *poetics* to the *poiesis* of textuality, a move from the analysis of the verbal text as autonomous artefact to much more complex understandings of the embodied and processual making of meanings in complex social and cultural contexts. I also argued that that process of change had been accompanied by a move from a belief in analysis and metalanguage to a refusal of the latter in favour of a performance and narrativity which would always acknowledge the embodied and interested participation of the no longer observer/analyst. Chapters 2 to 4 have been exploring the intertextual and textual traces of these dialogues between a theoretical poetics (structuralism, modernism) and a performative *poiesis* (poststructuralism, postmodernism), pointing to some of the constitutive elements of the former in the making of the latter, and to the essential differences between the two. At the end of the last chapter, I began to suggest that metaphors and narratives were also metalinguistic and could not be otherwise in theoretical contexts, and that the metalanguage of a certain kind of linguistics might at least be no less oppressive than the intellectual performance of metaphors seemed to have turned out to be in the effort to understand just how it is that readers, writers and texts go on making one another and the objects of which they speak. I also suggested that there is much that is metaphorical about the representation of linguistics – and of structuralism – in the discourses of current social and political theory.

In the contexts I have been exploring, linguistics and structuralism and semiotics have been found to be patriarchal (de Lauretis), to be objectifying science (Foucault), to have been guilty of the attempted colonisation (as metalanguage) of all other semiotic systems (de Lauretis, Eco), to have been responsible for the construction of the standard language as a 'takeover' of all other dialects (Deleuze and Guattari, Bourdieu), and in feminist discourse (Irigaray, Kristeva) for the oppression of all women. There have been some very strange things said about language and women, many of them fuelled by the now much more dominant discourse of psychoanalysis – more dominant, that is, than linguistics is, in feminisms – where the Lacanian symbolic (effectively *langue* in Saussure's sense) has been written as patriarchal, the law of the father and therefore as necessarily oppressive of women. I have written elsewhere about feminist narratives of linguistic oppression and the need to counter them with some more sophisticated linguistic understandings of the way language works (Poynton 1985; Threadgold 1988), but it is not just psychoanalysis that seems to be the problem here.

As I indicated in the last chapter, the common understanding of 'linguistic' is very much limited to certain logical, philosophical and American structuralist understandings of what 'linguistics' as theory/metalanguage might mean, so that, for example, speech act theory, on its own, becomes a theory of language *and* performance in some contexts, and all linguistics is rejected in others. On the other hand, linguistic structures themselves (the structures of the language we speak and write) come to be seen, in the abstract, as constitutive of oppressive social orders of meaning.

Judith Butler (1990) has argued that the humanist conception of the gendered subject is a product of 'what language constitutes as the imaginable domain of gender', 'a substantive person who is the bearer of various essential and non-essential attributes' (Butler 1990: 18–19) – for example, the noun and its adjective, the subject and its predicate. The grammatical categories, she argues, also produce the philosophical concepts of 'being' and 'substance': 'It was grammar (the structure of subject and predicate) that inspired Descartes' certainty that "I" is the subject of "think"' (Haar 1977: 17–18, quoted in Butler 1990: 21). Gender is not, she argues, thinkable in these grammatical terms. It is not something one is, but something one performs. For Irigaray, on the other hand, grammar/language is phallogocentric to the point where there can be no feminine subject in language at all, and 'this sex which is not one' is also a (grammatical) subject which is not one (Butler 1990: 11).

There are some extraordinary confusions here – between language as system (*langue*, the symbolic) and the practice of language, between the metalanguage of linguistics or philosophies of language (*subject* and *predicate* and *noun* and *attribute*), and the actual structures of the language itself, not as ordered and arranged by the metalanguage, but as lived and performed. Butler herself demonstrates the possibility of thinking outside the structures she says determine thought, and Irigaray is nothing if not a speaking and grammatical subject in her own texts. There is the need to contextualise the structure *subject and predicate* in the co-text in which it is articulated, a co-text which may very well unsettle any universal meaning that structure in and of itself may have. There is also the need to contextualise and frame these large assertions about the power of language to form and produce realities and subject positions. Butler does locate the constraints of the 'hegemonic' masculine signifying practices she is talking about in 'the regulatory practices' identified by Foucault as productive of gender norms (1990: 17) and in the history of philosophy, but Irigaray's statements about language are universalist and untenable in any actual context of language use.

The more fundamental point, however, is how to think resistance to phallogocentric linguistic norms if you have only *subject and predicate* as the linguistic arsenal with which to do it. Marcus (1992), as one example, has moved beyond the structure of the clause to the discourse category of the 'script', a 'gendered grammar of violence' which positions both men and women to behave in certain ways (1992: 392). Her response is to argue that women should rewrite the script, 'frighten rape culture to death', responding with female violence and the refusal to believe in the rapist's body as 'powerfully real and really powerful' (1992: 401). Metaphorically, this intervention is an important one because it finally stops constructing women as the victims of language or 'scripts', and suggests they have the power to rewrite them. However, this advice, based in an (at best) partial understanding of the powers of representation and signification, ignores the very real social and legal dangers in which this becoming-agent may place women, dangers which become very clear in the case of spousal murder, where abused women do murder their husbands (McCarthy 1995; Threadgold 1995). It is advice which shows no understanding of the difficulties and unpredictabilities of making an intervention at one level of what is in fact a very much more complex set of interlocking structures (Threadgold 1994; Frow 1995b). There are the discursive structures which produce the rape script in the first place, the institutional domains and cultural structures in which those discourses circulate and are regularly generically reactivated (Cameron and Frazer 1987), the sedimented and multi-levelled structures of legal practice in which any resistance to such a script would inevitably be next located, and the predispositions of bodily habitus in all those places. For that habitus, the existing 'script' is a way of living the body, a set of beliefs 'learned by the body' which are not things 'one has . . . but something that one is' (Bourdieu 1980/1990: 73), and which are therefore difficult, if not impossible, to change with a single one-on-one and dangerous intervention in a single local site. The concept of the 'script' here is close to Propp's understanding of the folk-tale or to a generic schema of a fairly limited kind (Propp 1928/1968; Labov and Waletsky 1967). There is little understanding of the fact that no one genre (script) of violence can be privileged as the determinant of all effects of violence.

Mills (1995) provides an excellent introduction to modes of feminist stylistics (McConnell-Ginet 1980; Burton 1982), making use of feminist work in sociolinguistics (Cameron 1985; Coates 1986; Coates and Cameron 1988), feminist linguistics (Lakoff 1975; Edelsky 1977) and critical linguistics (Fairclough 1992a) to develop modes of feminist reading of different textual levels, including the discursive and focusing on reading for gendered representations in texts. She also addresses the issue of women and writing in a chapter called 'The Gendered Sentence', which tackles the debate in feminism about whether women actually write or speak differently to men. Some time ago, struggling with feminist arguments about precisely this issue – about language oppressing women and feminist ideas of writing as woman, *écriture féminine*, which would subvert that linguistic oppression – I wrote about the stylistic similarities in the writings of Irigaray and Derrida, about the feminist struggle with meanings involved in writing at all in these contexts, and about the fact that men too had difficulties making language and texts mean what they wanted them to mean and making representations of the previously 'unthought' comprehensible to new audiences (Threadgold 1988). Newton struggling to make a new scientific register and genre (Chapter 2 above) is one example; Derrida's (1988) struggles to make Searle understand 'what he meant' is another. Elizabeth Grosz (1995a) has recently addressed a number of these issues again in ways that are useful here.

Rejecting the sex of the author, content or style as possible determinants of a feminist text (a feminine writing), she turns to the sex of the reader, and reminds us that even a gendered reader remains subject to the text's materiality, a materiality which exerts a resistance not only to the intentions of the author but also to the readings and uses it may be put to by readers. In the case of the author, the text is subject to what Derrida called *destinerrance*, a tendency to go astray, 'to never arrive at its destination' or indeed to arrive at an unintended destination (Grosz 1995a: 17). The signature of the author is no guarantee of anything, because it always requires a counter-signature, someone to sign for it, a reader, but the reader is not free to read or receive at will: 'writing . . . must be capable of functioning in the radical absence of every empirical receiver in general' (Derrida 1988: 8) and thus always has its own ways of offering resistance to the one who countersigns. All of this supplies support from an unexpected source – the Derrida who is accused of promoting a belief in the indeterminacy of meaning – for detailed and careful understandings of the materiality of texts. In this sense, Derrida, like the structuralists, places the burden of signification in the text, not in consciousness.

Returning to the issue of women and writing, somewhat loath to define the feminist text at all because of a 'Foucauldian anxiety about what power is invested in providing definitive categories' (Grosz 1995a: 18) and acknowledging the fact that the same text may be read as feminist in some contexts and not in others, Grosz nonetheless suggests some guidelines. Reading Benveniste's work on the relations between enunciation and the enounced with Derrida on the signature, Grosz (1995a: 18) argues that, while the subject of the enunciation and of the enounced cannot be presumed to be identical, they also cannot be definitively separated. This is because the process of enunciation is always inscribed in the act of utterance itself, producing what Derrida has called the fundamentally folded character of the writer/text/reader relationship: 'the fact that as a product the text is an effect of labour, a work on and with signs, a collaborative (even hostile) labor of writing and reading' (Grosz 1995a: 20). Grosz uses Butler's concept of the performativity of gender 'bodies and discourses producing one another' to suggest 'that there are ways that the sexuality and the corporeality of the subject leave their traces in the texts produced, just as . . . the processes of textual production also leave their trace or residue on the body of the writer (and readers)' (Grosz 1995a: 21). There are, then, despite her reluctance to categorise, and perhaps because of it, a number of 'relevant relations' that she argues need to be taken into account in thinking about what a feminist text might be and might accomplish. They are the following:

- The text will render visible the patriarchal or phallocentric assumptions governing the contexts in which it works, and question the power of those assumptions in the production, the reception and the assessment of texts.
- A feminist text will in some way problematise the standard masculinist ways in which the author occupies the position of enunciation, challenging the 'authoritative position of the one who knows'.
- A feminist text will not only challenge the patriarchal norms within which it works, but will help to produce new, sometimes unthought, discursive spaces – new styles, new forms of content, new ways of arguing, new genres – to contest the limits of current modes of textual production and reception and current modes of understanding these.

(adapted from Grosz 1995a: 22–4)

That said, there is no reason why such texts should not be produced by men, or any of women's others, and there is no guarantee that the text will not go astray and miss its destination or end up somewhere it was not meant to go. Nor is there any need to privilege particular modes of engagement with these aims or to privilege particular discourses or knowledges. Even the text of linguistics, of structuralism or of semiotics cannot rely on the signature in the kinds of 'enfolded' engagements with a feminist reader and writer that this Derridean metaphor suggests. The text will offer its resistances and it will bear the traces of the corporeality of its maker as will the text of any attempt to engage with it. It is interesting here, since I am endeavouring to foreground the intersections between structuralism and poststructuralism or postmodernism to remark an instance when Derrida's own text went astray in ways that are germane to these arguments. I am indebted to Kevin Hart for drawing my attention to this conjunction of events.

In the 1960s, Derrida was a philosopher in his thirties, writing for philosophers. He was invited to a conference in Baltimore, the 'International Colloquium on Critical Languages and the Sciences of Man'. The conference was intended to import structuralism into America. Jakobson's famous paper on 'Linguistics and Poetics' (1958/1981: 18–51) was presented at a conference on style held at Indiana University in 1958, and had been published in a collection called *Style in Language* (edited by Sebeok) in 1960.

Derrida spoke on the final day of the Baltimore conference (21 October 1966) and delivered a searing critique of structuralism in the paper called 'Structure, Sign and Play in the Discourse of the Human Sciences', a paper that was one of the first of many rereadings and rewritings of Lévi-Strauss's structuralist account of the 'scandal' of incest (Derrida 1978: 278–94; see also Chapter 3 above). The destination of Derrida's text was a certain French philosophical audience, but it was literary critics who, as it were, 'signed for it' and took it up. There was a certain 'errance', a tendency to wander, built into the codes, the genre, the vocabulary of Derrida's text, which enabled it to be taken up by an American audience of literary critics at Yale and elsewhere, whose 'reading formations', perceptions and investments intersected with its Jewishness, its Jewish modes of interpretation, its Europeanness. The dominant literary critical discourse of the time, not American philosophy, was the take-up point, and this removed structuralism from serious literary attention in a weekend. This had not a little to do with certain kinds of 'professional vision' and specific embodied histories. It was also largely an accident, and accidents are not to be taken lightly either in the histories of textual transmission or in the demise of structuralism.

Mills (1995), like Fairclough (1992a, 1995) in his critical discourse analysis, uses a version of functional linguistics in her feminist engagement with stylistics. Both she and Fairclough use a model of interdiscursive or intertextual relations (the interdiscourse or intertext being the trace in a particular text which makes possible the identification of other instances of the same sequence in other texts) (Mills 1995: 159), and Mills uses the concept of the gendered reader. Both are considerably influenced by poststructuralism and feminism. Others working in the Hallidayan functional tradition of critical linguistics in Australia have explicitly reworked the Hallidayan framework under the impact of poststructuralism and semiotics, and of all these things and feminism (Poynton 1985, 1990, 1993; Lee 1993; Wright 1993; Yell 1990, 1993). There was in that work much discussion about the fact that the theory did not have an adequate social theory to support the linguistics and the work of Foucault, and Bakhtin was an important influence in early attempts to rectify that (Thibault 1991; Lemke 1985, 1988; Kress 1985). What follows is my attempt to reread and rewrite Halliday in the context of that work and of the issues raised so far in this book.

LANGUAGE AS SOCIAL SEMIOTIC

In 1978 when he published *Language as Social Semiotic*, Michael Halliday sketched out what was then an extraordinarily rich proposal for a social theory of language and for a theory of language as a reality-constructing and reality-changing semiotic process. This is what I take a 'social semiotic' to be – a probabilistic, never entirely predictable system for making meanings which at once constructs and changes, and is constructed and changed by, social processes and social realities (Threadgold 1986). It is worth pointing here to the parallelism between Halliday's term 'probabilistic' and Derrida's term 'undecidability'. Both, in fact, derive from scientific discourses. Halliday's concept is from statistical probability theories. Derrida's term is not an antonym for 'decidability', but is derived from Gödel's work (Hofstadter 1980: 438) on metamathematics, which argues that any arithmetical system of any richness can generate at least one proposition that is true within the system but that cannot be accounted for in terms of the system. Derrida's point, then, rather like Halliday's, is that no system of interpretation (or of textual production) can ever fully account for the meaning of a text in a way that is both complete and consistent.

Halliday's theory of language as social semiotic (1978, 1985a, 1985b) needs to be clearly framed and contextualised in relation to its own intertextual history. A materialist theory of language which construed language in Whorfian (1956) and social-constructivist terms (Berger and Luckmann 1966) as a mode of representation which constructs social realities, social identities and social relations as well as being constructed by them, it explicitly rejected the Saussurean opposition between language as system and language as practice, tending to follow European linguistic, semiotic and functionalist traditions (Jakobson 1958/1981); Prague School linguistics (Matejka 1978; Mathesius 1911) rather than American structuralist ones (Halliday 1985b; Threadgold 1986). At the same time, the influence of Firth (1957) and British functionalist anthropology (Malinowski 1923), and work in the ethnography of communication (Hymes 1967; Cazden et al. 1972), constrained a very specific formulation of the relation between the textual and the social, or between the functions of language and the immediate contexts in which language was used.

Working with and against these traditions, Halliday developed his functional theory of language, seeing language as something that had evolved to serve the functions required of it by society, which were to represent the world, to allow interpersonal interaction and to construct coherent text. Thus the resources of the grammar of language were seen to be organised in terms of three metafunctions – the ideational (sometimes called the experiential), the interpersonal and the textual. These functions were constructed as 'realising', and producing, in a process of mutual action, the three elements of the immediate context in which language was used: the field (the ongoing-activity type or subject-matter being exchanged); the tenor (the role relationships and relations of power, status and affect involved); and the mode (whether the text was spoken or written and so on). These constituted the semiotic construct of context. More importantly for a feminist poetics, every clause structure in every text was understood as a complex polyphonic structure (Halliday in Thibault 1987: 611) of all three functions, conceived not according to the usual linguistic constituency models, but as a structure of particles (the experiential function) traversed by the interpersonal function and diffuse fields (prosodies) of interpersonal meaning and the wave-like, periodic structures of the textual function (Halliday 1979; Threadgold 1989):

> I sometimes use the metaphor of polyphonic music: that, in a sense, you have one unfolding melodic line from the experiential, another melodic line from the interpersonal, and another from the textual component. These operate through three major systems at the clause rank: the transitivity, the mood and the theme.
>
> (Thibault 1987: 611)

Halliday (1978) has suggested that it was the linguistic/anthropological tradition of Boas–Sapir–Whorf which contributed to his understanding of the experiential component, Malinowski–Firth and the socio-anthropological tradition (including Mary Douglas) to that of the interpersonal and Mathesius and the literary rhetorical tradition to his understanding of the textual function. There is in fact no direct influence here at all from contemporary cultural and social theory, although it would not have been absent intertextually in the texts he was reading. This may have protected Halliday from being positioned by some of its more problematic assumptions about the way the social and the cultural were constructed, but it also meant that, in effect, he constructed his view of the social and the cultural from the understandings of linguistic function he had gleaned in these other contexts. Halliday always called the combination of field, tenor and mode the 'semiotic construct' of context, and Hasan (1985) continues to refer to it as the 'contextual configuration'. It is also very clear from the influence of Malinowski, Firth and Hymes, among others (Halliday 1985b), that, however mediated by semiosis or construed through language, this was intended to be the actual material, corporeal, spatial, temporal context of the utterance. The language, the text as social action, and the practice/site are actually theorised as an integrated contextual configuration. It was the beginnings of a theory of the social, but one that was projected from a theory of language into that space and which therefore could never be adequate as social theory. There are material linguistic traces in texts of bodies and of spatio-temporal contexts, but they are only traces and never sufficient either to reconstitute their social 'origins' or to predict the ways in which the text may be 'taken up', signed for.

In many ways Halliday's theory of the social is also a projection upwards from language through the semiotic construct of context to the social system, again construed as three separate spheres: the *social structure, the context of culture* and *the adult linguistic system*. The *adult linguistic system* is mediated by the first two as an institution which accounts for linguistic variation and conflict. The account of the *social structure* (family role systems, social class and hierarchy, and status and role relationships) is very much overdetermined by Halliday's reading of Bernstein's (1971, 1975) work in the sociology of education, work which has connections with that of Bourdieu and Foucault (Threadgold 1987), and which introduced a materialist economic or class-based argument, and potentially a speaking subject, into the theory, in the form of 'a subject constructed in language' and possessed of 'semiotic coding orientations' (Bernstein's elaborated and restricted codes). This subject was derived from the 'critical socializing contexts' of the family in its different class configurations. Speaking subjects, in other words, were produced (made) by the class contexts of the family. Their ability to make meanings with the resources of the linguistic system was marked, at least in early schooling, by a context- and class-produced 'orientation' towards meaning.

It is thus the intersections between *social structure*, so defined, and *language as institution* that produces social dialect variation, linguistic variation of class and geographical kinds that derives from difference as a constitutive feature of social structure. Notions of embodiment and its relations to consciousness, of differential access to economic, cultural and symbolic capital, of the 'power takeover' of the dominant language, relations of power and discursively positioned subjectivity, even of habitus, are not incompatible with this construction. But they never quite emerge from the nominalisations of modernist social theory which structure Halliday's texts – *social hierarchy, social role, adult linguistic system, text, semiotic codes, coding orientation*, and so on.

The *context of culture* was configured very much as the context of disciplinary knowledges within which linguistics as discipline and knowledge operated (1978: 11). In this sense, it was comparable to Foucault's early understandings of 'discourse' as discipline but taken for granted, not seen as 'enigmatic' as Foucault saw it. Language as institution, in that context, was again subject to variation, this time the register variation produced, again probabilistically, in and through different knowledge formations. Register is a semantic or linguistic concept in Halliday; it is the effects of context on text that produce it. It is the traces of corporeality in the text, if you like (Thibault 1987: 610).

Language, then, is a social semiotic in the sense that its functional organisation as system (as the potential for language use in social interaction) is a symbol of (is a semiotic/interpretant [in Peirce's sense] of) the structure of human interaction in society. On the other hand, its function as institution (language shaped and formed in and through social institutions) symbolises social structure (including class structure) and the structure of human knowledges:

So language while it represents reality *referentially*, through its words and structures, also represents reality *metaphorically* through its own internal and external form. (1) The functional organisation of the semantics symbolizes the structure of human interaction (the semiotics of social contexts . . .) (2) Dialectal and 'diatypic' (register) variation symbolize respectively the structure of society and the structure of human knowledge.

But as language becomes a metaphor of reality, so by the same process reality becomes a metaphor of language. Since reality is a social construct, it can be constructed only through an exchange of meanings. Hence meanings are seen as constitutive of reality.

(Halliday 1978: 191)

It was, I think, this understanding of language as an interpretant, a metaphor for the social, powerful as I think that understanding itself remains, which effectively blocked, contained, attempts to understand the social in its difference to language.

What remains useful for critical work, perhaps particularly for the traditions of interdiscursivity, are Halliday's understandings of language and text themselves. Produced/made text in these Hallidayan formulations was already potentially *not* monologic text; that is, it was not in any sense text which spoke with one voice. Every text as linear wording involved the polyphony and the non-isomorphism of the three functions of language – the ideational/experiential, the interpersonal and the textual – and might also realise, mapped across these same apparently linear wordings, linguistic variation of the register and dialect type, the traces in the text of the social interaction, the social structure and the institutional contexts in which it was produced. The particular configuration of all these possible inflections of the language in realised text was what Halliday called 'register'. In practice the term 'register' was used to explore language use in institutional contexts, for example scientific English (Huddleston 1971), and the concept of 'coding orientation' was used in Halliday's interventions into primary school pedagogy (1978: Ch. 13). But the existence of both concepts of difference in language effectively meant that Halliday did not see the link between text and context as one of appropriateness, but as one of fundamental difference in which speakers with different coding orientations might behave very differently in the same context. This has not stopped the theory of register and text/context relationships, transformed into a doctrine of appropriateness, and written into curriculum documents, from being used in Great Britain and Australia to suppress linguistic difference in the classroom (Fairclough 1992a; Cameron 1995), yet another example of a text going astray and not being read the way Halliday 'might have meant'.

Halliday's was clearly not a theory of Bakhtinian heteroglossia, nor a theory of intertextuality or interdiscursivity in either Kristeva's (Threadgold 1986) or Foucault's senses (Fairclough 1992a), and it was in practice a theory of textual structure (a poetics) not of textual production or of readership (a *poiesis*). But it did provide a theory for thinking how it was that the details of lexicogrammar might be related through social interaction to social context, always implicitly and later explicitly (Halliday 1985b), including the likelihood of interdiscursive or intertextual interactions between texts as a consequence of that process. It is the complexity of what is involved here, on a number of levels, the multiplicity of potential recontextualisations between and among strata, a process that is at best probabilistic, that is able to protect the theory (although it has not always done so) from a stratal homogeneity or isomorphism between these different levels or orders of meaning-making and opens it up to rewriting in poststructuralist terms. This is no doubt what prompted a number of early rereadings of Halliday in Bakhtinian terms (Lemke 1985; Thibault 1984), and prompted my own early comparison of Halliday's work to that of Voloshinov (Threadgold 1986).

REWRITING REGISTER

Halliday's understanding of register as the total set of patterns of linguistic 'choice' in a text, patterns which located it in a specific, usually institutional context, was a good place to start. However, for different people, and for different reasons, it began to be theorised differently. What had been 'register', still as an explicitly textual phenomenon, was coming to be understood in the Australian context as heteroglossia and dialogism, with a developing distinction between what I now read as the position of the enunciation and the constitution of the enounced. The position of the enunciation was beginning to be articulated with theories of rhetorical purpose or generic schema (Longacre 1974; Hasan 1985; Martin 1985a, 1985b), and the enounced, what was uttered, was coming to be seen as an even more polyphonic structure than it had been in Halliday. Now, made text was seen to be potentially realising simultaneously the multifunctionality of Halliday's clause grammar, and the intertextual or the interdiscursive, including dialect or register patterns from other texts and contexts. Halliday himself did not use the concept of intertextuality until 1985 (1985b: 47), by which time it had become a part of the way he framed the relations between texts and contexts, relations which were becoming much less hierarchical and much more spatialised than the 1978 formulation of higher and lower order contextual relations had suggested.

Foucault's work on discourse was being used to think through questions of text/context relations and to identify the lexicogrammatical traces in texts of the 'places where the words/discourse had been before', to misquote Bakhtin slightly (Threadgold 1987, 1988; Lemke 1988; Kress 1985). Poststructuralist (or postmodernist) work on the narrativity of all knowledges (Lyotard 1979/1984), work on the metaphoricity of all language (Ricoeur 1978, 1986), and Derridean work on genre (both its inevitability and its iterability [Derrida 1980]) was influencing my own understandings of the kinds of interdiscourses/intertextuality that might be traceable in the lexicogrammar of text (Kress and Threadgold 1988). These would include traces of discourses in Foucault's sense, narratives, metaphorical configurations in Ricoeur's, and possibly traces of other genres as well as of other registers and dialects. Indeed it seemed to me that what Foucault had called discourses – the discourse of childhood, of sexuality, of penality, for example – might also involve, in their verbal modes, typical narratives, metaphors and even registers or embedded genres, as well as smaller units of text. Any of these might constitute the verbal statements of a discourse which were then only a part of all of the potential statements of that discourse that might be realised in semiotic media other than the verbal. None of these things were themselves texts (whole generic forms). They were configurations of the 'statements' of a discourse realised in and through other texts as the generic forms typical of some particular larger discursive formation (medicine, the cinematic apparatus, a particular discipline, and so on).

This, of course, changed the nature of the task that had been textual or discourse analysis. It now required, indeed, an immersion in discourse, in the discursive formations to which the text one was investigating belonged interdiscursively, and an active participation in the practices that were producing the texts, a self-reflexive and gendered ethnography and an awareness of the professional vision (Goodwin 1994), the practices of imaging (de Lauretis 1984), which might shape what one could see.

GENRE

Text, produced in social interaction, never occurs without a generic shape and some kind of interpersonal or rhetorical purpose. Poynton's (1985, 1990), Yell's (1993) and Thibault's (1991) work on the interpersonal function of language and on conversation within the Hallidayan tradition was beginning to unsettle the Hallidayan idea of the interpersonal as either 'an exchange of meanings or goods and services' or as *only* a diffuseness in and across all texts. This work was beginning to foreground the position of the enunciation (my terminology, not theirs) or 'voice' and to prioritise the personal, emotional aspects of language over the representational and the textual, insisting on the productive, meaning-making, aspects of interaction. This prompted me (Threadgold 1988, 1989; Kress and Threadgold 1988) to think of genre as sets of strategies or processes which shaped not only the making of text, but the remaking of discourse or intertextual resources as these were reactivated in some particular textual and generic encounter.

I came to understand genres (in the literary rhetorical sense used in Fowler 1982; Hauptmeier 1987; Bazerman 1988; Swales 1990) as text types which specified a position of enunciation, typical modes of address and possible positions for an audience, and constrained textual and intertextual labour, the work of making text. Socially, genres clearly had to be understood both as models for making texts and, once made, as models for understanding them. On the other hand, the interaction between genre and the complexities of a multifunctional and socially located and various language, and the intertextual resources of 'discourse' as I defined these above, meant that genres too were likely to be constantly reconstituted as they refashioned the ready-made stuff of intertextuality.

Van Leeuwen's (1987) work on 'Generic Strategies in Press Journalism' had analysed the way in which in the 'news story' 'many different, partly contradictory, partly overt and partly covert social purposes are translated into generic structures' (1987: 199). In his corpus of ten texts, he identified subgenres such as 'short reports', 'features' and 'editorials', including phases of narration, description, exposition, procedure and adhortation. Working in the newsroom he was able to bring together native informant type analyses/labellings of genres and modes with explicit linguistic accounts of the ways in which these are realised in actual texts. His conclusion, based on social and linguistic analysis, was that there is no evidence for a single generic schema of obligatory stages which could explain the genre of the texts. He saw the structure of the texts as better explained in terms of a network of generic choices or strategies which are available as the context-specific strategies which realise the social purposes of journalism in a specific context (1987). Van Leeuwen's work is not just about language or about narrowly defined text structures derived from folk linguistic labels. It is a critique and an analysis of those labels, and it is about social structure, cultural realities, and the socially produced and disciplined agents of social institutions and practices (journalists and the media).

Genres, then, as in the case of Newton in Chapter 2, also had to be related through their typical performances in context to institutions – the everyday, the family, the school, the law, the state, the bureaucracy, the media – to relations of power and ruling, and to questions of social difference – of sexuality, race and ethnicity as well as class (all but the latter questions that had never been addressed in Halliday's theory). Genres were processes, *poiesis*, not products, and constantly subject to negotiated constraint and change.

HABITUS: CORPOREALITY AND THE TEXT

Such conclusions called out for a theorising of the person/s who were performing these intricate textual manoeuvres in these various sites and that, finally, took me to social theory. I have been talking above about texts, genres, narratives, intertextuality and discourses. Such categories cannot do anything without people. They are the forms in which we recognise the material traces of bodies and contexts in texts, and they have been called by many other names. Some of the typical names include 'member's resources', codes, scripts and frames, dialogism, even intertextuality. My question is: How do they get into bodies, how do they brand and mark bodies, how is the gendered and differentiated body implicated in this relation between text and context? Mine is the same question that produced de Lauretis's sexed and habituated imaging subject in Chapter 3 above.

Poynton (1990: 248) argued that it was not only the immensely complex and probabilistic nature of semiotic systems themselves, but also 'the specificity of the linguistic (semiotic) demands made by the individual's personal history', which generated variability of forms and meanings. She concluded that the 'expressive/emotive' dimensions of language were little understood as semiotic resources for producing 'structures of feeling':

> The attachment of feeling to representation is of particular importance for the circulation of ideologies, because it involves *a virtual physical attachment of people to beliefs and values*, thereby ensuring a fierce commitment to those beliefs and values and resistance to attempts 'to take them away' by means of argument.
>
> (Poynton 1990: 251–2; my italics)

This is reminiscent of Bourdieu's 'belief is a state of the body not of the mind' (1980/1990), and both positions raise profound questions about centring attempts at social change on language or representation alone. Linguists (Rossi-Landi 1977; Martin 1985b) and social theorists (such as Habermas) who see ideology as the result of a failure of *intellectual* labour – a failure to work communicatively or critically on a text which has become reified, its processes of production forgotten – fail to theorise this folding of the body into its texts, this work done by texts on bodies. There is a considerable difference between forgetfulness as an intellectual phenomenon to be corrected by rational reminding, and a 'fierce commitment', a corporeal attachment to beliefs and values.

Rossi-Landi (1977), however, does provide some useful arguments. Like Halliday, Hjelmslev (1943/1961: 115) and Lévi-Strauss (1963), he believed that the systems with which linguists usually worked were far too narrow, stopping short at explaining the level of the sentence, 'so that various pieces of knowledge are left to wander about on their own, without any attempt to bring them together' (1977: 112). Rossi-Landi proposes an alternative view of the stuff of which we make cultural texts, a system of what he calls 'parking lots of artefacts' (paradigms), a constant mixture of verbal and non-verbal or non-discursive categories. Such parking lots include the possibility of 'ready-made' artefacts at sentence level and above (utensils and sentences, mechanisms and syllogisms, self-sufficient mechanisms and lectures or books, automated machines and subcodes and lexicons, special constructions and objectual and verbal programming codes, and so on), which parallel the ready-made nature of the phoneme at the lowest level of linguistic articulation (Rossi-Landi 1977: 107–10). 'Artefacts . . . *pour out of the productive process and stay there waiting.*' They are the coagulations of work and they are remarkably resistant to the 'entry of new influences from outside'. They tend to remain what they are even if they are used in new productive processes, and, 'of course, they do not lose their properties if they are *not* used' (Rossi-Landi 1977: 108). This is a position which is reminiscent of Derrida's insistence on the materiality and resistances of the text.

What he is talking about here is precisely the kind of Peircean networked semiotic space that Eco and de Lauretis describe, a space in which meanings are not confined to moving within the well-policed spaces of a single semiotic system (de Saussure's *langue*, for example), but can cross those boundaries. This was Eco's (1979) model of infinite semiosis. Like Rossi-Landi, Eco believed that it was the labouring subject of semiosis who could change this space. We have already seen (in Chapter 3 above) the way de Lauretis went back to Peirce to relocate that work in a sexed body marked by its previous encounters with semiosis. But Rossi-Landi's artefacts are also the genres, narratives, myths, metaphors and discourses I was discussing above.

The most useful aspect of Rossi-Landi's argument for feminism is that it provides support for the theory of the intertextual rather than only word-by-word construction of texts, and that it suggests that 'forgetfulness' can be remedied, the 'coagulated' products of cultural production can be rewritten. At the same time, it argues that that cannot be done without a re-membering (deconstruction) of the elements of which they were made in the first place. That, to me, suggests that feminist rewriting cannot work only at the levels of ready-made products (intertextuality). It must also work at the level of the words and phrases of which they are made. It must learn to know their grammar; but the grammar is in the body.

Rossi-Landi locates the parking lots of linguistic artefacts in the body, the labouring (but not gendered body) of the Marxist subject:

> Here the problem may arise of the nature or ontological *status* of linguistic parking lots as distinguished from material parking lots, and with it the question of finding their proper place or locus . . . Linguistic objects are a part of verbal sign systems. Now once one has admitted that verbal sign systems 'are in' the nervous system of individuals ('internal material dimension' and the question of differential traces: 2.4.1–2) and that they constitute moreover, groups of univocal sound stimuli commonly received and transmitted in speech-acts, as well as groups of the corresponding graphical stimuli listed in dictionaries and grammars and used in everything that is printed (5.1, 5.2.3, 6.5), one has said all that it is possible to say about their ontological *status* and about their locus at *this level of generality*.
>
> (Rossi-Landi 1977: 109, n. 44)

For Rossi-Landi, there is no question – as there was for Eco (1979) – about the material traces of texts in bodies, about the corporeal effects of texts on bodies. Those traces are 'in the nervous system' and presumably the musculature, the habitus of the body. The latter is something about which Rossi-Landi, this time a little like Eco, has nothing more to say. It is, however, relevant to the performativity of that body (Butler 1990, 1993), to the issue of just what complexities of a material kind (sinews, muscles, nervous system), as well as representational or discursive kind, might be involved in changing or redirecting that performativity. The question of how a body comes to know its own emotional investments and to recognise its own made habitus to the point where it wants (desires) to remember, to make itself differently, remains unanswered. In Chapter 6, I will suggest that the theatrical rehearsal room offers some ways of thinking about these issues.

Poynton's (1990) arguments begin, with the work of feminist scholars in other fields, to address these questions. Gatens (1989) has theorised resistance to change, explaining the incredible energies men and women expend in maintaining, rather than changing, their conditions of oppression. Her work explored the ways in which cultural understandings of bodies, the ways bodies are lived and constituted as part of a network of other bodies, the images we have of our bodies, affect the ways those bodies are lived. Her focus here was on the ease with which bodies could be made to signify as 'other', on the lived experience of alienation, and on the ethics of such questions of difference. Grosz (1995a: 63) writes of the way 'power actively marks or brands bodies' so that consciousness is 'an effect or result' of the making social of the body. Lloyd (1989), seeking a different philosophy to Descartes' story of disembodied, desexed minds, tells another story which comes from Spinoza. It is a story of mind as 'an idea of the body':

> The body is not an underlying cause of the mind's awareness and knowledge, but rather the mind's object – what it knows. And the mind knows itself only through reflection on its ideas of the body. Its nature is to be the idea of a particular body.
>
> (Lloyd 1989: 20–1)

Minds must, then, be sexually differentiated, multifaceted, realising the complexity and difference of the bodies of which they are ideas: 'Female minds will be formed by socially imposed limitations on the powers and pleasures of female bodies' (Lloyd 1989: 21). These feminist stories recall for me de Lauretis's theorising of the gendered semiotics of experience and habitchange and of the way those processes differ for different kinds of bodies and subjects. The feminist stories include power, pleasure, feeling, and the shaping and marking of the body and consciousness by the materiality of the social and of language. They also connect with Bourdieu's sociology of the habitus:

> The *habitus* – embodied history, internalised as second nature and so forgotten as history – is the active presence of the whole past of which it is a product. As such, it is what give practices their relative autonomy with respect to external determinations of the immediate present . . .
>
> Thus the dualistic vision that recognises only the self-transparent act

of consciousness or the externally determined thing has to give way to the real logic of action, which brings together two objectifications of history, objectification in bodies and objectifications in institutions, or, two states of capital, objectified and incorporated . . .

(Bourdieu 1980/1990: 57)

Later Bourdieu will argue that the habitus is the institution made flesh, the performance of institution, social class and sexual difference 'confirmed by social treatments' and by 'the act of marking' (1980/1990: 72). The habitus can be changed, he argues, by writing *the body* differently. At this point the focus has to be on rewriting the body, *re-membering* the body, to effect social change. But, if the body and the text are enfolded as suggested at the outset of this chapter, it will not be too circular an argument to insist that work on and with texts will also always be work on and with bodies. These are useful stories for a feminism seeking to accomplish social change and they have already proved productive in research into literacy as an embodied and not merely intellectual practice, research which has focused on the production of habitus and on the conditions and social practices that might be necessary to make it differently (Kamler et al.: 1994).

Part of what the body is is the history of the texts and the places and networks of bodies where it has been before: the ways in which it has been materially marked, 'branded' by and in practice, the sexed and coloured differences it has lived, the limits that have been imposed on its access to cultural and symbolic capital (Bourdieu 1991). But there is also the investment, the desire, feeling, pleasure and pain, the memories, and the possibility of negotiating the multiple positions which have interpellated the body in those histories, the things we sometimes nominalise as 'agency'. And that, it seems to me, is better accounted for, or accounted for as well, by de Lauretis's (1984) materialist and semiotic theory of a sexed consciousness produced in active interaction with perception and signification.

Between them, these theories begin to account for a social order which is *both* imbricated in language, textuality and semiosis *and* is corporeal, spatial, temporal, institutional, conflictual, and marked by sexual, racial and other differences. They also account for the fact that the texts produced in such probabilistic encounters are both constrained by, and always also exceed the limits of, the immediate context of utterance. What is in the body, inscribed on the body, lived through the body, cannot be contained by any present context and nor can we imagine how we access the 'higher order social semiotic' without recourse to theories of the body. This is why Halliday's understandings of those relationships remain useful as a way of starting to deal with the difficulties. But it also explains why, in the end, and as Foucault and de Lauretis showed, there can be no easy way of thinking the text/context relationship.

INTERTEXTUALITY AND THE TEXTUAL FUNCTION OF LANGUAGE AS EMBODIED PERFORMANCE

While the interpersonal function of language marks the overt presence of the body in the text, it is the textual function of language which most clearly marks the corporeal trace. Halliday's understanding of the textual function of language was a theory of the structures of coherence in text, but it was also a complex and potentially very valuable theory in a poststructuralist context such as the above, with an extraordinary interest in intertextuality (Halliday and Hasan 1976; Halliday 1985a). It was conceived in two ways, or in terms of two major systems of meaning. Both were seen as functional in relating texts to their contexts of production. The first, cohesion, involved lexical collocation (patternings of lexical words recognised on the basis of similarity, difference and part/whole or metonymic relations) and grammatical phenomena such as reference (e.g. anaphora, cataphora, reference back and forth in the co-text from a point in the text), ellipsis (again a metonymic relation involving the recognition of an absence and the ability to fill it from co-textual or contextual knowledge), substitution (recognition of this form, e.g. 'she' [pronoun], as a substitution for that one, e.g. 'the woman' [noun]) and conjunction (logical relations of connection within the text). What understanding these textual resources enabled was a tracking of the probabilistic making of text, of the patterns which made whole text structures (such as genres, for example) internally coherent and cohesive with and comprehensible in context. It was thus, and this it does not say, also connecting those patterns to contexts via an implicit reader who could recognise the patterns metonymically (for which read also indexically or deictically) or metaphorically, and move back and forth in the co-text of this text, and in and out of this text to context (presumably configured as knowledge of other texts, of language as system and institution, of genres, and so on – the kind of knowledge embodied in the habitus). It also implies a writer with similar resources who will produce text in a similar fashion.

Cohesion, then, has the potential to describe in detail some of the complex ways in which speakers and writers make text and are positioned by and in text in social interaction (discourse). It is already implicitly intertextual: lexical collocation, patterns of vocabulary in texts, particularly, is a kind of 'code' which speakers will only be able to access from their embodied experience of text in other contextual configurations.

The second system is that of theme–rheme organisation, the way in which the clause as message is organised to begin somewhere (theme) and to end somewhere else (rheme). Halliday describes this as a wave-like or periodic rhetorical feature of text. Specific genres generally have particular ways of patterning their theme–rheme organisation, for example, never using as theme what was rheme in the previous sentence, or always doing so or doing something else altogether. This system, however, although described as textual, also clearly has critical implications for understanding both the traces of corporeality, of writing, in text and the interpersonal negotiation of texts. In Halliday's work it is connected prosodically with the system of given and new information, so that what comes first (as theme) is typically given information (assumed to be known to writer and reader), and what comes last (bearing the focal stress in the rheme, the second part of the clause) is new information for the reader, but also tells a reader where the writer wants them to be positioned. There are many ways of changing that arrangement in social interaction in actual texts, but the point is that the performance of these systems, through the regularity of the patternings that performance produces in a text, consistently and simultaneously positions the writer (for a reader) and allows the writer to construct generic positions for a reader who, across an accumulation of clauses in a text, has to begin where the writer does and end where the writer puts her.

This is not, then, just a structuralist theory of the way texts are internally constructed. At least it does not have to stay that way. It is a theory which implies a reader and a writer, a speaker and a hearer, and has a good deal to say about how that reader/writer makes texts in a constant process of movement – back and forth within the co-text, in and out of the text to other texts and practices. If we assume from now on that anyone involved in this activity is also an embodied, sexed participant in these activities, therefore bringing different lived corporealities to the task, the probabilistic aspects of the exercise and the likelihood of texts 'going astray', being read and rewritten in multiple ways, increases componentially.

METALANGUAGE AND THE PROBLEM OF METASEMIOSIS

One of the most misunderstood elements in the poststructuralist and postmodernist critique of modernist theories, constantly evident in attempts to rewrite them, has been the question of metalanguage (Jakobson 1956/1985), language for writing about language. In much of the discussion about the objectifying nature of modernist theories (the grand narratives of Marx, Freud, Durkheim and de Saussure, for example), it is assumed that the problem of metalanguage is a problem for and of 'linguistics'. The amazingly consistent refusals of linguistics (or of semiotics), which I have documented in my accounts of various theorists in the course of this book so far, are evidence both of the widespread nature of these assumptions and of the fact that they are based on a very narrow reading of what linguistics might be. When there is recourse to theories of language, they arrive mediated through the texts of Derrida, Lacan or Foucault, or Kristeva and Irigaray. One of the now-taken-for-granted positions in these arguments is that there is no such thing as 'linguistic meaning' (Threadgold 1991); that is, that meanings are not somehow 'contained' in language. This position is usually directly derived from the work of Foucault and Derrida, who have argued convincingly (as have many linguists whose work Derrida [1967/1976a] at least has used) that it is not possible for signs, linguistic or otherwise, to refer in a fixed way to single meanings. This anxiety about meaning and language is helped along by Lacan's and Kristeva's work on the symbolic, where it is argued that there not only is a (single) 'system of language' (something linguists like Firth [1957] and Halliday [1985a], and semioticians like Eco [1979], would not accept), but that it is repressive, excludes the feminine, is based on the law of the father, and so on.

At the Strathclyde conference on the 'Linguistics of Writing' (1987), Halliday specifically addressed the charge that 'linguistics' imagines that it recovers from discourse a 'fixed and stable meaning', arguing:

> We do recover from discourse . . . a complex and indeterminate meaning. . . . The reason it is so hard to make this process explicit is that we can only do so by talking about grammar: and to do this we have to construct a theory of grammar: a grammatics . . . a designed system, a metalanguage.
>
> (Halliday 1987: 145)

Then, to paraphrase Halliday, the terms of the grammatics so constructed become 'reified'. We confuse the grammatics (the categories, or labels, we borrow from extralinguistic experience to describe the *for us* 'ineffable' experience of language itself [Halliday 1983]) with the actual grammar that is language itself. This is precisely what happens when feminist theory begins to argue that the subject/predicate construction of a grammatics is in (and of) itself patriarchal. Halliday invents the term 'grammatics' to deal with the fact that in English we are forced to call both things, the language itself and the linguist's metalanguage, 'grammar'. The problem is that the categories, or the terms of your metalanguage (Threadgold 1990), like the terms of the linguist's grammatics, are also essentially ineffable.

Halliday's (1983) account of how a child comes to have a performative (not metalinguistic) understanding ('belief is a state of the body') of the phenomenon the linguist's grammatics might categorise as the grammatical 'subject' of the utterance is as follows:

> Our ability to use language depends critically on our not being conscious of doing so – which is the truth that every language learner has to discover, and the contradiction from which every language teacher has to escape . . .
> Language is an active participant in the semogenic process. Language creates reality – and therefore its categories of content cannot be defined, since we could define them only by relating them to some pre-existing model of experience, and there is no model of experience until the linguistic categories are there to model it. The only meaning of Subject (or

Actor or Theme) is the meaning that has evolved along with the category itself . . .

Does a child, then, know what a Subject is? We cannot ask him – . . . nevertheless it is clear, surely, that a child does know what a Subject is, because he uses one a hundred times a day. We have only to listen to a five-year-old in ordinary, real life situations, and we will hear the categories of the grammar that we find most difficult to explain, deployed in their appropriate semantic roles . . .

Fundamental semantic concepts, like those underlying Subject, or Theme, Actor, New, definite, present, finite, mass, habitual, locative, are, in an entirely positive way, ineffable.

(1983: 10, 11, 13)

How, then, if grammatical categories are ineffable, are we to understand Halliday's other assertion, that the history of linguistics has usually regarded language as a system of forms with meanings attached to make sense of them (which would be the recovery of the fixed and stable meanings argument), while he wants to treat language as 'a system of meanings, with forms attached to express them' (1983: 13)? How do we access the 'system of meanings' except through language which gives them form; and, having accessed it, have we not still fixed it, given it a stable form?

REWRITING THE LINGUISTIC SYSTEM

It is worth remembering here that *system*, in Halliday's Firthian linguistics, is not system as used in an expression such as 'the linguistic system' (as in either de Saussure or Chomsky). Firth (1957) explicitly rejected the notion of *langue* (language as system), in favour of understanding the paradigmatic and syntagmatic relations that operated in a particular domain; the systems and structures that operated, for example, in the nominal group, or in newspaper headlines. The concept of 'the system of language' was meaningless in this context. Firth understood that structures (syntagms) and paradigms (systems of alternatives) characterised all the various domains in which language functioned – from phonemes, words and phrases to larger units. This system and structure concept is not unlike Jakobson's understanding of metaphor and metonymy (1957/1971b). Jakobson actually accuses de Saussure of not understanding the always simultaneous operation of syntagm and paradigm, of succumbing to the traditional belief in the linear character of language, '*qui exclut la possibilité de prononcer deux choses à la fois*' ('which excludes the possibility of saying two things at once') (1957/1971b: 243). Rather, according to Jakobson, the constituents of a syntagm (a structure and thus a context) are in a state of contiguity (metonymy – each element is part of the whole), while the elements in a paradigm (a substitution set) are linked by various degrees of similarity (metaphor). But every element in a linguistic structure then always has simultaneously two interpretants (Jakobson quotes Peirce's use of the term), a meaning that derives metaphorically from the system (paradigm), and another that derives from its contextual relations with other signs in a sequence. Reading and writing always involve these processes, the ability to 'gloss' the fact that this word, phrase or larger chunk of text is similar (metaphor) to that one (a statement of a discourse for example, a noun phrase), or that this piece or whole chunk of text is part of that whole context (metonymy) and can be made sense of accordingly. The 'systems of meaning' at the level of the clause structure have this simultaneity and already plural meaning built in. Halliday's understanding of system is a combination of this and Hjelmslev's (1943/1961) understanding of the sign-function and the relation between system and process, a framework which also proved productive in Eco's (1979) conceptualisation of a processual semiotics.

Elsewhere (1985a: xxvii), Halliday is explicit that his grammatics, the account of the 'systems of meaning' specific to the three functions of language, describes the functional meaning of the grammar of language, but that it is not a description of the semantic system of a language. It is not, in other words, an attempt to describe what Eco (1979) called the 'global semantic space'. The functions of the grammar are describable, the semantics is not. For Halliday, as for Firth and Jakobson, any particular linguistic item in a linguistic chain (the grammar of a natural language, for example) is simultaneously part of a structure (a context/concatenation) and part of a substitution set (a set of equivalent alternatives, concurrence). It always has at least two interpretants. Hjelmslev's very considerable advance over de Saussure – in the understanding of the workings of the linguistic sign as involving substance and form at the level of both the signified (the content-plane) and the signifier (the expression-plane) – is crucial to understanding this. Figure 5.1 (adapted to Halliday from the ideas of Hjelmslev 1943/1961: 28–60) clarifies why the lexicogrammar, the single wording of the clause, the apparently linear structure of language, carries so much baggage. It is the phonic or graphic realisation of connections to the physical process of making the sign-function, the trace of a corporeal making, and it is also the mark or trace which must motivate any corporeal labours of meaning-making the texts may engender:

What Halliday's grammatics does is to attempt to locate in particular domains of the lexicogrammar what kinds of grammatical meanings are at stake, what the systems of potential grammatical meanings might be in that context. Following Halliday's arguments about the ineffability of any such categories, we have at best a set of potential category labels, or rather a number of sets of interlocking networks of categories, which help to locate what areas of grammatical meaning may be at risk in particular contexts within a clause structure. They enable us to name parts of the clause structure in ways which then prompt questions about what those names may mean in

Language

Purport	Substance	Form	
content purport	content substance	content-form	**Content-plane**
('real world')	(semantics)	(lexicogrammar)	
expression purport	expression substance	expression-form	**Expression-plane**
(physiological/ physical body)	(phonetics)	(phonology)	

Figure 5.1 The sign-function (planes of realisation)

this context, uttered by this sexed and coloured body, not that one, in this disciplinary context not that, in this kind of genre and not that, and so on.

Such 'semantic labels' for elements of lexicogrammar, Halliday's grammatics, are already an interpretation, the linguist's interpretation, of the functions that grammars of languages need to serve. It is an interpretation that comes, as we saw above, from a long and complex tradition of such interpretation. In that they are not merely structural labels, they are already an advance on constituency models of grammar, which only describe the contiguous links to the structural context of the syntagm, with no understanding of the simultaneity of the metaphorical links to sets of alternatives which might have been used in that context. But we need more Hjelmslev to understand why the process does not stop there, and indeed to see where it might go next. Hjelmslev's other remarkable innovation, apart from his understanding of metasemiotics (e.g. Halliday's understanding of the difference between a grammar and a grammatics) and his rewriting of the sign (1943/1961: 114ff.), was his conceptualisation of the difference between denotative semiotics and connotative semiotics, something Eco (1979) combined with Peirce's concept of the interpretant to produce a model for thinking about what he called infinite semiosis, thus putting paid once and for all to the idea that all linguists and semioticians believed in fixed and stable meanings.

In this context, it seems to me that Halliday's understanding of the meaning potential of the lexicogrammar of language is just that: a modelling of a

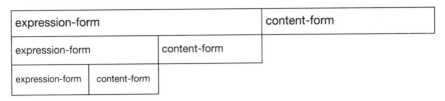

Figure 5.2 Denotative and connotative semiotics

denotative semiotic – a coming-together of independent elements (a content-form and an expression-form) from two different systems of two different planes to form a sign-function (1943/1961: 58) – establishing 'transitory correlations of elements' as the result of 'provisional coding rules' (Eco 1979: 49). Any sign-function is then, however, capable of becoming the expression-form for a further transitory correlation with another content-form to form a new *connotative* sign-function, and so on.

In Halliday's theory of language as social semiotic, some of the further connotative levels of semiosis are suggested in the theory of the semiotic construct of the immediate context of utterance and its relations to the higher order social semiotic of the social system, including social structure, context of culture, and language as institution. These 'skew' the probabilities available at the denotative level, constantly interacting with embodied histories to produce new and different, as well as reasonably static, meanings. Thus systems such as nominalisation (the packing into a noun form of many complex meanings, e.g. democratisation, poststructuralism), transitivity (the process types and participants in the clause), or projection (the process whereby a clause comes to function as a representation of a linguistic representation, e.g. in quoting and reporting relations), as well as the systems of cohesion and theme–rheme which we have looked at above, mean differently in different intertextual and generic configurations, and in different interactions with different readers and writers in different contexts.

To this extent, and understood in these terms, the metalanguage of a functional linguistics is no different to the metalanguage of Freudian or Lacanian psychoanalysis, the metalanguage of Marxism, the metalanguage of Foucauldian poststructuralism, or the emerging metalanguage of the archetypal refuser of metalanguages, deconstruction (the *trace*, the *arche*, the *pharmakon, différance, destinerrance*, the *signature* – one could go on). Linguistic theories *qua* grammatics cannot provide any 'objective' means of analysing texts. In using them as metalanguages, we are again, as in all other kinds of theoretical activity, doing what Greimas has characterised as 'making meanings by transforming meanings', or as a C. S. Peirce might have put it, moving always by means of an 'interpretant' which is only another sign towards an 'object' which is itself something that 'stands for something else' and is thus, again, a sign and an interpretant.

In every case, the embodied reader or writer maps from the language of the text being read or written to other interpreting codes or texts (metalanguages). There is no qualitative difference. The linguistic theory is just another code. The authority it carries, however, as Cameron (1995) has pointed out, means that we cannot discount its effects in interpretive contexts.

Linguistic metalanguage, then, a language to talk about language and semiosis, is a particularly useful resource for appropriation by a feminist poetics which has already recognised the typical monologic clause (subject/predicate) and text structure of introduction, conflict, climax, denouement (both as theorised and as practised) as masculinist, sexual, and potentially Oedipal and patriarchal (de Lauretis 1984). Here is a whole new set of ways of conceptualising, theorising textuality, and of producing new kinds of texts and meanings. The result is a new metalanguage available to be appropriated by a feminist poetics and for the performance of feminist critique. Most importantly, a feminist poetics will not be a feminism oppressed/repressed by language. The idea of grammar as corporeal trace offers many resources for a feminine and feminist subject at large in the networks of textual practices that constitute the genres, discourses and narratives, the dialogism of the culture, enjoying crossing boundaries, mixing spheres, changing identities and making meanings differently.

Chapter 6

Patriarchal contexts

If feminist social, political and cultural theory (Pateman 1988; Morris 1988; Yeatman 1990; Smith 1990; Gatens 1996; Grosz 1994, 1995a) has told us anything it has told us that what we do not need is *a* social theory, a single all-encompassing, totalising framework with preconceived categories and boundaries to keep us all in our proper places. This kind of feminist statement always strikes a certain note of alarm in the hearts of male theorists, particularly neo- or post-Marxist theorists, who like to characterise such thinking as the irresponsible and dangerous plurality, the indeterminacy and apolitical phenomenon they are wont to give the name postmodernism or even poststructuralism – and sometimes deconstruction (Norris 1992; Eagleton 1990; Jameson 1984; Butler 1992, 1993; Threadgold 1996). Donna Haraway (1991b: 181) once said, 'the production of universal totalising theory is a major mistake that misses most of reality, probably always, but certainly now'. Diane Elam, in a recent book on feminism and deconstruction, speaking of the positive values of 'undecidability' for women, has this to say:

> The affirmative potential of feminist politics is that such politics takes the undecidability of the multiple determinations of women, the clash of virgin, whore, mother etc., as the aporetic space within which a freedom arises.
>
> (Elam 1994: 84)

And, turning to Barbara Johnson on abortion, she adds:

> To win the debate on abortion would be to allow the undecidable, in so far as abortion would be neither a decision which could be made in advance, or made once and for all for all women . . . By acknowledging the undecidable, deconstruction and feminism allow us to imagine other spaces – spaces of political otherness. An ethical or just politics must recognise that this handling (of difference) cannot itself become the object of a contract, cannot be given a determinate meaning. A just politics must seek to handle these differences, to respect them, without

implying that what is other can be made identical by means of that handling.

(Elam 1994: 84–5)

She might well have been speaking of theories of text and context; for, in exactly the same way, decisions about context cannot be made in advance or made once and for all for all texts. They have to be made again every time, in every case, if we are in fact to be able to imagine the spaces of otherness, the differences, which a preconceived theory may very well inhibit us from seeing. That does not mean that, in all contexts where the analysis of language is at stake, it will not be useful to think about the ways in which intersubjective, text-forming and reality-constructing meanings are at stake. It does mean that you will not always be able to predict in advance which aspects of language will do which parts of that work or how textual activity, interventions into the world of semiosis, may change or probabilistically skew *the worlds* into which they intervene. Halliday's theory thought of contexts as skewing the probabilities of register in texts. In fact, it seems to me essential to see both text and context as essentially processual and transitory categories. Then, the likelihood that textual processes and intersubjective interventions will skew, or change, worlds, is every bit as likely as the reverse operation. In fact, in most situations what happens is, as Deleuze (1986/1988) said in the context of thinking about the interaction between the verbal and the visual in film, 'a mushy mixture' of the two. That was probably always the case, but it is certainly the case now in a postmodernist world.

HABERMAS: GENDERED THEORIES OF THE SOCIAL

When Pateman rewrote the social contract as the 'sexual contract' (1988), she was foregrounding the objectifying theory which underpins so many of our social institutions. Gatens (1991) was dealing with the same issues when she deconstructed the masculinity of the 'body politic' itself. Habermas (1981) is a social theorist who has become known as a discourse theorist because his social theory foregrounds communication. This is not a theory of language, however. It is a theory of context. His discourse theory (with no linguistics) differentiates social life into three tidily different spheres – the scientific, the aesthetic and the moral spheres of knowledge – and is paralleled by the cognitive, normative and expressive spheres of interest, and related to a further division of the 'world' into the objective, the social and the subjective. Habermas argues that 'the claims raised in the context of modernity' arise in these three differentiated spheres of value. His theory is in some ways a typical example of the kinds of masculinist theory Pateman and Gatens were contesting. As Ricoeur (1986) has shown, Habermas's work stands at the end of a long tradition of German philosophy and social theory, from Kant, Fichte, Hegel and Feuerbach, through Marx, to Weber, Mannheim, and Marcuse and the Frankfurt School (Wiggershaus 1995). His 'utopian' interest, for Ricoeur, lies in the fact that he tried to read Freud and Marx together, suggesting that the concept of 'alienation' in Marx has its correlative in Freudian 'desymbolisation'. The process of psychoanalysis is a process 'by which we go from desymbolisation [*frozen symbolic relations/reification*] to resymbolisation through the intermediate stage of transference' (Ricoeur 1986: 230, italics are my addition). This, for Habermas, is like Marxist critique (Ricoeur 1986: 27). It is a reversal of a reversal, which takes all those entities that were falsely *projected* upwards in Hegel from concrete material reality to the abstract world of thought and representation, and relocates them, reverses those projections to their initial basis in material reality. Projection is an early term in Marx for the developing concept of ideology (Ricoeur 1986: 29–30). For Ricoeur, as for feminists writing more recently of Habermas (Meehan 1995), Habermas's most useful contribution is his own critique of Marx's understanding of production/praxis, to include not only instrumental rationality, but also communicative action, an inclusion which makes the critique of instrumental rationality possible.

Because there is some similarity to Halliday's tripartite divisions of the social as projected from his theory of language – itself part of a long tradition of theoretical accounts of the social – it is important to stress here just how totally autonomous from each other these spheres are in Habermas. There is certainly no polyphony of the spheres in this account. It is a typical case of post-Marxist masculine and modernist anxiety about order, arrangement and keeping everything in its assigned place – perhaps especially women. We cannot communicate successfully, Habermas (1981) argues, without associating the appropriate claim with the appropriate sphere. Nancy Fraser (1995) has pointed to the extraordinary gender blindness of a theory which separates mothering from paid work, labour from maternity, and money and power from the family, and which assumes, on the one hand, that there is *only* 'symbolic reproduction' in the home and, on the other, that there is *no* 'symbolic reproduction' in the 'system-integrated action contexts' (ruled by the media of money and power) of the capitalist economy and the paid workplace. The participants in this fictional world of Habermas's construction are the worker, the citizen, the consumer and, later, the welfare state client.

The role of worker as provider, breadwinner, earner of the family wage (Fraser 1995: 33), the feminine subtext of the consumer role (1995: 34), and the masculinity of citizenship based on the dialogical capacities central to becoming a participant in political debate and public opinion formation (Fleming 1995) are the focus of Fraser's (1995) feminist critique. This masculinity of citizenship is irretrievably connected with a specifically German liberal intellectualism, with a strong prejudice towards rationality and a firm belief in the legal bureaucratic state, and accomplished through the supposedly gender-neutral medium of power. Adding to the above the 'soldiering aspects' of citizenship, the conception of the citizen as the protector of women, children, the elderly and the polity, Fraser shows how femininity is constructed in Habermas as dissonant with paid work and citizenship, and always confined to the life-fostering, child-rearing space of the family, the silent place (not engaging in the debate of the public sphere) of the one who is cared for and protected (Fraser 1995: 34–5).

Habermas's separation between the official economic sphere and the private sphere of the lifeworld may have some *'prima facie* purchase on empirical social reality' (Fraser 1995: 27), but it makes it impossible to see the subordination of women to men in both spheres. Setting up the male-headed nuclear family as having only an incidental relation to money and power is, moreover, not only counterfactual. Feminists have shown that, in relation to abortion, child abuse, wife battering and family law, families are thoroughly permeated with the 'media' of money and power (Graycar and Morgan 1990; Cornell 1995; Kirkby 1995). There is in Habermas a complete failure to recognise the false universality of a citizenship based on property ownership, public debate and the location of the family outside the force of law (so that those protected have no access to law) (Fleming 1995). Nor is there ever any questioning as to why 'consensus' has to be the goal of a democratic state, or whether it is a useful one (Weir 1995: 263). For Fraser, it is the issue of gender which makes this separation of spheres both counterfactual and 'ideological'. For her, social motion and causal influence are multidirectional and

> feminine and masculine gender identity run like pink and blue threads through the areas of paid work, state administration, and citizenship as well as through the domain of familial and sexual relations. It is one (if not the) 'medium of exchange' among them, a basic element of the social glue that binds them together.
>
> (Fraser 1995: 36)

Because Habermas has projected his own inflexible story of separated spheres on to the realities of classical capitalism, in a typical example of what Bourdieu has called 'objectivism' (1980/1990), he is totally unprepared for welfare state capitalism. Welfare state capitalism finally forces him to see the breaking down of the boundaries he has erected, but again because he cannot 'see', except within the frameworks of his theory, he can only read this as the 'inner colonisation of the lifeworld' by money and power. His is a typically anxious representation (Norris 1992) of what others have seen as the breaking down of the tightly compartmentalised spheres of the modernist state into a postmodernist reality (Harvey 1989). Haraway (1991b: 161) speaks of the 'comfortable old hierarchical dominations' and the 'scary new networks'. For Habermas, the welfare state is devastating.

Communicative contexts are 'desiccated', 'symbolic reproduction is destabilised, identities are threatened and there are social crisis tendencies' (Fraser 1995: 39). New conflicts develop which 'differ from class struggles' (with which he could deal) contesting 'reification and the "grammar of forms of life"' (e.g. fundamentalism, peace, ecology movements, feminism) (Fraser 1995: 39). Even in the face of such obvious excesses, his theoretical framework, on the defensive, attempts to contain what it could not have anticipated. Subversive movements will only be deemed 'successful' if they succeed in 'decolonising the lifeworld'. And, since feminism does not (indeed, cannot) do that, it is at best a 'defensive' movement. There is, it seems, only one kind of change that this framework will allow Habermas to see (Fleming 1995).

Fraser suggests that what Habermas reads as 'colonisation', 'erosion' and 'desiccation of contexts of interpretation and communication' (Fraser 1995: 43) have meant something very different for women. Women have been 'interpellated in contradictory ways, as workers, clients, mothers, citizens', but the meanings of the 'roles' themselves, previously protected in their separate spheres, have been opened up to contestation, in ways that have been both ambivalent and productive for women. 'Colonisation', then, is not an adequate explanation for what has happened here, and nor is 'decolonisation' an adequate answer. There are many more kinds of change than this, and if the family has been the site of struggles over money and power, at least since the Hardwicke marriage act in the eighteenth century (Threadgold 1995), then colonisation is hardly an adequate description of what is now occurring. It is the inability of Habermas's modernist, masculinist theory of the social world (with its differentiated spheres) to 'communicate' with postmodernity that is at stake here – it is, after all, an emancipatory discourse which argues that communicative action is the 'cure' for instrumental rationality, for ideology. This is the typical language of critical theory, a critical theory derived from Freud and Marx via Horkheimer, Adorno and Marcuse, the story of culture and subjectivity constructed by the Frankfurt School (Luke 1992). Habermas's theory of communicative action is based on the theory of the speech act.

DERRIDA AND THE SPEECH ACT

Speaking of his debate with Searle about the limits of the speech act, Derrida argues that 'the values of propriety and of property, of the proper name, and of copyright (the rights of the author)' are 'the axiomatics' presupposed by speech act theory (1988: 113). This supports in another context Silverstein's (1979) Whorfian arguments that speech act theory is a projection upwards from 'real life' into theory of all the ideologies of what we do when we speak that are built into the grammar of language itself and the social life in which it is used. In this reading, the 'speech act' which is to be the 'cure' for ideology would itself be constructed on all those ideologies of the separate spheres which Fraser (1995) does such an excellent job of deconstructing. And this is precisely why the question of consensus (as achieved through the politics of the speech act) is itself ideological. This, it seems to me, adds another set of problems to Habermas's work which, on the whole, the feminists debating with him in 1995 (Meehan) do not see. And they do not see it because they are not actually concerned with what theories of language which are theories of language in use (unlike Searle's and Habermas's work) could tell them. Again, Derrida is very clear about what the issue is: that of 'marginality' and 'parasitism' (1988: 112):

> Of what does speech act theory speak? Of what should it render an accounting? What should it describe and from where does it draw its objects and examples if not from 'real life'? And if it excludes, even provisionally, methodologically, what goes on there ('all sorts of marginal cases . . .'), what is left for it? To what does it refer? Why determine as marginal what can always go on in 'real life', which is, to my knowledge, the only place from where a theory of language can draw its 'facts', its 'examples', its 'objects'?
>
> (Derrida 1988: 125)

It is this process of exclusion, this attempt 'to simplify . . . and . . . raise a hue and cry about obscurity because they do not realise the unclarity of their good old *Aufklarung*', which Derrida characterises as 'no less dangerous (for instance in politics)' than 'those who wish to purify at all costs', and as the 'violence . . . at work in academic discourse' (1988: 112). Derrida is referring, in what he says above, to both Searle and Habermas, arguing that these theorists of communication, dialogue and consensus are precisely those who will not communicate, who will not read what the other (Derrida) says, who are afraid of dialogue and communication:

> Exposed to the slightest difficulty, the slightest complication, the slightest transformation of the rules, the self-declared advocates of communication denounce the absence of rules as confusion. And they allow themselves then to confuse everything in the most authoritarian manner.
>
> (Derrida 1988: 158)

This is why so much feminist labour has been devoted to the rewriting of certain kinds of objectifying, exclusionary masculinist theory, because, until you do that, there is no place, no story, in which a feminist pedagogy or a feminist poetics can start. This feminist work has read the texts of masculine theory as texts, just like other texts, denying them their status of objectivity or theory, and rewritten them as metanarratives, just another story. One of its most important rewritings has been the rewriting of the universalist subject of these enlightenment theories as a specifically masculine, sexed subject, whose perceptions and constructions of the worlds he observes are marked at every point by his embodied subjectivity, and are therefore at best partial representations. It is the construction of a specific kind of masculinity in the texts of critical theory that is the focus of Luke's (1992) argument.

Her argument is that what the Frankfurt School theorists conceived as the psychic and social development of the subject within capitalism was in fact a specifically male experience 'translated into epistemology' and represented as universal. Luke's analysis of this position focuses on the centrality in the theory of the Freudian notion of the 'death-instinct'. Marcuse, for example, postulates a universal desire for social order and for freedom from repression and domination (of the kind institutionalised, for example, in the family and the school). For him, this desire is what enables the psychic dynamic for negative (ideology) critique which produces freedom. But the Freudian-derived death-instinct, mediated by the pleasure principle ('the need to resolve tension'), is still a primary autonomous drive in this theory, and subjectivity is conceptualised as founded in the life/death opposition. This is reminiscent of the oppositions between the masculine soldier/protector, citizen speaker/breadwinner roles and the roles of life-fostering child-rearing and being protected that structure Habermas's discourse.

The oppositional life/death binarism, along with a whole range of other binarisms – self/other, nature/culture, subject/object, thesis/antithesis, antithesis/synthesis – has a long history in Western philosophy, which is much older than Frankfurt School critical theory, and has been critiqued extensively by poststructuralist and feminist theorists (Lloyd 1989; Gatens 1991). Hartsock (1987) speaks of the masculine subjectivity constructed in Hegel's analysis of the self-conscious subject, and of its complex and intimate relations to epistemology:

> Hegel's analysis makes clear the problematic social relations available to the self which maintains itself by opposition: each of the two subjects struggling for recognition risks its own death in the struggle to kill the other, but if the other is killed the subject is once again alone. In sum then, the male experience when replicated as epistemology leads to a world conceived as, and (in fact) inhabited by, a number of fundamentally hostile others whom one comes to know by means of opposition (even death struggle) and yet with whom one must construct a social relation in order to survive.
>
> (Hartsock 1987: 170)

Benhabib (1987), relating the construction of masculine subjectivity to the Freudian and Oedipal story of the male ego – in which the making of masculine selves involves the construction of strong boundaries between self and other (the female parent), and a sense of separation and isolation – comments on the projection of this constructed and troubled masculinity into theoretical constructions of the public and the social, such as the social contract and the law:

The saga of the autonomous male ego is the saga of the initial sense of loss in confrontation with the other, and the gradual recovery from the narcissistic wound through the sobering experience of war, fear, domination and death. The last instalment of this drama is the social contract: the establishment of the law to govern all . . . to reestablish the authority of the father in the image of the law.

(Benhabib 1987: 84–5)

Luke (1992), following Hartsock, suggests that this masculine experience is specifically different to female embodied experience, which sets up all kinds of challenges – for example, menstruation, coitus, pregnancy, childbirth and lactation – to the notion of the body as bounded, autonomous, or to the self as separate from the other. Irigaray (1977/1985a) has made the same case for the specificity and difference of female embodiment in more metaphorical and deconstructive ways, also based in psychoanalysis, arguing for the specificity of the female experience of the body by telling it within different stories – for example, a geometry of fluids instead of the Euclidean one of solids and bounded entities.

If the gendered differences are even half as great as these stories would suggest, then we cannot start from such social or speech act theories to build a radical or a feminist theory, pedagogy or poetics. The generality of the points made about the nature of masculine subjectivity in the arguments above are, of course, only valid in specific and historically located sites (Buchbinder 1994; Connell 1995). Masculinities are as myriad as femininities. And yet there are a whole range of cultural and social sites where the feminist arguments rehearsed above do seem to be borne out in the masculine repetition of the pattern of death and killing in the search for unity, peace, harmony and life in a wide range of cultural sites. Luke (1992) mentions the phallocentric institutions of the military, cultural myths, fables, narratives and literary texts that construct masculine heroes who pay the price of death for their quest of love, and the 'brutal inscription' of the life/death conflation in pornographic texts which superimpose imageries of violence and death on 'the fundamental life-giving act of sexual intercourse' (Luke 1992: 32). (The whole of this discussion on masculine subjectivity is greatly indebted to the arguments in Carmen Luke's paper.) The institution of the social contract, and the law to control unfettered nature in order to produce harmony, order and consensus, is only another version of this story (Pateman 1988). The myth of consensus and of universal (disembodied, desexed) individuals, equal and impartial and engaged in normative and rational discussion, which permeates neo-Marxist and post-Marxist social theory as well as the law's vision of itself, is thus a masculine construction, and completely elides the difference that actually constitutes the social order. At the same time, it is a construction which justifies control and power, even violence, of a patriarchal kind, by rewriting subjection and slavery as freedom (democracy), the economic exchange of women (prostitution) as marriage, sexual relations as social relations, and violence and control as Care and Protection (Pateman 1988).

It is the 'cure' that is called Care and Protection that I want to investigate in the last part of this chapter.

PERFORMING GENERIC VIOLENCE AND THE MAKING OF SEXUAL DIFFERENCE

The story I have told you so far is a feminist story of the theoretical construction in narrative of an archetypal masculinity, and of discourses associated with that narrative which construct masculinist interventions in the social world as Care and Protection. It is not the only story one could tell of masculinity, and it is not to be confused with the stories of actual masculine subjects who, like all embodied subjectivities, are constructed at the intersections of a whole complex range of generic, discursive and narrative positions, of which this story and these discourses are only a part. It is also a story which contributes to the making of feminine subjectivity, and to the making of the subjectivities of all those who are the incomplete and lacking 'others' of patriarchy's male hero – children, people of colour, homosexuals, those of other ethnic and cultural backgrounds, those of lower socio-economic or educational status. For all of these, this masculine story offers only the position of the goal, the recipient, the affected participant (these are all names for 'participants' in Halliday's functional grammar). If any of these positions is accepted, lived and embodied as habitus, then this is also a story which contributes to the construction of an internalised and unconscious compliance with the structures of the patriarchal order (Gatens 1996). The latter depends precisely on those who are its objects, those who are *subjects to it*, recognising, acknowledging and living what patriarchy constructs as *their* lack in ways which make them desire *its* cures.

It is a story which, as I have already suggested, is realised in a wide range of sites, but it is also realised, in ways which I have not yet talked about, in a plethora of conflicting ways – sometimes obvious, sometimes almost invisible. Its structure and its intersections with the discourses of Care and Protection are not even always to be located tidily within a single text that we might want to call a genre. Sometimes the story structure maps on to the generic structure, so that at least two structural readings are possible, and the two are coextensive; sometimes the story is embedded within another genre; and sometimes the story structure binds texts in different genres together into a larger narrative – to give just three examples. And the discourses of Care and Protection can be (and are) constructed within a wide range of diverse and different fields. Analysing the specificities of those fields, linguistically or in any other way, even locating this analysis within institutional practices and relations of power will not necessarily tell you they are there, unless you are prepared to look across a wide range of texts for intertextual patterns and are already reading from a position within a feminist or other story which has alerted you to the possibility of finding them. One finds, after all, what one's theories or stories allow one to find (Goodwin 1994), which is why feminisms cannot countenance the idea of one theory, particularly a patriarchal one.

Text 6.1   High Court Appeal, 1986–1987 [162 C.L.R., 447–65]

J. (APPELLANT)
LIESCHKE AND OTHERS (RESPONDENTS)
ON APPEAL FROM THE SUPREME COURT OF NEW SOUTH WALES.

Infants and Children – Neglected and uncontrollable children – Crimes and offences by and against – Summary proceedings involving infant – Right of parent to be heard – Serious allegations against parent in relation to child – Natural justice – Child Welfare Act 1939 (N.S.W.), s. 72.

Legal Practitioners – Solicitor and client – Retainer – Duty solicitor system – Assignment to represent infants – Non-criminal proceedings – Absence of instructions from parents or guardians – Absence of court order appointing person to give instructions.

Held that in proceedings before a magistrate relating to a 'neglected child' within s. 72 of the *Child Welfare Act* 1939 (N.S.W.) the parents of the child have a right to be heard. The right depends, not on the exercise of the magistrate's discretion, but on principles of natural justice that entitle parents, whose authority over their children and access and duties to them are challenged, to be heard on every issue of fact relevant to a decision affecting those interests.

Twist v. Randwick Municipal Council (1976), 136 C.L.R. 166, at pp. 109–10, applied.

Reg. v. Worthing Justices [1976] 2 All E.R. 194 and *Humberside County Council v. The Queen* [1977] 1 W.I.R. 1251; [1977] 3 All E.R. 964, distinguished.

Per curiam. The practice is to be deprecated of appointing duty and other solicitors to represent infants in non-criminal proceedings in the absence of instructions from parents or guardians or of a competent court order appointing some other person to give instructions.

Decision of the Supreme Court of New South Wales (Court of Appeal): *Shales v. Lieschke* (1985) 3 N.S.W.L.R. 65; 16 A. Crim. R. 384, 10 Fam. L. R. 261, reversed.

APPEAL from the Supreme Court of New South Wales.

The appellant was the mother of five infant children (the third to seventh respondents) whom the first respondent had apprehended and brought before a Children's Court, alleging that each was a 'neglected child' as defined in s. 72 of the *Child Welfare Act* 1939 (N.S.W.). In ensuing proceedings before a magistrate (the second respondent), the appellant applied as of right to appear as a party. The magistrate, in respect of one child concerning whom serious allegations were to be made against the appellant, agreed 'to permit the parents to appear by leave at the commencement of the proceedings'. The magistrate refused the parents leave to appear in relation to the other children, but stated that they would be allowed to call evidence if he found a prima facie case. The appellant applied to the Supreme Court of New South Wales for prohibition and mandamus and an injunction restraining the magistrate from refusing to allow her as of right to appear. Cantor J. dismissed the application. The Court of Appeal (Kirby P., Mahoney and Priestley J. A.) dismissed an appeal: *Shales v. Lieschke* (1). By special leave the appellant then appealed to the High Court.

D. M. J. Bennett Q.C. (with him *J. P. Hamilton* Q.C. and *P. J. Saidi*), for the appellant. In proceedings to remove a child from the custody of a parent because of that parent's conduct in respect of the child, the parent has a right of audience. The Court of Appeal erred in discerning a legislative intention in the *Child Welfare Act* 1939 (N.S.W.) that a parent should not have that right. The reference in s. 18(2) to a parent's entitlement to appeal on behalf of a child does not mean that a parent cannot appeal or be a party on his own account: *Houssein v. Under Secretary of Industrial Relations* (2). The Act does not exhaustively prescribe the persons who have a right of audience and when. No question of parties arises where proceedings are non-adversary and protective. Where proceedings are adversary, they are treated as civil proceedings and necessary parties must be joined. The present proceedings are protective, but that is not inconsistent with an accused parent's right to be heard and to test allegations to defend custodial rights to the child. There is a right to be heard based on natural justice: *R. v. Board of Appeal* (3); *Commissioner of Police v. Tanos* (4); *Twist v. Randwick Municipal Council* (5); *Corporate Affairs Commission v. Bradley*(6); *Rushby v. Roberts* (7). That right arises here from the possibility that the proceedings will end in an order affecting the appellant's rights to custody or guardianship and the mutual interest of parent and child in the continuing relationship of custody and guardianship. If the magistrate had a discretion to permit the appellant to appear, his decision failed to take account of the possible loss of custodial rights, took into account irrelevant considerations, and was so unreasonable that it should not be allowed to stand.

(1)   (1985) 3 N.S.W.L.R. 65; 16A Cran.R. 384; 10 Fam.L.R. 261.
(2)   (1982) 148 C.L.R. 88, at p. 94.
(3)   (1916) 22 C.L.R. 183, at p. 185.

(4)   (1958) 98 C.L.R. 383, at pp. 395–96.
(5)   (1976) 136 C.L.R. 106, at p. 109.
(6)   (1974) 1 N.S.W.L.R. 391.
(7)   (1983) 1 N.S.W.L.R. 350, at p. 353.

This legal text is what I would call the first phase or section, the introduction/setting/thesis to a whole genre – the genre of appellate court judgement – in the High Court of Australia. It would be perfectly possible to describe that genre in some detail, using a variety of linguistic, rhetorical or literary traditions (Threadgold 1991, 1993a). The legal genre of judgement, the rhetorical, syllogistic tradition, which is the one the profession itself is trained in, might well be the most relevant. This text, then, would be the thesis in a generic structure which follows up with antithesis (debate and argument, in most cases involving several actual voices, since appeals are frequently heard by more than one learned judge) and synthesis (the actual judgement, usually delivered by the most senior judge, which summarises and incorporates the different voices of the antithesis, restoring monologic order, the law speaking with one voice, and effecting closure of the debate). It is a genre in which all the preceding *written* legal process is embedded in that practice of gentlemanly acknowledgement of precedent and previous judgement that Bazerman argued Newton developed in the scientific article (see Chapter 2). If I look at it again, however, from my feminist story, I read it as the archetypal narrative of masculinity, the story of public men (but, in the end, that of *one* public man), faced with conflict and argument which threatens order, and acting logically and according to the legal rules of masculine consensus to restore harmony and order (introduction/setting–complication–resolution). Nothing very violent about that, you will say. Well, no – but that is not the whole story. I have not told you what the genre is about; I have not talked about what it is that these learned men are arguing about or indeed resolving.

They are arguing a point of law, whether a parent (she is actually a female parent in this case, but the issue, and she, quickly become universalised and desexed in the legal discourse) who has been accused of being an 'incompetent' parent should have the right to speak, 'to give evidence' in the case brought against her by, or on behalf of, her children who are correspondingly accused of being 'neglected children'. The argument is therefore about legal precedent, what the statutes say (the Child Welfare Act in this case), and a whole range of legal issues to do with the conflicting discourses (my language, not theirs) in that Act, the discourses of Criminality and Protection; that is, whether to be a neglected child is a *criminal offence* requiring punishment, or a *social problem* requiring the Care and Protection of the state and the law. You see how the discourses themselves already involve conflicting stories of what it is to be neglected. What it boils down to is that, if it is a criminal matter, then precedent will not allow the mother to be heard, the parent to speak. If, on the other hand, it is a matter of Care and Protection, then precedent is thrown to the wind, and so are the statutes, in favour of arguments belonging to the discourse of natural justice, which allow a single judge to decide that it is the right of parents, according to natural justice, to be heard in cases involving them and their children. God may no longer serve as fountain-head and source of law, but natural justice, embodied in appellate court judges, still does. This judgement, then, is one that allows the parent, and this woman, to speak. Again, you will say, that this is not very violent.

Well, no – but that is not the whole story either. Embedded in Text 6.1, in the introduction to the masculine narrative or the thesis to the legal judgement, there is another story. Martin (1991) does not like the 'irresponsibility' of my poststructuralist arguments which postulate the embeddedness of narratives in genres. Halliday, on the other hand (1985a), has provided imaginative ways of thinking and explaining the functions within genres of this embedding. Speaking of the clause complex, he argues that clauses which are embedded are, in terms of the mood structure of the grammar, unarguable. The function of the embedding is to make the embedded material dis/appear to be part of another larger structure which is presented as the main clause or argument and thus made available for questioning or debate. As with clauses, so with genres and narratives. In this case, the story of the woman and her children is literally incorporated into the first part of another genre, and forgotten as an issue thereafter. It ceases to be a matter of argument. It is this embedding/forgetting which enables that beginning to be constructed as a beginning and the judgement to be constructed as an ending, when in fact the story began long before that beginning and has still not ended when the judgement allowing the woman to speak is 'handed down'. You will note the way the genre positions the woman as recipient, and effectively silences her for its duration – she has not, after all, yet spoken, although she has now been given permission to speak – and public men, debating in the public sphere about Care and Protection for her and her children, have been talking *to one another* for four years.

The embedded story is a story of patriarchal violence, of child sexual abuse. Now, because I will have male readers, I want to make it very clear here that the violence I am talking about is not that of men as child abusers, but that of a patriarchal structure which produces child abuse both by women and by men, and which very possibly, because of the discursive and narrative nature of what constitutes the construction of the child abuser and the evidence of abuse, actually focuses on masculine abuse of protector power and 'screens out the multitude of seductive relationships which feminine protectors have established with their children' (Yeatman 1987). What I do want to emphasise is that that patriarchal structure is here realised in the structure of the nuclear family, or at least the heterosexual family, and that that itself is deeply embedded in (and reproductive of) the masculine narrative and the discourses of protection discussed above. The story of the family is that of a masculine parental hero (protector) who defends and protects those within his power (care) from those who might harm them.

The embedded story is a sketchy story about a man and a woman who are said to have engaged together, and separately, in some unspecified form of child sexual abuse involving the woman's four children, three girls and a boy. Before the case ever came to the magistrate's court, where the processes of appeal recorded in the judgement genre were set off by the magistrate's decision not to allow the woman to speak, the woman had been deprived of her children. This decision was made before any evidence had been heard other than that involved in the narrativity and discursivity of the original accusation of abuse by a person or persons unknown in terms of the written records, a process totally unprotected by the rules of the legal discourse of hearsay or any other rules of evidence or truth. The children have been put in foster homes, and there they remain for four long years while legal men decide, speaking all the while of the urgency of the matter, whether the woman may be allowed to speak. The woman and her children are tried, judged and sentenced, *and by hearsay*, which is what the four years of debate are all about (can a parent's evidence *as hearsay* be admitted to the court?), long before the legal processes which claim those functions for themselves, and consistently erase this story, ever begin. There is a brief moment in the transcript of the original proceedings in the magistrate's court when the magistrate and a policeman decide *sotto voce* that the woman should not be heard because it might prejudice their case against her. Four years later the High Court Judgement, giving her the right to speak, reprimands those public men for their less-than-public behaviour:

> The magistrate in the course of argument evinced some concern that the 'complaint' might not be established if the parents intervened and 'that could be said to be working very much against the interests of the children'. The concern was misplaced. The magistrate's refusal to accord the parents a right to be heard lest their appearance prevented the making of an order presumed the existence of facts which would show that the children were neglected children and presumed that it was in the children's interests to prevent a parental attempt to challenge the proof of those facts.
>
> (Brennan J. High Court Appeal at 457)

You will note that by now 'she' is 'parents' generically, and that neither the children nor she have yet been allowed to speak.

This violence done to a family is done in the name of that same masculine narrative that structures the nuclear family and the discourses of Protection. When the parental protector uses the power of that position to harm rather than protect, or is perceived to have so done, then the State or its agents steps in to repair the narrative, to replace the protector, replicating the structures of domination which made the abuse some sort of reality in the first place. And the Law, the ultimate patriarchal protector, replicates the structures again, adding to the violence of child abuse itself, and the violence of the protection of welfare agencies, by performing the generic violence of erasing the whole story of child abuse, turning it into a patriarchal story about a point of law, and offering four long years of further violence to a woman and her children in the name of Care and Protection. Never in any of this are the narrative and discursive structures, the embodied realities and subjectivities, who live the patriarchal narrative and perform the discourses of protection, the structures of domination which are the cause of the problem, ever even addressed. The judgement of the High Court, in re-establishing the rights of parents, as natural justice, actually perpetuates and affirms the same structures. Like Freud, when he systematically denied his own scientific evidence of the child sexual abuse of his women patients, and rewrote it as hysteria (Yeatman 1987), a problem with women, so this court turns the problem into a problem with a woman, a woman who wants to speak. The law cannot admit the problem of child abuse, because it would mean rewriting the narrative of the male hero protecting his others which the law tells about itself, in which the law itself is deeply and unconsciously involved, and which is embodied and performed in this judgement as disciplined legal masculinity.

I tell this story at some length because it is one of those stories in which the business of violence, and of masculine protection as violence, is not at all obvious, where it has to be looked for and written about in a number of complex ways, where what we call a genre is fundamental to the performing of the violence but will itself actually tell you very little about the way it is performed. Nowhere does the law's own institutional story tell of the narrativity of the construction of an affidavit, of the countless storyings and retellings of stories that may be involved in the production of a genre that, as a finished product, its narrative history elided and erased, is said to be a piece of factual evidence. Nowhere are the effects of narrative – of narratively constructed memory or of desire – accounted for. Dorothy Smith's (1990: 12) 'anatomy of a factual account', which juxtaposes the kinds of narratives and memories involved in arriving at the decision that 'K is mentally ill', was the kind of scenario I was looking at here. However, if the agents of the law, those who embody and enact it as practice, who perform their masculinity in the courts on a daily basis (Threadgold 1993b), believe that the public written genres of the law (the judgement, case precedent) constitute justice and the doing of justice, then they enact and perform that belief so that it does so function. That function of these written canonical texts cannot be discounted despite the fact that the unspoken spoken texts of everyday life, of police activities and of the lower courts give the lie to this belief. There were several stories to be told about these texts, not just one, and they needed to be told from a number of different places at once. And this is not the end of the story, because we still do not know whether she ever spoke and we do not know whether her speaking made her guilty or not guilty. My second story is the same story, but it is also a very different story.

It is located in a theatrical rehearsal room, another place of performance where people are actually trained and work hard to perform themselves differently. It is impossible in this space to believe in copyright, in the force of the proper name, or the value of the signature. It is impossible to keep the play text within the covers of a book, impossible for the text not to go astray and miss its destination. Here there are real bodies, real spaces, real interactions – all at work remaking this text, rewriting it from a multitude of different perspectives and embodied and disciplined positions, and in a variety of different media, as acting bodies, set and costume designs, and lighting and musical scripts. Here are a whole range of different and multi-medial literacies, and it is suddenly obvious that the aesthetic intersects in myriad ways with the economic, the professional, the institutional, the political and the making of policy, and that all of them contribute to the making of gendered subjects. The whole process of rehearsal foregrounds the centrality of the body to the business of making meanings, the fact that texts only mean as embodied and enacted texts, that text and context cannot be formalised as separate, that they exist as a semiotic chain of events, enacted on and through bodies, in which meanings are made now in one media, now in another, and then superimposed upon, and embedded within, one another.

It is also very clear that all performance texts have histories – histories of rehearsal and repetition, of the systematic embodiment of the discourses of the other (the playwright's story) or of the erasure of the discourses of the other by a different embodiment, another story (a different interpretation, a discarded rehearsal run). Crucially, it is apparent that to analyse just the verbal play text, or just the performance text, would be to analyse a carefully crafted and, to some extent, finished product (although the performance text always gives the lie to the idea of a finished story), but it would also mean missing most of the story, most of the time, of the complex histories of production of either or any of these texts. It would also be to miss the fact that most stories actually do not end, that they have futures as well as pasts, and that what they construct as endings are often merely the beginnings for others' and other stories. The business of theatrical embodiment and performance as realised in rehearsal, the labour and pain of making meanings with the body, have become for me a metaphor of the much slower and less visible processes by which genres, discourses and narratives are embodied or rewritten as history and habitus in the business of everyday life and in the processes we call education.

Text 6.2 Centre for Performance Studies, University of Sydney

Director, and two actors playing Othello and Desdemona, technician and two project academics observing – November 1990

B Director

O Othello/Actor

D Desdemona/Actor

TT/GM academics

Rehearsal (extract of Director's instructions to actors)

B: I want to use that thing – of Shakespeare's in the text – the idea of poison through the ear – coming into people's lives – one of you will sit in the chair – and the other two of us will whisper lines from the play into your ears – one on each side of you – it will be the voices in *your head that you are hearing – and *you can respond with lines from the scene – we'll be the inner voices – from the text – one in each ear.

The Desdemona improvisation (extracts from approximately the last third of the transcript)

O: . . . that cunning whore of Venice.

B: Why should he call her whore?

D: Have mercy on me. Send for the man and let him confess a truth.

O: . . . cunning whore of Venice. What? Not a whore? Are you not a strumpet?

B: Why should he call her whore?

D: My Lord! Send for the man and let him confess a truth! Bring him hither and let him confess a truth –

O: Oh thou black weed – why art so lovely fair? Thou smellst so sweet that the sense aches for thee – would thou hadst ne'er been born!

D: Have mercy on me – Have mercy on me –

O: I took you for that cunning whore of Venice – you, you, you, . . . We have done our course – there's money for your pains – we have done our course –

D: By my life – No!

O: There's money for your pains –

D: Send for the man and ask him – I fear you –

B: Why should he call her whore? Why should he call her whore?

O: Thou black weed –

D: Oh banish me! (*Screams out in real anguish as she crumples and her head falls to her lap. B and O crouch over her and come in closer.*)

O: I took you for that cunning whore of Venice – Thou public commoner – Ay, you, you, you, . . .

B: Why should he call her whore? Is it not the husband's fault if wives do fall?

D: What do you mean?

B: Is it not the husband's fault if wives do fall?

O: We have done our course. There's money for your pains. Ay, you, you, you, –

D: What do you mean by that?

O: Not a whore?

D: No, by my life and soul.

O: Are you not a strumpet?

D: Send for the man and ask him –

O: Was this fair paper, this goodly book made to write whore upon? Oh thou public commoner – There's money for thy pains –

D: Oh, let me live!

O: Oh thou black weed –

D: Let me live –

O: Would thou hadst ne'er been born –

D: Let me live –

B: . . . Hell gnaw his bones –

O: There's money for thy pains –

D Finally breaks down uncontrollably and weeps. Othello/Actor and Director stand awkwardly, silent, behind and to each side of her – hands on her shoulders.

Silence for about two and a half minutes – she gradually weeps less violently –

Discussion (following straight on from this 'end' of the improvisation)

B: Would you like a tissue? . . . Can you use that?

D: Yes, sure – it's horrible isn't it?

TT: Masochistic – awful –

B: Well we didn't mean to be so cruel – but *she* went with it – it is cruel, yes – we – we should be able to use that – that thing of the accumulation of all those things he's been saying to her –

D: Yes, it's an amazing journey 'cause she does – it's the bewilderment – she's so bewildered – and it's the outrage –

GM: And he's so mad – there's nothing *you can do –

D: No – and the torment –

B: If there's nothing to build it on – to build a defence on – that's the madness isn't it – *you don't know where it's coming from – that's the problem –

TT: And *you don't know where to start to answer it –

B: But I think it's important that we get that quality of 'She *doesn't know where* it's coming from' –

D: Or *how* to deal with it – and that it becomes a torment too – *she* becomes as tormented as he is – you see – *I* never got that before – and that banishment is better than this –

B: I think *she* hears those voices when – in the scene before – a lot – and when she wakes up – yeah –

D: Yeah – 'Who's there?'

O: Once again it's that image – his speech is like poison that's poured into the ear –

B: And we can use that for you, too – maybe – in the ear – and poisoning what's there between you – I must write this down – that's it for today folks!

*Who are these 'you's': Desdemona, or the women in the rehearsal room? There is a complicated transference going on here.

Whatever other things we might be able to say about the genre of Shakespearean tragedy, and whatever other stories this text tells and has told to various people at various times, one of the things that is in this case fairly obvious is that this text tells again, and has told and told again for some centuries, the same narrative of masculinity and the same discourses of Care and Protection that I have been reading in this chapter in other texts. On at least one level, *Othello* is a story about a femininity which is constructed by men as a problem, written by men as deceitful, cuckolding, adulterous – as whore – as the source of disharmony and of a terrible personal and social masculine tragedy. The problem is dealt with by men, and ultimately by Othello, in the violent murder of the offending feminine, Desdemona, a murder which is again written as Social Duty and Protection, the restoration of order and harmony. Desdemona is killed 'Lest she betray more men'. The real source of betrayal, the masculine figure of Iago – the embodiment of patriarchal and misogynistic violence, and the narratives and discourses which produce his and Othello's troubled and dangerous masculinities – are again erased and left intact in this protective act of violence against a woman. In performing the narrative and its discourses as theatre, actors constantly re-embody, re-enact, as the genre of theatrical performance, the misogyny and racial hatreds of centuries of different embodied and historically located and socially specific stories of these things, which cluster around and find new realisations in and through this one. So do readers and young performers in school classrooms. They are not exactly the same discourses and narratives from time to time and from place to place, and they depend on what the performing bodies know, can know, in these different contexts, but they are constantly remade in the labour of performance (Wayne 1991).

Text 6.2 both is and is not *Othello*. It is a transcript of a rehearsal text, of an improvisation performed, and lived, as part of a workshop at the Centre for Performance Studies at the University of Sydney in November 1990, and designed to prepare for a performance of the murder scene in *Othello*. As such it is a text which is a small part of the history of that performance text. Some of the words of Shakespeare's text are embedded within this rehearsal text, appropriated for use in another genre. They are the words Shakespeare projected as Desdemona's and Othello's words, now mediated again through the voices of actors and a director in another text, another story, another genre. The rehearsal improvisation is a genre designed to assist actors in the embodiment of the discourse, the habitus, of the other – the discourse of the character, or of the author through the discourse of the character – which the actor must embody in order to live the character and make the character live for an audience. It is a genre which demonstrates in microcosm, which makes visible in poignant and accessible ways, what happens in that other process of rehearsal and improvisation in classrooms where little girls and little boys are disciplined to take up their assigned positions in the genres and the discourses and the narratives of a patriarchal order (Kamler et al. 1994). It offers a place to read the disciplinary effects of patriarchal discourse on the bodies of masculine and feminine subjects, the violence which attends the making of masculine and feminine subjectivities.

The nature of the improvisation is explained by the Director at the beginning of Text 6.2. There are two improvisations, one involving the character/actor Othello, one involving the character/actor Desdemona. In each case, the other actor and the Director engage in pouring verbal poison into the ears of the character/actor, poison derived from Shakespeare's text, in ways which the Director says explicitly are like the voices in your head, the tapes that keep running in your head in everyday life.

The rehearsal situation typically involves an apparent, and linguistically (often pronominally) and corporeally marked, split subjectivity – where the actor's role as character and as self/actor are explicitly 'spoken'/'written' and performed differently and in intersecting ways. The same body speaks/performs both in different languages, with different bodily hexis, simultaneously, and frequently one merges into the other. The following is a brief example of an actor and director discussing, in rehearsal, the consummation of the relationship between Jean and Julie (which occurs off stage) in Strindberg's *Miss Julie*:

DIRECTOR: How would *he* feel afterwards?
ACTOR: Well *he* must have enjoyed it . . .

DIRECTOR: Yes, but how did *you* feel, straight afterwards, after you'd
     fucked her?
ACTOR: Oh, *I* enjoyed it, but it was really frightening with his
     Lordship's boots there . . .
     (from a rehearsal transcript, *Miss Julie Project*, Centre for Performance
     Studies, University of Sydney)

he = the character
you/I = actor as character

In the *Othello* improvisation the actor playing Othello continues to play a
role throughout the improvisation. On the other hand, the actor playing
Desdemona is herself as woman as much as she is Desdemona, and part way
through the improvisation, approximately where your text of that improvisation starts, Shakespeare's words, mediated by the voices and selves of actor
and director, begin to affect her body, do violence to it, as the body of
woman/actor, quite directly. It is not just Desdemona's *enacted, performed*
body that is affected.

In the improvisation with Othello as subject/object, the two women mostly whisper into his ears. Only towards the end does Desdemona/Actor say
Cassio's name loudly enough to be audible on the video recording.
Othello/Actor begins by sitting upright in the chair and remains upright
throughout, while the women stand, leaning forward slightly to reach his
ears, in an almost perfect embodiment of Bourdieu's description of the bodily hexis of sexual difference:

> The fundamental oppositions of the social order . . . are always sexually
> overdetermined, as if the body language of sexual domination and sub-
> mission had provided the fundamental principles of both the body lan-
> guage and the verbal language of social domination and submission.
> (Bourdieu 1980/1990: 72)

The actor begins by enacting a weeping, and rocking back and forth in
response to their whisperings – all of it text about cuckoldry and being
deceived and cuckolded by Desdemona – but he begins this as soon as they
start, acting it as Othello. As they continue he responds by enacting his
speeches as Othello in the murder scene, eloquently declaiming them as he
has been trained by now to do (as disciplined literate acting body), articulating and embodying from seated position the Othello he now performs.

The words from the text are all that is needed to reactivate that embodied
habitus:

> What is 'learned by body' is not something that one has, like knowledge
> that can be brandished, but something that one is . . .
> Every social order takes advantage of the disposition of the body and
> language to function as depositories of deferred thoughts that can be

triggered off at a distance in space and time by the simple effect of re-
placing the body in an overall posture which recalls the associated
thoughts and feelings, in one of the inductive states of the body, which, as
actors know, give rise to states of mind.

(Bourdieu 1980/1990: 73, 69)

The speech Othello/Actor performs, enacts, includes the lines:

It is the cause, it is the cause my soul . . .
Be thus, when thou art dead, and I will kill thee,
And love thee after. Once more and this the last, . . .
It strikes when it does love: she wakes.

(V.ii.1–20)

Therefore confess thee freely of thy sin . . .
            Thou art to die

(V.ii.54–7)

Othello/Actor is visibly upset by the whisperings, but he enacts Othello's
response without hesitation, performs the intention to do violence to that
which hurts him: to kill her. And the scene, Shakespeare's text, gives him
plenty of words with which to articulate this intention and his pain. He is
never at a loss for words and he is always in control, able to act and do.

The brief discussion following the improvisation is light-hearted and
Othello/Actor is not visibly upset by the experience:

B: I enjoyed doing that –
O: I couldn't hear what you were saying (*To B*) – I could only hear
      this side at first –
B: Oh and I was saying such *nasty* things to you –
O: Oh I know – I got it finally –

The improvisation with Desdemona/Actor as subject/object is very different.
This time the voices of Othello/Actor and the Director are mostly audible.
Desdemona/Actor responds with the few lines she has in the scene to
respond with (V.ii) – but this leaves her with only the possibility of denying
accusations, pleading for mercy or banishment, or asking for Cassio to be
sent for to speak on her behalf, to declare her innocence – 'M'Lord? What
do you mean? By my life – No!' She has no words with which to speak her
innocence – her guilt has been, and is being, written on her body, in her
body, by men's speech, and she has no words – Shakespeare's text gives her
no words – with which to deny it or to act. Nor indeed, as we saw above in
the child abuse case, does this society or its social structures. And her
embodied innocence, her love performed, is not enough. This masculinity
needs words, arguments, proofs, evidences, the public forms of debate and
consensus, which she cannot give. When they are given by duplicitous masculinity – Iago and the handkerchief – Othello misrecognises deceit as

evidence and truth, as he has been disciplined as masculine subjectivity to do, and destroys himself as well as her. His is a typical patriarchal problem, his highly valued genres are precisely those of evidence and truth. They blind him to all other genres and they destroy him. I am reminded here of Derrida's comment above about the dangerous nature of those who would purify.

In the Shakespearean text, the only words of defence for Desdemona offered by the text are given to Emilia – and the Director articulates these from time to time in Desdemona/Actor's right ear (but always as questions – 'Why should he call her whore? Is it not the husband's fault if wives do fall?') as Othello/Actor articulates a series of selected speeches about her worthlessness, whoredom, etc., in her left. Desdemona/Actor begins by sitting in an upright position, but her hands are already clenched in her lap, and her toes are turned in in a very vulnerable posture. As the voices continue, she gradually drops her head on to her chest, then into her lap in an almost foetal position. She gradually loses control of the Desdemona role – which gave her no control anyway – although she continues to speak Desdemona's words. At one point, where she is clearly very personally upset, her two tormentors pause, and then crouch behind her, lean closer and come in for the kill. This improvisation becomes *her* torment, *her* punishment – and in the end she weeps uncontrollably. There is a long period of silence, while she weeps and recovers – the two women academic observers and the male technician are also tearful.

The whole improvisation is extremely painful to watch, even on video. It is far too close to home, not nearly clearly enough a performance, verging on those other performances which rehearsal simulates, the voices that keep on running in your head when you are a woman brought up in a patriarchal society – and that you cannot answer, that you have no words to answer. What happens to the male actor is equally damaging. What one witnesses here is the construction of that masculinity which fears and hates femininity, is damaged by his fears about femininity, embodies and enacts the belief and the narrative that violence is justified in the name of protection – but he seems less damaged because of the patriarchal violence he is able to speak and act to deal with it. The whole construction of masculine and feminine subjectivity in patriarchy is rehearsed here – visibly, audibly and corporeally.

Theatre-trained practitioners do not always read this text the way I do. They see it, like the Director in the transcript, as a very productive piece of improvisation which can be used to make a performance. Like the genre of the judgement, it is that too, but it is also an instance of the very real pain and labour that is often involved for women in rehearsal, where, as part of their everyday working lives, they have to learn to perform the effects of the violence and misogyny in the texts of male playwrights (Gibson Cima 1993). Performance always involves a labour of making the self, a muscular, emotional labour, a labour of constructing memories for the body, which 'brands' the materiality of the body and leaves its corporeal traces in the text of performance.

This is why the complexities of genres, narratives and discourses must be studied, but also why it is important to be able to focus closely, linguistically, on relevant bits of the whole performance, and again much more widely, ethnographically, on the social histories of participants and processes. Neither poststructuralist theories of intertextuality, nor linguistics, nor ethnography alone can deal with the kind of complexity I have been trying to explore in this chapter, and no single patriarchal social theory can deal with the very different positions that are needed to read and write as women, as people of colour, as any of patriarchy's others. A whole range of theoretical fictions are necessary, a whole range of different positions to let us see around the corners of our theories and the stories in which we are entrenched, because they are in our bodies. We have somehow to teach the pleasure of storying, and thus the desire to see what it might be like in someone else's story, and to try to understand when we get there. And we have to subvert, not fulfil, the desire for tidy endings and clear beginnings, and to stress the scientific and ethical importance of never being satisfied with half the story or with the silences in stories. Telling many stories at once may be unsettling, and not very tidy, but it may just protect you from that monologic discipline which will otherwise keep you in your assigned place, speaking in the voice of the master, remaking the patriarchal order and the generic chains which bind you and keep you there. It is certainly a strategy which is neither apolitical, nor irresponsible, nor patriarchal. It is a feminist strategy for performing a politics of gender, race and class, which will not be built on the basis of patriarchal theories, and it is a way of telling differently the story of femininity, and a multitude of other stories, including those of masculinity. But it will only work as strategy when men read its stories as serious theory, and engage with it on those terms. Until they do, a whole range of serious gender issues will simply be left off the agenda.

Chapter 7

Poiesis, performance, (his)tories
Black man, white woman, irresistible impulse

I am producing too many stories at once because what I want is for you to feel, around the story, a saturation of other stories that I could tell, or maybe will tell or who knows may have already told on some other occasion, a space full of stories that perhaps is simply my lifetime, where you can move in all directions, as in space, always finding stories that cannot be told until other stories are told first.

(Calvino 1982: 88)

The abduction of Koorie children for enslavement became organised in NSW in 1893 . . . Threats of prosecution under the Neglected Children and Juvenile Offenders Act were used to coerce parents into compliance. In most cases children were just kidnapped – Koorie parents taught their children to run and hide when they saw a government vehicle or whites approaching . . . Children abducted from their parents were housed in the compound where they were to be deculturalised and were to learn a limited vocabulary in English. The speaking of their own language was banned.

(Fesl 1993: 112, 113, 114)

Implicit in her desire was racial self-loathing. And twenty years later I was still wondering how one learns that. Who told her? . . . I focussed therefore on how something as grotesque as the demonisation of an entire race could take root inside the most delicate member of society: a child, the most vulnerable member: a female . . . In exploring the social and domestic aggression that could cause a child to literally fall apart, I mounted a series of rejections.

(Morrison 1993: 167–8)

'THE BODY ENACTS THE PAST . . . WHAT IS "LEARNED BY THE BODY" IS . . . SOMETHING THAT ONE IS' (BOURDIEU 1980/1990: 73)

The discourse of Care and Protection associated with the public sphere and with the performance and constructions (*poiesis*) of a certain kind of white masculinity is particularly relevant to the subject-matter of this chapter. My concern here is with the rewriting across a period of almost a century, in many different institutional sites (the police, the media, the law, government, literature, film, tourism, pedagogy and the family) in many different genres and media of expression and by many differently embodied and coloured subjects, of the stories of the Governor murders in New South Wales in 1900. The stories culminate in some ways with the documentary by Frank Clune (1959), the novel by Thomas Keneally (1972/1978) and the film directed by Fred Schepisi (1978), but they do not end there. They go on beyond my last chapter.

The discourse of Care and Protection is central, it seems to me, to the present framing of those past events in the context of the 1992 High Court Mabo judgement on Aboriginal land rights, a judgement that was the culmination of Eddie Mabo's legal argument that ' "Australia" is morally illegitimate to the extent that it is founded on European denial of prior ownership by indigenous people' (Rowse 1993: 2). It is central to the continuing issue – even after major public enquiries, including a Royal Commission – of Aboriginal deaths in custody. It informs the infamous Aborigines Protection Act (1909–1936), as well as the related tragic issue of 'lost generations', the generations of Aboriginal children 'taken into state protection', removed from their families with no way of finding their way back (no records were kept which would enable them to be 'found' [Fesl 1993: 115]). It is distantly heard, too, in the partial records of 'frontier massacres' of Aboriginal people (Reynolds 1982, 1995), massacres aimed at 'protecting' white settlers.

Aboriginal people tell us they remember and continue to live many otherwise lost stories: 'I remember all of my mother's stories, probably better than she realises' (Huggins 1993: 61). They remember what Fesl has called 'the invisible text': 'unseen because it was scattered like lost pieces of a jigsaw through the pages of colonial archives' (Fesl 1993: 1). They do not 'have' these memories like knowledge to be brandished about – they live them, enacting a history that is never articulated by the white voices who have projected into the present James Governor's story. Their lived stories are the corporeal traces that precede (although their articulation follows) everything I will have told you. Theirs are the stories of 'what it has been like to be "on the other side" of assimilationist policies' (Huggins 1993: 61), stories of the embodied experience of the patriarchal structures of institutionalised racism which made James Governor, the white woman he married, the white women credited with inciting him to murder, and the legal subjects who, having passed judgement on them all, then weave their narrative of protection and closure to erase their embodied and disciplined involvement in that guilt. The one story that is never told – not discursively, not narratively, not generically – in all that will follow for some time in this chapter, is the story that holds all the others in place, that enables and produces the huge stabilities and intersecting complexities of the narrative and discursive patternings I will explore below – the story of whiteness and the story of Care and Protection.

Among the many things that are at issue in the tortured and difficult histories of the Governor murders are questions of how it is that subjects (identities), realities, beliefs and allegiances (what I have called above genres, myths, narratives, metaphors and discourses) are involved in the construction of our common-sense and theoretical understandings of culture, nation, race and sexuality or gender, how in fact they constitute the difference on which notions of culture are based. The Governor murder stories allow an exploration of the ways in which identity- and reality-constructing discourses and genres, dialogism and debate, are constantly remade, rewritten and recontextualised by differently positioned writers and readers across a range of genres produced in a diversity of institutional sites and in relation to complex networks of knowledges and reading and writing practices. And yet they also allow an understanding of how, with all that rewriting going on, deliberate political rewriting or merely everyday argument and difference, the same otherness, the same differences, the same marginalities, go on being reproduced as they are challenged and made differently. They allow an exploration of both the productive and the negative aspects of concepts like culture, nation and identity. They allow a different kind of exploration of the business of rewriting with which this book began.

FRAMING WHITE AUSTRALIA

Here is the question: Rivière's crime, in which the frontier between rationality and madness is hard to establish and which seems therefore to take its place in the sequence of crimes which had held the judicial stage in the 1820's [sic] – crimes disproportionate, excessive and incomprehensible, for they seemed to violate the natural and social order (parents killed, children killed, the criminal feeding on his victim's flesh, while the criminals seemed to have acted without apparent motive and to have been in possession of their full intellectual faculties).

(Foucault 1973/1975: 272–3)

I have quoted Calvino, Fesl, Morrison and now Foucault at length, as a way of introducing and framing the issues to be raised in this chapter. In their mutual contradictions and intersections they signal and anticipate the complexities and the legal and everyday fictions that surround the Jimmy Governor murder case in Australia in 1900. Narrative, hallucination, madness, rationality, history and memory, truth, objectivity, gender, class and race are just some of the issues at risk in the telling and multiple retellings of this story within and outside the law, tellings that challenge and confront the public face and presence of the law, and tellings that ultimately deny the possibility of the category 'extra-legal' precisely because the legal is always constructed and lived in the very space defined as extra-legal – the space of what law defines as its 'others'.

I will take as my starting point Michel Foucault's (1973/1975) *I, Pierre Rivière, Having Slaughtered My Mother, My Sister and My Brother . . .* In this text, Foucault and others set out an agenda for the exploration of the discursive construction of criminality: both the making of the criminal self and the categorising of that self as criminal, mad or deviant by the law and its agents. What this work demonstrates are the inevitable and consistent intersections between, on the one hand, the rationality and the contradictory practices of the law, medicine and psychiatry, and the contradictory rationality and insanity of the self that is Pierre Rivière, and on the other, the inevitable and consistent intersections between the apparently implacable, scientific and neutral faces of the law, medicine and psychiatry and their subjective, fictional, dialogic and feminised 'others' – the institutions of the media, popular and oral narrative culture and literature.

What is most interesting in all of this is the extent to which all of these practices, the embodied realities, the talkings, and the writings which are the traces we have of them, are limited and constrained by what can be said and written and indeed meant at a given point in time. Here I want to relate the Rivière case to Foucault's work on the discourses of the social sciences where he showed how official knowledges work as technologies or instruments of 'normalisation', providing the disciplinary structures which produce populations with carefully controlled and limited notions of what the 'normal' or the 'true' might be at a given point in time. Any disciplinary structure such as the law, medicine or psychiatry participates in these processes, so that what is to count as 'truth' or 'knowledge' – the truth about a person's health or criminality or sanity – is always the result of the kinds of institutional and discursive practices which constitute a discipline on the exclusion of its others (Foucault 1973/1975). Expert knowledges thus discursively produce the objects of which they speak and simultaneously exclude those categories which cannot be accounted for within the established 'truth'. Such categories include knowledges and discourses like those of the madman, the pervert, the patient, the peasant – knowledges and discourses that cannot be heard by the established order, or that have been subjugated, made 'marginal', by official histories.

In the case study of Pierre Rivière, Foucault makes it clear that he regards it as an act of resistance to the dominant systems of knowledge, a critical activity in itself, to simply 'quote' these unruly positions, without commentary (Foucault 1973/1975), thus publishing and making visible what is otherwise located below the level of 'science' (Foucault 1980: 81–2). Thus we read Rivière's 'confession' along with a number of the original nineteenth-century documents surrounding the case. There is no immediate commentary, but the documents dialogue effectively among themselves, juxtaposed so as to provide a study of the way techniques of normalisation, surveillance and punishment actually work. Rivière is a paradigm case in understanding how the modern criminal is produced.

He is a multiple murderer, with a history of apparently 'odd' behaviour, a peasant with little formal education who writes an apparently rational and 'educated' confession. In the course of the series of events which begin with the murder (or the murder/narrative – he writes that he had meant to write the narrative before the murder, that it was 'written in my head' before the murders), and proceed with his capture, the trial where he is found guilty and sentenced to death, the appeal where the sentence is commuted to life imprisonment, and his suicide in prison some years later, he is caught up in the contradictions, oppositions and 'indecisions' (McHoul and Grace 1993: 19) between a number of expert discourses and practices. First there are the contradictory arguments of the medical and proto-psychiatric experts who find him mad or sane, depending on whether it could be argued that a disease called 'monomania' – in which sufferers are mad for a short period and then completely recover their sanity – could be said to actually exist. If it did exist, then was it possible to argue extenuating circumstances and thus to find the culprit not guilty of murder? These indecisions already involve a second set in the form of two incompatible discourses on punishment. These discourses evidence a temporal discontinuity between the eighteenth and nineteenth centuries. Is a murderer to be executed – the visible and public punishment of the body – or to be sentenced to life imprisonment, with the associated implications of panoptic control (Foucault 1975/1982) and the becoming object of the subject who is then an object for scientific surveillance? But this is not yet the limit of the indecisions. At the level of popular knowledge, the witnesses contradicted each other. At the level of expert knowledge, so did the doctors – and the jury could not reach a decision.

Rivière committed these murders in 1835 at a time when revolution and murder, official and illegal killings, were endemic. At the same time as Rivière's trial for parricide was in progress, a trial centring around attempted regicide was also in process and being reported in the news. The parallels between the killing of a parent and the killing of the symbolic father of the body politic then entered the discursive fray, via the route of further indecisions about the relative roles of the legislature (and the sovereign) and the judiciary. The revolution had attached punishment solely to the legislature. 'Extenuating circumstances' might have appeared to be a reversion to the pre-revolutionary arbitrary discretion of the judiciary. There were political indecisions here as well: the judges could not deliver a verdict of 'extenuating circumstances' in a case of parricide with its links to regicide without offending the sovereign. They thus refused that verdict and then appealed to the king for commutation. This is just one aspect of the struggles for power that were enacted here in and around Rivière's statement – his murder/narrative/confession. In the course of this case psychiatric knowledge was introduced into the enforcement of the law. The criminal madman, as a being harmful to the social order, had to be condemned, 'but his status as madman took precedence over his status as criminal' (Foucault 1975/1982: 215). This paved the way for the development of the theory of limited responsibility and the introduction of all the degrees of insanity into the concept of responsibility before the law. It made it possible for not only psychiatry, but all the social and human sciences, to intervene in judicial procedure and to reduce, as did the presence of the jury as the representative of public opinion, the power of the judiciary. Thus the domain of the 'extra-legal', at the level of expert knowledges and public opinion, begins to enter the domain of the legal. These complex processes constitute the discursive construction of the criminal.

Through all of these procedures the account of the crimes which Rivière himself composed in prison continues to occupy a kind of non-space. There is no space for it in the deliberations and the discourses which surround it. 'The official discourses (law, psychiatry, medicine) simply do not know how to *treat*, in both senses, Rivière's memoir' (McHoul and Grace 1993: 20). One of the major problems is its indeterminacy, its genre, as narrative and/or confession, as diary, as plan of action even. Not the least of these imponderables, as Foucault has pointed out, is the way the murder and the murderer and the narrative/confession keep changing places (1975/1982: 202). The complexities of the relations between act, identity/subjectivity genre and discourse here are considerable; and they are not issues which the 'experts' in this case ever begin to *treat*. They persist in looking for a truth, for a certainty of knowledge in a discourse which has little to do with 'truth':

It was this (Rivière's memoir) that had to furnish the proof, fill the gap, and make it possible to re-establish knowledge in a certainty regained.

But what in fact happened? The subject who had fallen into a trap set a trap in turn; he behaved so as to raise the doctors' and lawyers' uncertainty to a sort of undecidable universal of madness instead of furnishing what was expected – the proof of the true and the false. In the event, the proof doubled back on itself as soon as they thought they had grasped it. One sentence is amply sufficient to demonstrate this: 'I was arrested with a bow and though I said I had made it in order to pass for mad, yet it was not exactly that.'

(Foucault 1975/1982: 285)

What is paralysed by this discourse in which the question of true or false remains undecidable is the experts' will to truth.

Speaking of their own attempts to discuss the question of murder, and anticipating criticism of the fact that their book is a text about texts about murder, and not about some ultimate reality, Deborah Cameron and Elizabeth Frazer (1987: xii–xiii) ask: 'What would constitute "the heart of the matter"?' – the absent ultimate reality. Their answer is that 'The discourse by which sex-killing is made intelligible to us, whether it comes from the killer, a psychiatrist or *The Sun*, is not parasitic on some higher truth: it is the heart of the matter and the rest is silence.' That is, the accounts that people give of killers, or that killers give of themselves, are not the 'truth', they are constructions, and, like all constructed texts, they depend on what Cameron and Frazer call 'the codes of the culture' to give them meaning.

When a killer writes, or speaks, a confession, he cannot do it except within the limits of his own experience, within the limits of the discourses and texts to which he has had access. His understanding of the events he records, like his representation of them, is always mediated by that kind of coded understanding and discursive and intertextual limitation. Thus, the 'truth' of the subjugated discourse, like that of the expert knowledge, is culturally, socially and historically specific, a cultural construction. It offers no blinding insight into the workings of the killer's mind. The explanations the killer provides are generic conventions which he has learned in society to be associated with that kind of event and which others recognise as probable accounts of it.

It is within this kind of explanation that Rivière's confession/memoir finds its place. Foucault argues that it is a place in a particular discursive tradition and the knowledges that go with it – a tradition of 'narratives of crime', circulating as broadsheets and true confessions, in which the people, speech and rumour, local narrative and news and great events, came to produce history:

> All these narratives spoke of a history in which there were no rulers, peopled with frantic and autonomous events, a history below the level of power, one which clashed with the law.
>
> Hence the relations of proximity, opposition, and reversibility set up by the fly sheets among the 'curious' news items, the 'extraordinary' facts, and the great events and personages of history. For the broadsheets narrated both contemporary crimes and episodes of the recent past; the battles of the Empire, the great days of the Revolution and the war in the Vendée, 1814, and the conquest of Algeria rubbed shoulders with murders . . . Murder establishes the ambiguity of the lawful and the unlawful.
>
> (Foucault 1975/1982: 205, 206)

Thus it was that Rivière 'came to lodge his deed and his speech in a defined place in a certain type of discourse and a certain field of knowledge' (1975/1982: 208). That historical field 'was the condition which made this premeditated murder/memoir possible' (1975/1982: 209). The representations available to him enabled him to envisage his act of slaughter as meaningful and justifiable. 'They shaped the form of his killing and the way he understood it' (Cameron and Frazer 1987: xiii). Desire, text and action were inextricably linked because they were 'produced' by a particular discursive practice made up of Bible stories and history learned at school, murders recorded in flysheets and broadsheets, and confessional autobiographies, and his lived experience of the contemporary social order, shifts in 'what historians awkwardly call mentalities' (Foucault 1975/1982: 183). 'He became aware that a snare lurked somewhere. What called itself order was a lie, or rather the existing order was the reverse of order. Pierre Rivière assumed the stance of a questioner of the straight and the crooked, the just and the unjust' (Foucault 1975/1982: 181). This is precisely what Cameron and Frazer (1987) demonstrate much more fully in their account of murderers as 'heroes' and 'deviants', taking up both kinds of discursive formation articulated in the Rivière case, the tradition of crime narrative and the expert knowledges of the normalising tradition. It is their explanation of the construction of the murderer as deviant and as hero, as 'produced' within a specific set of discursive practices, that foregrounds the relationship of these stories to the case of Jimmy Governor.

NED KELLY, BUSHRANGING, THE DORA DORA MURDERS AND SANDAWARA

Jimmy Governor's behaviour and self-construction has connections to this kind of lived 'reading formation'. The bushranger Ned Kelly had been at large in Australia from 1869 to 1880 when he was hung in Old Melbourne Gaol (Morgan 1994: 6). Sandawara, Tjandawara or Pigeon, an Aboriginal resistance fighter from the Kimberleys, was killed in 1897 (Muecke 1992: 66ff.). Muecke records two versions of the story of Pigeon, an Aboriginal version in which it is his cousin who defeats him by magical means, and Pigeon dies a hero, his gear carried off to 'be exhibited on an effigy in the museum in Perth' (Muecke 1992: 69). The white version, derived from Ion Idriess's account based on contemporary police records, has Pigeon cornered by police, trying to escape like a wild animal, and finally buried in a tree by tribesmen (1992: 66–8). Muecke points out that the 'black' version is said to derive from 'a man who was there', while the white versions all rely 'on the "official" printed word' (Muecke 1992: 70). The white version is committed to representing Pigeon as a defeated man and to the 'othering' of the Aboriginals (their strange burial customs); but, as Muecke points out, the Aboriginal version too exoticises events (the museum story). The white story belongs to the 'discourses on Aborigines as they have been formed in the intensely real and bloody struggles of history' (1992: 71).

In 1987, Colin Johnson published a novel, *Long Live Sandawara*, in which Sandawara survives as a fictional hero, but, perhaps more importantly here, becomes a hero for a group of young urban Aboriginals who set out to emulate the Sandawara myth, committing a bank robbery in which all are killed. Clune's documentary (1959) suggests connections between Jimmy Governor's 'voluntary confession' on capture and the story of the Dora Dora murders and murder chase, which began with the murder of a white man in 1891 and ended, after a three-year chase, in 1894. Like Pigeon, Jackie and Willie, the Dora Dora murderers, were black 'trackers', these two from Queensland. They had been employed by the Victorian police, but had been turned loose 'after their services were no longer required' (Clune 1959: 15). Clune's argument is that the fugitives passed through the Gulgong and Liverpool Plains district on their way northwards and 'may well have been helped by the "blacks" of the Gulgong district' (1959: 16). Jimmy Governor would have been 19 in the year they were captured, and would, according to Clune, have lived 'this marathon manhunt, as police and trackers in dozens cast around to overtake or intercept the fugitives' (1959: 16).

Jimmy Governor himself was appointed a tracker at Cassilis Police Station on 15 July 1896. The role of police trackers in the history of black/white relations in Australia is a complex one. There is only one account of that relationship which allows the tracker's own stories to be heard – the story of Jack Bohemia, published by Jack Bohemia and Bill McGregor in 1995. McGregor, in his introduction to the book, suggests that that relationship may have been very different to the way it is often stereotyped:

> He was not merely my 'informant': I was his scribe. In many ways the relationship that developed between us over the years . . . resembles the relationships which developed between Jack Bohemia and the police constables he worked with. He and I each had our own separate agendas to pursue; but we each had to make compromises . . . Our relationship was mutually exploitative, like the relationship between the tracker and the police constable. To regard it as simply me (powerful, white) exploiting Jack Bohemia (powerless, Aboriginal) as an 'informant' is at best to trivialise it, and at worst a serious misrepresentation . . . As will emerge from Jack Bohemia's narratives, he was not a man to be used by white people merely on their say-so.
>
> (Bohemia and McGregor 1995: 13)

There are very few places in the long and convoluted rewritings of Jimmy Governor's story when we hear his voice, and we never hear it except projected through the written words of white reporters. But when we do, in what is called a 'voluntary confession' on capture, he speaks of bushranging:

> During this time Jacky Underwood, Joe, myself and Mrs Governor were talking about bushranging at night after our work was done. I told them that if I was a bushranger I supposed I would take some catching. Jacky Underwood said: 'Oh no, Jimmy could not be a rider through the scrub like me; you would have to follow.' Joe said: 'I'm as good as any of you.' I said to them: 'I don't crack myself as being any good, but perhaps I could do as well as any of you.' Underwood said: 'What do you say if we go bushranging?' I said: 'I don't care.' Then Underwood said: 'I shot a blackfellow in Queensland. You had better come with me.' Two or three days before the Mawbey business I broke up our plates and saucers and everything in my own camp, and was to go next day, but didn't go. My missus, Jackie Underwood and Joe laughed at the idea of bushranging. They said to me: 'You are not game to go.' I said: 'That is forcing me to go.'. . . . During that time they had been talking about bushranging every

day. I had never read any of Deadwood Dick's novels or any books about bushranging till we came out that night.

(Sydney Morning Herald, 3 November 1900: 1040)

At his trial, he is reported as repeating this story, much more briefly, and saying: 'so I thought I would show them I was game and could lead them' (*Sydney Morning Herald*, 24 November: 1130). There are many narratives which may have positioned Jimmy Governor in 1900: but it seems extremely likely that the ones Jimmy himself knew about and articulated belonged precisely to that tradition of white romanticisation and eroticisation of masculine violence, the bushranging tradition, and to the complexities of the masculinities constructed in the tracker traditions of Australia's early histories, black and white. They are not traditions or discourses that are taken up in the later masculine literary and filmic attempts to rewrite the story, but they do not die. In many of the newspaper reports which the Keneally novel and the showing of the film reactivated in the 1970s in Australia, the romanticised bushranger story surfaces again (*National Times*, 2–7 January 1978: 5–10; *Sun*, 22 June 1978: 33; *Sunday Telegraph*, 20 April 1980: 9). The *National Times* piece is typical:

Trackers were despised by the whites and hated by the blacks.

Jimmy had been talking a bit about going bushranging. Ned Kelly had been dead only about twenty years.

Jimmy and Joe Governor hoped to be black Ned Kellys and as such they failed. Jimmy knew it . . .

He would never be anybody's hero.

(National Times, 2–7 January 1978: 6, 10)

In this 1978 story, the black man is denied access to the myths and narratives of bushranging visually as well as verbally. In one of the illustrating photographs the captured Jacky Underwood (Mort in Keneally's novel) is photographed flanked by four much larger policemen with the caption: 'Bushranging's not the game it's cracked up to be'. On the previous page three-quarters of a century of myth-making produces an image of a black man with club pursuing what appears to be a very ugly woman into what look like flames – the fiends of hell perhaps? This white denial of black access to Australia's bushranging history effectively also denies the history of black bushranging and the part those white masculine traditions of violence might have played in the production of a black murderer. Such a man has to be 'outside' white culture; but there is in fact every indication that he may have been positioned by, 'inside', these cultural stories of masculinity.

THE CULTURAL CONSTRUCTION OF MURDER

Cameron and Frazer explore the whole range of cultural representations of murder from Gothic models to nineteenth-century broadsides to the emergence of detective fiction and its associations with the pleasures of crime and horror stories such as *Frankenstein* (Cameron and Frazer 1987: 51). They point to the gradual emergence of a blurring of fact and fiction in the similarities between the generic characters of horror fiction and the murdering fiend of the tabloid press. They conclude that this is related to the development of sado-eroticism, the link between cruelty, domination and the erotic, and the existentialist construction of fiends and libertines as rebels. They find that there are two kinds of murdering heroes in these stories: the fiend/beast/monster whose terrible desires and deeds remove him from the pale of society and reduce him to the status of animal, nature before the social contract; and the libertine or rebel, the 'outsider', whose desires are also outside social norms, but only because of the repressive and restrictive nature of society. In both versions the murderer is essentially a man in a state of nature. There is either a pre-social-contract brutality and anarchy or an idealisation of the state of nature. As they point out, these two versions seem opposed, but in fact are not so dissimilar. In placing the killer in a state of nature, both versions explicitly 'deny that he could be in a "state of culture": *that is a product of society not an outcast or a freak*' (Cameron and Frazer 1987: 67; my italics).

Cameron and Frazer's argument is that the state of nature explanations cannot be sustained when questions of gender and power, which these explanations omit, are introduced in the context of social and cultural analysis. The culturally determined nature of sexual murder emerges from its connections with cultural ideas of sexuality and gender. Man's 'beastliness' is a specifically late-nineteenth-century phenomenon. They argue that there have to be reasons for this, and they find them in a potential for sex murder that is profoundly embedded in Western culture and has been so since the eighteenth century:

> The eroticising of domination, cruelty and death is by no means *natural*: it arose at a specific point in history. But it is also not confined to a few abnormal men: its imaginary forms are ubiquitous in the West, pervading both highbrow and popular culture, contributing to a taken-for-granted stereotype of masculine sexuality as intrinsically sadistic, intrinsically desiring to take the Other by force. In a culture which thus conflates sex, power and death, the sexual killer is hardly an exile.
>
> (Cameron and Frazer 1987: 68)

While the sex murderer that they deal with is explicitly one whose acts have a sexual or erotic aspect, there seem to me to be parallels with the murderers I am concerned with here – Pierre Rivière and James Governor – who murder women without an *apparent* erotic or sexual motive. I say 'apparent' because in both cases the *implications* of eroticism in the way men write about the murders are very real. In the case of Rivière, the link between eroticism and domination is made explicit by the doctors whose professional vision allows them to see that there is a problem of incest associated with Rivière's fear of women (Foucault 1973/1975: 148). Eroticism is constructed into the literary version of the Governor murders by Keneally, for whom the murderer of women must be motivated by lust after that which is the possession of the dominating white male – the full, ripe, Mrs Healy. It is also there in the novel in the Presbyterian minister's lusting after black flesh, the embarrassment of white father and son who discover they have been fucking the same black gin, and the exposure of the patriarchal phallus to Gilda, Jimmie Blacksmith's white wife:

> She stood still, remembering the day Mr Newby had come across her and her baby by accident . . . Gilda always avoided him if she could, but he rolled up to her on his horse, vaulted out of the saddle and exposed his patriarchal blunt genitals, slug-white and sitting in his hand for her information.
> 'When yer find a bigger'n that on a nigger, Mrs Blacksmith, let me know.'
>
> (Keneally 1972/1978: 69)

In many important ways, then, the Rivière case anticipates, contextualises and frames the Governor murders in Australia at the turn of the nineteenth century. It raises all the complex issues of discursivity, narrativity, subjectivity, memory and history that intersect with the law in the Governor case. Part of my aim will be to relate the terrible acts of the murderer to his being not deviant or out of control, not primitive and in a state of nature, but in a 'state of culture' and to understand how the 'hallucinations' (Goodrich 1991: 174) of the common law are also inevitably 'in a state of culture' outside of which they cannot in fact exist at all.

READING THE ARCHIVE

In this context, then, the body of texts I will 'use as evidence' is not to be read as an empirical data corpus. It serves rather more the function of what Foucault called the 'archive', in which the collection of texts, conversations, documents, are actually what represents the organisation of a discourse or set of discourses (their statements), a discursive formation. What they reveal are the conditions by which it is possible to 'know' something at a specific historical point and by which this knowledge changes. Foucault defines the archive as follows:

> I mean the set of rules which at a given period and for a definite society defined:

1 the limits and forms of *expressibility* . . .
2 the limits and forms of *conservation* . . .
3 the limits and forms of *memory* . . .
4 the limits and the forms of *reactivation* . . .

(Foucault 1978: 14–15)

In the case of the Governor murders, these issues are directly related not only to gender, but also to race. In this case, the murderer was black and the women murdered were white. Again the murderer is caught up in the contradictions and intersections of a number of sets of conflicting discourses and power relations in which the law is always and inevitably involved and which give the lie to any notion of linear progress. To be writing of these murders in the 1990s, inevitably, is to recognise the unruly and unseemly parallels between that other *fin de siècle* and this one. In 1988, Australia celebrated a bicentenary which symbolised a national identity and a homogeneity which were conceived at exactly the period when Jimmy Governor first behaved in ways that declared them to be dangerous and dominant fictions:

> The *fin de siècle* of the nineteenth century figures in British historiography not only as a crisis of empire and the rule of property, but also as a turning point between a society in which the 'New Woman' provoked a frisson of desire and dread, and the society that succeeded it, a society that considered individual rights so differently that it could within decades grant women the vote.
>
> (Magarey et al. 1993: xiv)

It was, however, a society that failed to do the same thing for its Aboriginal peoples until many decades later, a society that in 1988 had still not come to terms with the 'human costs of unified constructions of national identity' and whose Aboriginal peoples again on that occasion demonstrated that 'assertions of national identity, unity and community are constructed by means of exclusions and repression' (Magarey et al. 1993: xv).

FEMINIST VOICES: OTHER STORIES

Bell hooks, writing much more recently about the connections between gangsta rap and the culture evoked by the film *The Piano*, or a number of popular movies 'that are seen by young black females' – e.g. *Indecent Proposal, Mad Dog and Glory, The Romance, One False Move* – argues that they:

> All eroticise male domination that expresses itself through the exchange of women as well as the subjugation of other men through brutal violence.
>
> A racist white imagination assumes that most young black males, especially those who are poor, live in a self-created cultural vacuum, uninflu-

enced by mainstream cultural values. Yet it is the application of those values, largely learned through passive, uncritical consumption of the mass media, that is most revealed in gangsta rap. Brent Staples is willing to challenge the notion that 'urban primitivism is romantic' when he suggests that black males become 'real men' by displaying the will to do violence, yet *he remains resolutely silent about the world of privileged white culture that has historically romanticised primitivism and eroticised male violence.*

(hooks 1994: 121; my italics)

It is precisely these aspects of white masculinity that none of the masculine tellers of the Governor stories – in the press, the documentary, the novel, the film, the personal letter – ever see. Nor do they understand their own romanticisation of the primitive, or their eroticisation of male violence, and this is why these stories of James Governor are as much about whiteness and masculinity as they are about Aboriginality.

Australia's national identity has been built around explicit racial exclusions, both in terms of the limits imposed on Aboriginal peoples at home and the boundaries constructed against racial 'others' from overseas. This process of exclusion is inseparable from the conceptualisation of white women 'as producers and guardians of a white nation' (Knapman 1993: 125). It is the resilience of these patterns of racist thought and behaviour, and their complex intersections with an institutionalised sexism, that the retellings and reactivations of the Governor stories across almost a century indicate most clearly. The public and published versions of the story effectively work to silence many other stories, some of which emerge around the margins of the dominant story in a number of contested and unpredictable ways. Recent feminist revisions of the history of the construction of the Australian nation and national identity have much to offer in providing archaeologies of the discourses that speak the murder story in the 1900s (Magarey et al. 1993; Grimshaw et al. 1994). They demonstrate very convincingly just how much more varied and contested were the social, sexual and racial relations of the period than the public texts and narratives that are the traces of the Governor murders would indicate.

Of particular importance here are their discussions of institutionalised misogyny in the 'men's press' of the period and its associations with the bushman mythology (Lake 1993). Also significant are accounts of the complexity of class relations between women in the domestic sphere as depicted in the popular press (Hamilton 1993), where the complex 'servant problem' of the 1890s was often assessed in 'a fundamentally misogynistic way': 'Responsibility for the "problem" was shifted to the "tyrannising" mistress, with the male household head as mediator' (Hamilton 1993: 77). Even more interesting are Castle and Pringle's readings of political cartoons of the period depicting aspects of the arguments for Federation and the 'birth' of the new nation. They argue that, at the time of Federation, the cartoon images

of, for example, the prime minister dressed as a nurse, nurturing the baby
'Commonwealth', are an indication that

> No full-blown masculine image had emerged . . . to represent the spirit
> or identity of the new nation. The masculine image is 'disguised' in
> women's clothing. The questions broached in these cartoons are not only
> concerned with the form of independence. They also bring into play sexu-
> al anxiety, and fears regarding the fitness for autonomy or self-sufficiency
> of Australian manhood.
>
> (Castle and Pringle 1993: 147)

All of these new histories are directly relevant to the question of the representation and construction of masculinity and femininity in the period;
issues which are central to the way the law deals with, is able to 'read', and
constructs the Jimmy Governor case in 1900.

LEGAL FICTIONS

> The hallucinating mind is in strict terms a mind that wanders, that 'luci-
> nates,' that goes astray. That is the source of common law, of unwritten
> law, it is the meandering of the legal mind, a temporal and geographic
> nomadism that snakes its path across the justificatory texts, the judge-
> ments, of the year books and the law reports. Here we can understand
> how the text is also the unwritten structure of everyday life, a reality
> which time treats badly and transmits very slowly over long periods, how
> reason itself becomes a mask 'worn by longstanding historical and politi-
> cal facts, the memory of which men [have] retained over centuries'
> (Braudel 1958: 26), how the limits 'marked by reason' have nothing rea-
> sonable about them.
>
> (Goodrich and Hachamovitch 1991: 174–5)

What is at issue in this murder story or stories – because there is more than
one version – is the way the telling of stories at all levels in a social system
becomes a huge machinery for the construction of social realities, social and
cultural institutions and the people, men and women, black and white, who
inhabit them and make them in their turn. For they are made, not given, as
black, white, feminine, masculine, and the law is but one of the factors
involved in this making. Exploring this involves a social semiotics of the
interactions between institutions, people, texts, discourses and behaviours,
between law and society, and an understanding of the ways meanings are
made and transmitted. This begins to explain how apparently just, impartial
and 'truthful' institutions, like law, 'make' the worlds they think they merely
represent – and do it in talk and in writing – in discourse as social process.
   Jimmy Governor was, according to Clune (1959), a 'half-caste', 'half-
white' Aboriginal who married a white woman, and worked, very much

within the white masculine tradition of the Lone Hand described by Lake (1993), as part of the white bushman/mateship myth. He worked as solitary fencer, shearer's hand, itinerant farm worker. This was a social location and a tradition in which the black Jimmy Governor is clearly an intruder. At a certain point in this history he murdered the wife and children of his employer Mawbey, and their governess. The dominant contemporary public version of the story – in the media and in the courtroom – foregrounds a problem with women. In all the public accounts the real cause of the murders is attributed to the difficult domestic relations between the Mawbey women, their governess and Mrs Governor, the white wife of Jimmy Governor. These are both class and sexual relations. The women are said to have 'taunted her' because she had married a black man. Two crimes then are signalled here – both perpetrated by women.

First Ethel Governor, a white girl of doubtful parentage, has exchanged herself in marriage in quite improper and subversive ways. Second the Mawbey women have engaged in typical 'tyrannical' behaviour towards their 'servant', have nagged and harassed in typical feminine fashion. Part of this construction is also related to Anne Summers' conceptualisation of Australian wives and mothers, particularly where the white mistress rules over 'blacks' and 'savages', as the moral guardians of society, as 'God's police' (Summers 1975). These women are perceived to have expressed and enacted a racism that is nowhere attributed to the white head of the Mawbey household. The rest of the story is that the Mawbeys withheld supplies and rations – payment for the fencing Jimmy Governor was employed to do – because members of Jimmy Governor's Aboriginal family had set up a 'blacks' camp' on their property. The Mawbeys reneged on the contract to pay, with the argument that the job was not well enough done. But the women nagged and are, in the end, responsible for their own murder. How, you might ask? Well, it seems that their moral guardianship over her, their nagging femininity, is the cause of her nagging in turn. Ethel Governor becomes a nagging and hysterical wife, stirring up her already 'primitive' and problematic black (he is never referred to as half-caste) husband to take revenge on her behalf. Thus do women bring murder upon themselves.

The violence that is unleashed by her complaints – in the form of the first murders and then a number of subsequent killings – is easily explicable within the binary categories of the law, categories that were beginning to be established at the time of the Rivière case. When Jimmy Governor says in his statement to police, 'I got out of temper, and got hammering them, and lost control of myself. I do not remember anything after that', he categorises himself as irrational, subject to uncontrollable passion, and liable to a defence argument of diminished responsibility, manslaughter not murder, passion not premeditation. The possibilities of the adversarial arguments in the courtroom are constrained by the limits of a discourse that both silences and appropriates the stories of the everyday, the community and its others.

But it is more complex even than this. The Jimmy Governor story becomes a part of a much larger story, a media story, a story of the making of a nation, of masculinity, of subversive and unruly women and dangerous racial others, and of the need for masculine control and protection to resolve these issues. In this context the arguments and oppression of the courtroom at the Governor trial are inevitable. They are also partial and constructed and it is the nature of that construction, that making of the black criminal and his guilty white wife, that I want to explore now.

MEDIA, NATION AND NARRATION: 'THE THRILL OF HORROR'

Jimmy Governor first earns notoriety when the events of the murders are reported in the *Sydney Morning Herald* on 23 July 1900. They are reported as a small paragraph in the 'Country News' column. The day after the murders, a number of pieces of a murder story, not even connected so that one would know they were part of the same story, are sandwiched between two very different kinds of local events – accidental death and a flood. The local loss of livestock at sea in bad weather sits between a number of international items – the Boer War, the Boxer Rebellion in China.

As the events escalate and the story develops, it occupies more and more space in the daily newspapers. Gradually, from day to day, cohesively and intertextually, a more and more alarming state of affairs is constructed. In a pre-television, pre-radio age, it seems that the newspapers functioned very much in the way that Patricia Mellencamp has suggested that television does now:

> Anxiety is television's effect . . . TV time of regularity and repetition, continuity and 'normalcy', contains the potential of interruption, the thrill of live coverage of death events. It is here, in the potential and promise of disruption – a shift between the safe assurance of successive time and story and the break-in of the discontinuity of the real in which the future hangs in the balance, the intrusion of shock, trauma, disaster, crisis – that TV's spectatorial mechanism of disavowal, which is retroactive, operates most palpably.
>
> (Mellencamp 1990: 80)

This is a perfectly articulated description of the discontinuities, the disruption of narrative order, and the intrusion of disaster that occurs on the newspaper pages in 1900. Towards the end of the three-month chase to capture the murderers, the *Sydney Mail* (November 1900) gives the story full-page spreads, with photographs and maps of the route followed by the Aboriginals and their pursuers. The story occupies half the columns in a full double-tabloid-size page of the *Herald*. It also occupies much of the space in the *Bulletin* and other local newspapers and magazines at the time. As the story develops, it appropriates and intersects with other stories and is recontextualised by them.

Colin Mercer, writing of the function of newspapers in producing the nation as habitus – a 'specific way of being in the world' – at the time of the bicentennial celebrations in Australia in 1988, describes the way the various subgenres involved in reporting that event operate 'to classify and delineate different phenomena, to enable certain forms of social identity and affiliation to be established and to establish in tangible forms the existence and arrangement of groups, classes and communities' (Mercer 1992: 28). He regards the newspaper as a 'civilising technique':

> It is possible to follow some of the paths flagged by him [Elias] in the relationship between a regular material cultural form like the newspaper and the elaboration of techniques for forming and mannering populations and citizens in the much more complex, extended and diverse national societies which emerged in the nineteenth century. Following this route, we can propose a concept of the nation itself not as a static structure, a container of dominant ideologies, a simple 'invention', or indeed a 'myth', but rather in terms of the rituals, daily practices and techniques, institutions, manners and customs which enable the nation to be thinkable, inhabitable, communicable and thereby governable.
>
> (Mercer 1992: 27)

The newspaper is one such technique, then – and a crucial one – in constructing the limits of what could be said and communicated about the Governor murders. At one level that did indeed involve the communication of 'high anxiety', the construction of a state of 'intense feeling' and 'alarm' which the authorities, the law and the reporting agencies of the media could then step in to allay. Thus, what keeps being told in and through the loosely organised fragments of the newspaper stories is actually the same story: the story which enables the nation to be thinkable, another 'invisible text' which you have to construct by reading across generic and textual boundaries. It is a story of masculinity confronted with considerable social disorder or disharmony, violently restoring order in the name of the protection and care of its others; a story of a certain kind of exclusive white masculine citizenship.

The distinctive repertoire of images and narratives in the Australian press in 1900 produces a characteristic construction and representation of the nation at the time of Federation. The Jimmy Governor story is always accompanied in the papers of the day by a small group of other topical stories. There are stories of war, and of masculinity engaged in war – the Boxer Rebellion in China and the Boer War in South Africa. These stories intersect with the myth of the Australian bushman and the complexities of the discourse of property, sexuality and protection which emerges around the dangers to women and children that are always present in war. They are also explicitly racist in their treatment of the racial other. Many of the Boer War stories in the newspapers stress the prowess and invincibility of the

Australian bushmen in the foreign space of South Africa. The problem with the Governor 'Black Fugitives' is that they seem, as racial and inferior others, to be able to elude the invincible bushman on his home ground. This activates – the body remembers – the dialogic construction of a discourse of the 'black' as 'nomadic/wanderer', one who 'goes bush', as the 'primitive' who, alone and close to nature, can evade capture in nature's own realm: the bush. These are statements of the discourse of race, but they are motivated, activated here by a particular problem, the racial 'others" disruption of the dominant story of the invincible white bushman. This is addressed specifically and dialogically in the following account/recount in the *Sydney Mail*:

> Not only is the country being put to a heavy expense, but the whole of the social life of the settlers along the murderer's tracks has been in a disorganised state, these black fiends having created a terrorism which is almost difficult to understand. Then there is another phase of the question which will likely escape attention. It is *the reputation our bushmen* now hold in the eyes of the outside world. That two men should be able to elude capture for three months is what will not be readily understood by outsiders. But whilst mistakes were made in the arrangements for capture, the nature of most of the country through which the Governors travelled was such that *only blackfellows who knew the wild and perilous nature of the hills would have any chance of capturing the fugitives.*
>
> (3 November 1990: 1056; my italics)

Only the black tracker, 'the superiority of Aboriginal knowledge and sorcery over whites and their weapons' (Bohemia and McGregor 1995: 69), will now be able to capture the Governors, and indeed the trackers from Queensland are called in. Thus does the capture of the Governors become a question of intertextually constructed national and masculine pride, a question of the reassertion of the values of culture over nature, civilised over savage. But, ironically, it is achievable only with the help of the black man in white man's clothing – the black tracker. The collocation intertextually of these stories of war and the developing narrative of the chase after black murderers at home, the visual and verbal genres, story and photograph, begin to parallel one another in the different geographical and newspaper spaces. Ranks of armed men in Africa look very like the photographs of the captors of Jimmy Governor, or even the ranks of men who form the jury which will judge him.

Thus the *Sydney Mail* account of the capture of the Governors on 10 November 1900 includes a very brief verbal text and almost two whole pages of photographs. These include the photograph of the prone, uncovered dead body of Joe Governor, full-face to the reader; an artist's impression of the shooting of Jimmy Governor, the body falling, face down, hands outstretched, towards the reader, in a virgin bushland setting, his white captors in the background, half concealed by a clump of trees; and three photographs which have to be 'read' as having an intertextual relation with the Boer War account and photographs on an earlier page of the paper on the same day. These include the photograph of John Wilkinson, holding his rifle, bearded and hatted (the man who shot Joe Governor). Generically and visually it is unmistakably similar to the photograph of three armed men entitled 'Boys and Men Were in the Boer Ranks' in the Boer report. Then there are two photographs, one of the ranked 'Captors of Jimmy Governor', one of 'The Jury' to try him. The genre is familiar. The photos are exactly parallel to that entitled 'Group of Burghers' in the Boer War report of 3 November; a group of armed men, defending their country from attack. The masculine 'esprit de corps', the solidarity of masculine bodies (and arms) united in a common cause, the individual who emerges from the crowd as captor, the reassertion of juridical and social order over the disruption created by black murdering bodies and feminine murdered ones, is all constructed in the ordered ranks of masculine bodies in these photographs. The genre, the medium (here visual), the site for the construction of the discourse, is different, but the discursive fields and their semantic potential are constant.

RACE AND UNRULY WOMEN

The only photographs of women in these pages of the *Sydney Mail* are of murdered women or problematic women, like Ethel Governor, a white girl who married a black, so that her photograph becomes a sign of the existence of the unthinkable/the unmeanable in this discursive field of gender and race and class relations. It is in some ways a more disruptive element than the murderers or the murders, since she has single-handedly disrupted the system by which women are given in exchange by men to one another, the system of protection. She has given herself from her position as 'white trash' and broken the rules of the framing and classification systems (Bernstein 1990) which should govern such exchanges. As such, she stands on the page as 'evidence' of a feminine desire to speak, to act, and of the doing and the consequences of it, head down in shame, eyes hidden by her hat, with no direct eye contact with the reader. The murdered 'respectable' women all gaze directly at the reader.

These photographic images of dead women, shamed women, who spoke when they should have been silent, are statements in the discourse on gender of which the stories on female suffrage are also a part. Juxtaposed with the stories of masculinity, war and aggression, the stories of protection, the woman suffrage question is constantly being debated. This is a story which constructs women very differently. It is juxtaposed in turn with stories on the question of the imminent Federation of the Australian States and the choice of a site for the National Capital. Again the genre of photograph which depicts the founding fathers of the nation is the same as that which depicts men at war saving the nation and men at home doing likewise. There is a

very real sense in which the unruly women in the Governor story are intertextually implicated in, and constructed by, a constant reference to (and
deferral and fear of) female suffrage in the new nation. The need to deprive
women of citizenship, to keep them out of these new public spaces, is very
real. So, the Governor murders, like Australia's convict past, are a very real
problem for imminent nationhood. In some way the story has to be made to
be a narrative of masculine control and power, of national success, not failure. This, I suggest, is why women have to be seen to have caused their own
murders and why institutionalised masculine white racism cannot be
acknowledged. As Claudia Knapman (1993) demonstrates, this is unfortunately not an uncommon narrative. Women and non-whites had no voice of
their own in our histories and narratives, and were always constructed in
terms of the stories that could be told, stories that were themselves constructed in terms of racial and gender ideologies. For her,

> This colonisation of historical explanation is the most significant of all
> the ways in which race and gender intersect. It is particularly obvious in
> the way in which a stereotype of the dependent and peripheral white
> woman has been brought into the action of the male colonising endeav-
> our to 'explain' white racism and racial conflict.
>
> (Knapman 1993: 135)

The media narrative, carried on in a variety of specific sites over a period of
months, is a narrative of masculine protection and the mobilisation of masculinity against the irresistible passion of the primitive and the irrational,
women and the racial other. It is a reassuring story which attempts to contain and eradicate (by hanging), and quickly (before Federation and the
public ceremonies which must argue for unity and identity), and by innuen-
do (women out of place are the cause of this unrest), those elements of its
own masculinity which it cannot speak and will not acknowledge. In fact,
Jimmy Governor was arrested just three weeks after Federation. But, just as
in the case of the political cartoons surrounding Federation (discussed
above), this masculinity is extremely problematic in the case of this media
and legal narrative, a masculinity indeed ' "disguised" in women's clothing'
(Castle and Pringle 1993: 147).

THE MEANINGS OF PROTECTION

I want here to quote from just three stories which surround early reports of
the Governor murders and are juxtaposed with these on one page of the
Herald in order to illustrate some of the points I have been making about
masculinity and nation.

> From China the news contradicts itself day by day. It is not more than a
> week since the world was filled with horror at the news of the slaughter of

Europeans in Peking. Only on Saturday last we received detailed accounts of the stripping and hacking of European women in the streets and the ruthless massacre of children. Shortly before that there was a circumstantial story of that last stand of the refugees at the legations, when white women and children were pistolled by their defenders at the last extremity to prevent their falling alive into the hands of their Chinese Assailants. It would now appear, if the latest of these reports is to be believed, that all this is officially denied.

(Sydney Morning Herald, 27 July 1900)

Here is the discourse of protection in full force – women and children as property; sexuality and death and the fear of the racial other. Here, protection is murder. This has uneasy and troubling connections with Cameron and Frazer's account of murders by husbands, and suicide murders, where the notion that the woman and/or her children are extensions of the male self, his property – 'if I go she goes' – is very common (1987: 15). What is even worse, as they point out, is the extraordinary judicial attitudes that emerge in trials following such murders, where statements like 'I regard this as a sad case. I am satisfied you were deeply devoted to your wife' (1987: 15) are not uncommon. That this discourse of protection by murder was common and often associated with racism is also illustrated by its appearance in the newspaper *Boomerang*, in a story published in twelve weekly parts in 1888. The story was called *The Race War* and is about white Australian fears of Chinese immigration. In it, a man speaking to the father of a girl he wants to marry repeats the discourse we have noted above: 'I'd sooner kill her with my own hands than have her live to raise a brood of coloured curs.' Her father replies that he knows 'the fate of a white girl among those leprous minded Asiatics' (quoted by Robin McLachlan, Charles Sturt University, in a lecture entitled 'The Past Invents the Future'; see also Dixon 1995). They are quite similar in some ways to the kinds of stories that were serialised in the *Sydney Morning Herald* in close proximity to the reporting of the Governor murders. The titles of two such stories were 'A Burgher of the Free State' (Rudyard Kipling), which was serialised in three parts at the end of July, and a story by Barbara Grand, 'Babs the Impossible', which began on 7 November.

As if this were not sufficient, the second quote from the *Herald* goes like this:

The burghers who after submission went away to join the raiders left their wives and families at Pretoria, to be maintained there by the British . . . These undesirable inhabitants were now ordered to join their husbands so that the capital may be relieved of their presence – dangerous as well as expensive. When they are encumbered with their wives and families the Boers will not be so eager in their guerilla warfare.

(Sydney Morning Herald, 27 July 1900)

Foreign women and children, it seems, do not warrant the kind of 'protection' given to one's own, but the consequences are probably similar. Juxtaposed with these two reports is the following:

> So far as the objections to womanhood suffrage are concerned which base themselves on the unfitness of women to vote, they are answerable in the same way. Fitness comes with exercise, and once the privilege of franchise is asked for, there is no valid abstract reason against its being granted. The remarkable fact about the situation as regards womanhood suffrage however is that so far no representative majority of women has asked for the franchise.
>
> (*Sydney Morning Herald*, 27 July 1900)

The representation of the 'unfit' woman voter stands curiously, and yet entirely appropriately, beside the women in need of protection and the fear of the racial other in the examples above.

Framed by the stories of these women who have not asked for the franchise and global reports of masculine protection elsewhere, a very similar discourse is being constructed at home in and through the daily reporting process. it is realised in the cohesive, thematic and logical links between individual reports and whole pages of newspaper text. The early reports have a characteristic set of transitivity patterns (verbs and the roles of the participants that go with them). Black men are actors and white women are goals (*Murders by Blacks*). As white masculinity mobilises, it becomes actor and black men become goals (*Surrounding the Blacks*; *Gloucester: Search Parties Leave for Singleton*; *Dungog*). This grammar of action and pursuit is supported by visual and narrative elements – the spatial, visual representation in map form titled 'Track of the Fugitive Blacks' (*Sydney Mail*, 3 November 1900: 1049) and the narrative 'A Chase of 81 Days', reported as the real story of one of those who had been pursuing the by-now outlawed Governors:

> I started off on July 22 last in search of the Breelong blacks, and followed them on day after day until Wednesday last, a period of 81 days. I have been fourteen years following station life, droving, &c., but I never undertook a thing in my life in which I had such experiences as I had during this chase. I would not undergo a similar trip again if I were offered 350 pounds, let alone the chance of capturing Jimmy Governor.
>
> (*Sydney Morning Herald*, 1 October 1900: 8)

About the same time, there is the beginning of a different use of projection (to construct fear and panic) so that what is thought to be in black heads (intentions) is reported in headlines as nominal or verbal fact: *Intention to attack other settlers*; *Blacks intended to attack*. Between 27 and 30 July, there is an extraordinary increase in activity (the 'blacks' are perceived to be everywhere), black trackers are called in, a reward is offered, and Kieran Fitzpatrick is murdered. This is accompanied by a whole new lexical pattern

– *rumour, excitement, gossip, anxious, unease, intense feeling* – which is thematised and cohesive across reports on the successive days. Stories reported as fact turn out to be fiction, projections of someone's fears and anxieties. Thus the Fitzpatrick murder is reported in contradictory ways in different columns of the same page of the *Herald* on the same day (28 July 1900):

'*Rumours Afloat*'
All sorts of rumours are afloat and it is not easy to separate fact from fiction. The most extraordinary stories have been circulated especially on the coach routes. *One of the most circumstantial was that an elderly man named Fitzpatrick, had been killed at Pogga, twenty miles west of Mudgee.*
(*Sydney Morning Herald*: 6, col. 3)

'*Excitement in the Country*'
In connection with the recent murders the people in the outlying districts are becoming terrorised, and are arming themselves with weapons and ammunition. Mr Fitzpatrick who *was murdered* at Wollar is a brother of Mrs George Brown of Wellington.
(*Sydney Morning Herald*: 6, col. 4)

Here, under different headlines in two adjacent columns of the paper on the same day, there are contradictions which seem to derive from the dynamic effects of lexical cohesion in the making of text. *Excitement* produces *terrorisation*, and in that context killing will have occurred. In the lexical set of which *rumour* is a member, *killing* will turn out to have been *circumstantial*, *story*. On 30 July, there is another generic reclassification; the killing 'story' will, after all, have been *fact*, but the details have changed under legal and medical scrutiny. The stories that are constructed through this report genre are partly 'factual' reports of events and partly realisations of the meaning potential of an intertextual discursive field that operates through bodies that remember, fear, anticipate. These textual traces are all that is left of the materiality of those bodies, the reality of those anxieties. This discourse they remember and have lived has considerable predictive and constraining power and bears little relationship to the 'congruent' or the 'real'. Yet the generic interpersonal relations of report consistently present the whole (including the reclassification of fact as rumour) as if it were objective fact, and attempt to position the reader to accept it as such. It is the regularity of the sequencing of these events, day after day, and the anxiety produced by the uncertainty of gossip, that produces compliance with the dominant story of chase and capture.

The construction of anxiety, and of the desire for the removal of the cause of the anxiety, continues with each new set of headlines and events:

Tragedy
Child killed *in mother's arms*
Finding the *bodies*

A *Terrible Experience*
Funeral of the *Victims*
A *panic* amongst the settlers
Female teachers in the country
(my italics)

This interpersonal semantics of anxiety is what may seduce the reader to comply with 'real' attempts (generically constructed as proposals/suggestions) at eradication of the danger to the social order:

Proposal to use bloodhounds
Reward *should be* increased
Settlers *should be* given arms and ammunition
(my italics)

Women in the country are in need of protection again. The cohesive and logical consequences of that in this context are once again masculinity rampant. The wave-like patterning across the texts from the thematising in first position of the masculine world, the agents of capture and pursuit (*the resources of every police station, everyone is armed with Winchester rifles, carbines and revolvers*) to the end-focus in sentences and clauses on the verbal and mental activity (encoded in projecting nouns – *speculation, discussion, alarm, ridiculous stories*) in the social world which now takes on a life of its own, is absolutely consistent across a number of separate reports on these days. These projecting nouns, mental processes, are constructing realities which have to be deconstructed by *authentic news* in order to maintain social order (*to allay alarm*). This dialogism and activity, together with the *affect* associated with *panic/alarm*, now become the focus of the overall narrative. Under the heading, 'The Work of the Police', sub-heading, 'Intense Feeling in the District' (28 July), the consequence of reward and the theme of danger to female teachers in the country is picked up cohesively and dynamically and generalised to all women:

Theme (writer's starting point)	*Rheme* (end-focus for the reader)
1 *Every man* [[who can leave his women-folk in safety]]	is joining *in the pursuit*
2 *Everyone*	is armed
3 *There*	is practically *a panic* *among the women-folk*

4 *Anxious fathers and brothers* have hastily
   returned from Sydney and Maitland . . .
   to allay as much as possible
	*the uneasiness which is
	felt on all sides.*

Women are relegated here to embedded clauses (postmodifying adjectival/relative clauses) as masculine possessions ([1] *his* women-folk) or become the site, at the other end of the clause, of the panic/alarm which has to be controlled (see [3] and [4]). In a very interesting way the *fathers and brothers*, the *everyone* of this text, have the same function as *authentic news* in *allaying* fear and *alarm*, which in this report takes a specifically feminine form. This seems to map back retrospectively, cohesively and intertextually, on to the *rumours/gossip/ridiculous, pernicious, stories* of the earlier account. These lexical items have connotations of femininity. They anticipate and collocate with the solidarity of the feminine 'taunts' adduced by the case for the prosecution in the law court. Men are the active forces in this social world, women take cover in the enclosures of the towns and are protected. Their hysteria is controlled by this means, although in fact it is men who are rushing about the countryside giving chase and effectively leaving the women to their own devices. He who discusses or protects by rushing off to give chase is always white and male. The thematic choices inscribe this into the text. The themes also serve as the starting point, the 'given' for the reader, and thus construct a reading position that is unlikely to unsettle that dominant masculine perspective, even though there are alternative and contradictory stories:

> This unprotection worried many. Everyone would have liked a policeman sitting on his doorstep. W. F. E. Cole, JP, wired the Inspector General of Police from Coolah on July 30, 'Town without police protection for ten days. Black murderers reported twenty miles from here. Many men away. Panic in town. Meeting of whole population unanimously request me to ask that at least one policeman be sent here immediately.'
>
> (*National Times*, 2–7 January 1978: 8)

Women must be kept in their place, and that place is not the public space of politics and voting. What we have here is a representation of femininity and masculinity which permeates the newspaper reports of the Governor murders and the accounts of the trial with which they conclude. In all of them, sexuality and race are inextricably intertwined. In all of them, women and people of colour are marginalised, silenced and oppressed. In all of them, the masculinity of the black murderer is an issue. In all of them, the controlling and protective masculinity which represents, constructs, reports, judges and condemns is problematic in the extreme. In all of them, there are traces of the institutionalised racism which would produce the White Australia Policy and a nation that in 1988 would still be struggling with the issues signalled here. One is reminded of Cameron and Frazer's (1987) comment that, in a society where death, sexuality and property are so inextricably linked, and here one could add racial hatred and fear, the sex murderer, the black murderer of white women, are both hardly 'exiles'. There is a fine line between the violence perpetrated by a Jimmy Governor on the white race and the violence that is legalised and socially ratified in war against foreign women and children and in a crime scenario where the criminal is 'outlawed', outside the law, and therefore able to be murdered with impunity. The masculinity that is at stake here is, indeed, not 'outside the social and the cultural', deviant, abnormal, but absolutely 'in the social and the culture', culturally, socially constructed, and the men of law are no exception.

I want to turn briefly to another set of discursive or narrative constructions of femininity and black masculinity before I look briefly at the summations in the Governor trial as reported in the *Sydney Morning Herald* in November 1900. It is the construction of Ethel and Jimmy Governor that concerns me here. The newspapers do not concern themselves with her. It is only when the case comes to trial that she is constructed as the ultimate cause of her husband's violence. The law, then, is directly implicated in producing this explanation as the conclusion of the media narrative. It is only when the transcripts of the court proceedings become available for publication that the narrative of nation and masculinity can conclude with the accusation of the feminine, a conclusion produced and constructed by the ultimate in masculine and paternal protection, the law and the State.

WAIF, WITCH, WHORE: WHITE WOMEN WHO MARRY BLACK MEN

In the public versions of the Governor stories there are a limited number of narrative explanations of Ethel Governor. It is important to recall here that the story circulates and escalates well beyond the confines of the newspaper and legal narratives in 1900. In the 1950s, contextualised by debate over the White Australia policy, Frank Clune's documentary, *Jimmy Governor* (1959), was published. In the 1970s the issue of Aboriginal rights, including finally the issue of Aboriginal suffrage, contextualises and reactivates the story in Keneally's novel, *The Chant of Jimmie Blacksmith* (1972/1978). The film version of the novel was directed by Fred Schepisi and screened in 1978. The novel and the film in turn reactivate a series of newspaper accounts of the events of the murders in 1900. The closing of Dubbo and Wollar gaols during this period, and the transforming of the former into a tourist museum, has a similar effect. New versions of old stories appear in the press and a new anonymous, ballad, *The Breelong Blacks*, which had been in circulation in pamphlet form ever since the murders, is reprinted in the booklet produced to commemorate the closing of Dubbo gaol (Hornadge 1974). This ballad again tells a version of the story that is different from the public constructions of the events. In 1990, my own interest in these events led to contact with the family of Kieran Fitzpatrick. Family papers and photographs, including a letter written by S. G. Ellis, a hawker who knew the Mawbey property at the time of the murders, provided a further set of variations on the public story. An interview with a family member whose memory of the events, constructed through oral family narrative and newspaper clippings, as well as the novel and the film, also offered a very different version of the story to that available through the legal and media construction of the events. In 1994, I taught these materials in a first-year course at Monash University. One of my first-year students who had helped in her final year of school with the editing of an Aboriginal students' magazine provided me with a narrative of the events written by a Year 9 Koorie girl student in 1993. The story obviously continues to circulate among black and white families, and it continues to bear the marks in both places of the versions of events that constituted the public and national narrative in 1900, a sexist and racist narrative told by men. In all of these versions, pre- and post- the actual trial of Jimmy Governor, the law remains implicated. It remains implicated through its judicial construction of the black murderer, his irresistible passion to kill, and his guilty white wife.

Ethel Governor is a problem. Why would a white woman marry a blackfellow? One explanation is class. As Clune puts it, 'an ignorant young woman who had taken an irrevocable step so far down the social scale that, in the opinion of the scornful, she could sink no lower' (1959: 27). Her father was a miner and she was pregnant and 16 when she and Jimmy married. This was a girl who was 'no better than she should be'. Frank Clune's 1959 story goes like this:

> Probably she was a waif, in domestic service in the township, or at a farmhouse, earning the wage of five shillings a week and keep that was usual at that time for young domestic servants or nursemaids, and with little romance in her life. Jimmy Governor was handsome, athletic, honest, sober, a steady worker, a fine horseman. Why shouldn't she fall in love with him?
>
> (Clune 1959: 25)

Clune's story is sympathetic, a Mills & Boon romance version of events. But there are already contradictions which emerge in his account of Jimmy: 'Why shouldn't he marry a white girl? Their children would be three-quarters white, and legitimate. Why not?' (1959: 25). And then: 'Jimmy Governor had done the right thing by a white girl he had seduced. He had made an honest woman of her, and had given her child his name' (30). Was she the victim of her own irresistible passion for the black man, or a victim of his desire to ally himself with the white race, his seduction? In the Keneally novel and in the film she is represented as a slut, a girl who sleeps around, the only kind of girl a black man would find to marry him. The stereotype of the white woman's irresistible lust after black flesh is also mobilised in some versions. A popular misogynistic version of these complexities, which begins to rewrite her as witch and murderer herself, is to be found in *The Ballad of the Breelong Blacks* (1974):

Now Mawbey he had no right
In touching those posts at all.
No doubt he thought he was cunning:
But it stuck in the Darkies' gall.
And there is that brazen faced woman,
I'm alluding to Governor's wife.
Who prompted them on with the murder.
She ought to be jailed for life.
For the lies and the yarns she told Jimmy,
Of the things that the Mawbeys said,
That for living her life with the blacks,
Both Jimmy and her should be dead.
That's how she worked up a row,
A scheme that was worked some time:
And if ever the truth gets known,
She coaxed Underwood into the crime.

She is even depicted as taking part in the actual murders:

But they were seen by Governor's wife,
'Look Jimmy, there go the girls!'
Were the words that vixen said.
The criminal ran them down.
With his Bondi killed them dead.

This anonymous text is very like the pamphlets and broadsheets circulating around the vicious and violent crimes of Pierre Rivière. Its very existence indicates a whole other oral history of talk and text-making around the crimes of which we have hardly any trace – the only public recognition of it the reference to rumour in the newspapers. It has interesting connections to public texts. Frank Clune records that Mrs Newby's dying deposition actually linked Ethel Governor to the murders. There is otherwise no evidence that she took part and every evidence that she did not. Clearly, though, someone heard that dying deposition and in time it became mapped intertextually, cohesively, thematically, on to other narratives of nagging, troublesome and dangerous women to produce the ballad as we have it in the 1970s.

Even Clune has her nagging hysterically, constructing her words from the transcripts of Governor's account at his trial:

Ethel's voice was shrill, scolding him. 'They rub it in. You let them insult me, and they do what they like with you!' . . .

'No', said Jimmy. 'I'll put a stop to it . . . I'll tell them what I think of him and his missus and that giggling schoolteacher. I'll get even with them.'

(Clune 1959: 52)

Clune is also instructive in elaborating on the details of the relationship between Ethel, Mrs Mawbey and Miss Kerz. The schoolteacher, he says, is jealous of this much younger woman who is already married and a mother. The mother cannot encourage this 16-year-old while her own daughters must be discouraged from imagining that mixed race marriages are either acceptable or possible. All the elements in Hamilton's (1993) account of relations among women in mistress/servant relations are present here. So are all the elements of the impossible position of the white women in inter-racial marriages described with such feeling by Carmen Luke (1994). All of these representations of Ethel are constructed by men. Ethel's own version of these events is not something we can know. That it might, however, have been very different is suggested in the hawker's letter (1900) sent to a member of the Fitzpatrick family, again a story told by a man. He represents her as working alongside her husband of whom 'she was very fond', and confirms that the Mawbey women 'sneered' at her, and that she became 'spiteful towards them and gradually embittered the blacks towards the women at the homestead'. His account of her marriage, however, is very different:

> Mrs Governor told me the history of their courtship and of how many white girls she beat to him and what a heroine she thought herself when she became legally married to him in the Church of England at Gulgong. She fully believed in the sanctity of their marriage. They took it as part of their tribal laws and were just as sincere about it.

This is not, I think, another of those stories of white women lusting after black flesh. It is a story of women and courtship and of the desirability of a good-looking man, and of feminine competition and victory. In this story Ethel has some agency, some control.

She also seems to have acted independently after she had left the camp on the night of the murder to go to Dubbo when she gave a warning that the murders were to occur: 'She said she was Jimmy Governor's wife and that the blacks were going to murder the Mawbeys that night. McDonald thought she was queer, but did not treat her seriously, but Percy McDonald investigated in the morning' (Ellis 1900). She and her black husband remain shadowy figures in all of these conflicting narratives. It will remain for Aboriginal writers to offer alternative stories which will subvert the discourse of racism which otherwise remains largely intact in all these generic and dialogic 'turns' in this very long conversation.

IRRESISTIBLE PASSION: READING AND WRITING THE OTHER

Thus the trial proceedings, reported in transcribed form in the *Sydney Morning Herald*, focus on her role in inciting her husband to murder. This is the story on which the defence counsel builds his arguments of diminished responsibility and around which he constructs the murder as a crime of passion. The adversarial nature of the courtroom requires that the prosecution argue the opposite case, premeditated murder. This binarism which plays itself out in the panoptic context of cross-examination and summation in the courtroom appears to revolve around Ethel Governor's hysteria and arguments about a tomahawk. Why would one have one, if not to use it? But there are traces here of another set of arguments, and another binarism, that revolve around Jimmy Governor's ancestry, his blackness and his whiteness, the same contradictory elements that weave their way through the representations of Ethel Governor.The defence arguments construct Jimmy as black, a man who, because black, cannot help himself: 'a man who by his environment and nature had not learned to control himself as other men had'. Miss Kerz (the governess) sneered at him and 'that was the turning point; when those words were spoken to him the sudden passion rose and that was the last of self-control. The savage heart, tainted with the thirst of blood, burst through reason and one of the foulest crimes was committed' (*Sydney Morning Herald*, 23 November 1900: 7). The defence argument is about femininity and its fatal effects when it acts through a primitive black man; 'a better man than most blacks'.

This argument depends on Ethel Governor's evidence, and yet there is some doubt about Ethel Governor's complicity with the defence story at the trial. Jimmy Governor testifies that his wife had complained to him about the Mawbeys and what they had said to her, and this is in all versions of the story, but when she is cross-examined she effectively denies it until the defence counsel reminds her of the story she is supposed to be telling. There is a sense in which she seems not to understand any of the procedures in which she is involved, or in which for reasons of her own she subverts them. Told that she does not have to give evidence against her husband, and asked whether she understands, she replies: 'I am not well enough educated to understand' and proceeds to give the evidence. Cross-examined by the defence, it is as though she has been trained, rehearsed, to follow the defence argument and then forgets the script, or perhaps her own voice is heard briefly and then silenced:

> I was living in Gulgong with my mother before I married Jimmy. He was very fond of me. He was particularly 'touchy' about his colour. He did not like to be called a blackfellow. It is true I had to put up with a great many taunts because of my marriage. Some people said I ought to be shot for marrying a blackfellow. Mrs Mawbey and Miss Kerz never said anything to me about Jimmy. They said it was a wonder a nice girl like me would throw myself away on a blackfellow. They only said that once to me. It did not make me unhappy, nor did I grow unhappy at Breelong because of the taunts. It made no difference between me and my husband.

At this point the defence lawyer prompts her to remember the story she is supposed to be telling:

MR BOYCE: I do not mean that. I mean did it make a difference to your own private happiness?

WITNESS: Yes it did. Once in the camp I went down on my knees and prayed: 'O Lord! Take me away from here; I cannot stand what these people are saying about me.'

It is these lines, probably the words of the defence lawyer, not Ethel Governor, which go on record as her position at the trial. It has to be remembered here, I think, that this is a 17-year-old single mother whose own story is not only never heard but not even particularly relevant to the adversarial arguments in this courtroom. It has also to be remembered that the only text we have is a report of a transcription of courtroom events which already occludes a whole set of embodied histories – police interviews/verbals, conversations between solicitors and their 'clients', briefing of counsel, and so on.

The prosecution case is not interested in Ethel Governor. The argument here is that 'The case of a blackfellow could not be regarded in any different light from that of a white man, no matter how his habits of life differed.' This is an interesting and profoundly ironic statement of equality, but one whose ironies parallel the paradoxical arguments in Clune, much later, that Jimmy Governor's violence and 'irresistible passion' were a result of his white pride:

If he had the aristocratic blood of the haughty Grosvenors and the fiery Fitzgeralds in him, inherited from the scions of those two noble families, who had demanded 'droit de seigneur' from Aboriginal damsels, then it is no wonder that he would avenge insult, regardless of consequences.

(Clune 1959: 10)

For Clune, trying to use the documentary genre to dialogue with the discourse of racism in the media reports of 1900, the only possibility was to reverse the binary opposition black/white and to privilege the white side of Jimmy Governor's character. But the discourse remains racist, even though the genre is not, just as it does when it is taunts about his prowess as a bushranger, delivered by his Aboriginal companions, which the prosecution adduces as the reason for his premeditated attack on white women and children. It is the questioning of his masculinity, in these arguments, that results in his determination to take revenge. What I am suggesting here is that, for these legal subjects, premeditation is inevitably associated with whiteness (just as pride and the need to take revenge are for Clune), and blind, unthinking passion is collocated with blackness. It is the stories that can be told about race and racial conflict, with all their binary contradictions and racist and sexist limitations, that structure the legal arguments.

The judge's summation participates in that gentleman's agreement which Keneally's novel will make explicit much later – the agreement to dispatch these matters as quickly and quietly as possible in a country that has just become a nation.

> The sweetness of it carried him through a swift trial in December. In the
>   dock he told how innocent Jackie and Mort and Gilda were.
> Then Australia became a fact.
> It was unsuitable, too indicative of what had been suppressed in the
>   country's making, to hang two blackmen in the Federation's early days.
> Press cartoonists sketched the nascent motherland. She was young, with
>   shoulders like a boy, and a firm mouth . . .
> She rather resembled Miss Graf.
> Easter came and filled centre ring at the Showground . . .
> People laughed in their state of grace, the old crimes done, all convict
>   chains a rusted fable in the brazen Arcady and under the roar of
>   buskers in temperate April 1901.
> And the other viciousness? The rape of primitives? – It was done and past
>   report.
>
> (Keneally 1972/1978: 177)

The judge assures the defence that he has done his duty by his client, that his conduct of the case has been admirable. He tells a lengthy tale of 'the horror that passed through the community' when the murders were committed, and of the 'weeks or months' of excitement that followed. He then makes the usual and generically proper address to the jury which asks them to view the case, despite all this, 'apart from their prejudices', to try the case 'on the sworn evidence presented to them', and to consider nothing outside of that.

It is the impossibility of this injunction, with its belief in the myth of objectivity and rationality – despite its own complicity with the subjective and very public memories that the 'thrill of horror that passed through the whole community' have constructed for the judge as well as the jury and the prosecuting and defending counsel – with which I want to conclude this section. Legal processes and legal agents are people, and they cannot be immune to the networks of meanings and beliefs which they live as part of the rituals and practices of daily life. The law cannot be, and must not construct itself, as separate from these processes. It is essential to any concept of justice that the semiotics, the gender and racial bias, the struggles over meaning and for power, and the narrativity of all legal process, be understood. This was not a story of unruly women and innocent white men. It was a story about institutionalised racism and sexism, a story about the way those things are constructed through the textuality of everyday life, a story about the way the law participates in these processes and a story which the law in Australia in 1900 could not speak or read, any more than the law in nineteenth-century France could speak or read its own complicity in the production of a Paul Rivière.

Chapter 8

The other side of discourse
Traces of bodies at work

In what follows I shall use linguistic terminology sparingly, explaining and defining as I go and when I introduce new terms. In general, as I have done above, I will use the term *discourse* or *discursive field* to refer to what Foucault called discourse – all the *statements* that you might make about race or gender or protection (or anything else) for example, in this context at this time. I will assume that such statements might be made in verbal, visual, corporeal or spatial forms or, indeed, any other forms. In what follows, discourse, in Foucault's sense, is further defined grammatically and visually as constituted by:

- certain typical, socially valorised semantic dichotomies (black/white, feminine/masculine, irrational/rational, nature/culture, and so on)
- patterns of lexical or image cohesion and intertextual links between image and text (Halliday and Hasan 1976; Halliday 1985b)
- a number of basic transitivity patterns in which certain participants are typically realised in specific ways (men as actors and sayers, women as goals or sensers, and so on)
- particular kinds of predictable narrative sequences.

I will use Halliday's functional grammatical terminology, referring to categories of grammar that he identifies under the three functional headings of experiential, interpersonal and textual (e.g. cohesion, lexical collocation, theme–rheme, transitivity, etc.). However, I will basically argue that the last two of these, the *interpersonal* and the *textual* modes of making meaning, also offer the dynamic strategies that are necessary to *perform* generically. They enable the shaping and reshaping, and the recontextualising, of the ready-made textual products of an interdiscursive or intertextual field. Texts are constructed as much from paradigms of intertextual resources as they are from paradigms of words and phrases. Thus 'ready-made' textual products may be as small as a lexical collocation (*white* with *superiority*) or a transitivity pattern (actor + material process + goal), 'chunks' of another narrative or genre, or as large as a narrative or genre itself. Here I am regarding the logical function of language – the ways in which we structure the sentence into main, subordinate and co-ordinate clauses, and the semantics of projection, the ways in which we quote or incorporate the speech and thoughts of others into our discourse (direct, indirect and free indirect speech) – as part of the textual function, the text-making function. But, in essence, I see both interpersonal and textual grammar as intimately related to the overt resources of the embodied subject who speaks and writes, reads and listens. Genres clearly offer explicit interpersonal strategies for positioning oneself (mood structure, modality) and explicit textual strategies for positioning others (the movement from theme to rheme). The position of the enunciation is usually associated directly with the generic strategy adopted, leaving clearly marked corporeal traces in the grammar of the text. Less obvious, less conscious, and thus folded into the text as corporeal traces that are harder to locate, are the positions of enunciation enfolded in the enounced. These are the traces of iterability, of intertextuality, of the places where the language and the body has been before.

However, it seems to me that this does not in itself explain some of the strategies individuals adopt when they actually choose to dialogue or debate with a previous writer or text. Thus, for example, the starting point of a novel, or a film, or of a little conversation, may be determined by the last 'turn' in an ongoing conversation – one which, in this case, has been going on for almost a century. If one is to look for the traces of corporeality in texts, among them are traces of 'authorship' and of this kind of dialogism; that is, not only the meanings which come from where the words have been before (Bakhtin 1981), the meanings that constitute a 'reality-maintenance' way of saying or knowing, 'a fashion of believing' (Whorf 1956), but also the semantic reversals, the semogenesis or new meanings, that occur in dialogic exchanges between texts and readers and writers and which constitute new constructions of reality (Mukarovksy 1977: 109). I am wanting to recognise that the subject of the enunciation does have effects in texts, effects which often shape the subject of the enounced, corporeal effects that can be traced in the materiality of the text, be it verbal or visual.

All writings are rewritings. Rewritings always have connections with readings, sometimes rereadings. And the sequencing of the readings and writings matters. Dominant readings and writings can and do mediate less dominant ones. Sequencing may structure what can be read and written (Smith 1990). Dominant forms may in fact silence others altogether, the story of the anonymous participant may be rewritten, silenced by the story of what Smith calls 'public textual discourse', the grammar of socially ratified and 'mandated courses of action' (Smith 1990: 241). It is silenced only in the sense that public discourse, because it never hears it, makes no record of it. The difference is a little like de Certeau's distinction between strategies and tactics, but with a very real difference in power in the public sphere. Strategic interventions into the Governor story have survived (in Derrida's sense of *sur-vivre*), tactical interventions are much harder to trace, although there are indications that there were many of them. Many or not, the intentions of these tactics to change what was being said and written do not have the *force* of institutionally supported forms of professional vision. In these public reading formations, readings and rewritings are also mutually supportive and therefore remarkably stable.

KENEALLY: THE NEATNESS OF THE STRUCTURE

When I was writing about Jimmie Blacksmith, our troops were in Vietnam, there was a lot of debate about that. At the time of the Blacksmith murders – the Governor brothers' murders in real life – we were in the Boer War; there was a lot of emotion about that. And there was a surge of nationalism which the New South Wales Crimes Act of 1900 was instituted to prevent: it says that whoever promotes the idea that there will come a time when the Monarch is not the sovereign of Australia is guilty of High Treason. Basically, without being whimsical, there are parallels between Australia in the late 1960s and Australia in 1900 – a sense that the question hadn't gone very far in that time, in those sixty years, and a sense that those events were extremely dramatic. In 1901 the indigenous people of Australia had no place in the Constitution, and just before I wrote the book they were given a place, in so far as the Federal Government was given the power to legislate for them – all these parallels seemed too good to be true.

(Grenville and Woolfe 1993: 189)

Thus it was that Keneally constructed the two subplots of Mr Hyberry the hangman and Dowie Stead and his companions. Dowie Stead is the fiancé of the murdered teacher in the novel. These representations of masculinity allowed Keneally to weave through his story of Jimmie Blacksmith the threads of nationalism and masculinity rampant that are associated with the actual historical context of Federation and the Boer War in 1900. Keneally made the novel from his gendered reading of the newspapers of the 1900s, reading, like de Lauretis's perceiving subject, selectively, his perceptions of what was pertinent mapping on to his own lived masculinity and his involvement in the political issues that surrounded him as a political man in the 1960s and 1970s, his habitus. It is clear from Keneally's own statements that he intended *The Chant of Jimmie Blacksmith* to be an anti-racist text or, more precisely, 'a picture of the ruinous impact of European culture on the Aboriginal' (Keneally 1982: 45). Indeed, he claimed that 'there is in Australian writing only one novel which examines the impact of the two cultures from within an Aboriginal mind, and that is my own *The Chant of Jimmie Blacksmith*' (Keneally 1982: 35). Keneally seems later to have recognised the arrogance of writing about Aboriginality 'from within' – 'Yes, I'd always wanted to write about aboriginal people on tour, not in the arrogant way of *The Chant of Jimmie Blacksmith*, from within, but by writing from the point of an observed travelling companion and tour manager' (Keneally 1993: 191). My focus here will be on that arrogance, on the way he constructs Jimmie Blacksmith as miscegenation of black and white, at home in neither space, and on the way the narrative voice of the novel colonises black minds and bodies. Keneally calls the novel a 'historical novel' and he used the intertextual resources I have reread and rewritten in the last chapter to write it.

When he was asked 'What started *Jimmie Blacksmith*?', Keneally responded 'It was the idea – the neatness of events as they existed in history . . . the neat, the nifty ways the historic tale encompassed Australian problems' (Grenville and Woolfe 1993: 189). Frow (1982: 295) wrote of the 'obtrusive stylistic neatness' of the narrative voice. It is the neatness of Keneally's construction of history, the tidy, always oppositional construction, the parallelism, the narrative control which organises and projects the message, which produces this sense of realism. It is a tidy structure which accords well with a certain white Australia's view of itself. The story of *The Chant of Jimmie Blacksmith* covers Jimmie's life from birth to execution, but the narration covers exactly one year and is neatly framed by two visits made to Jimmie, one by Jackie Smolders in June 1900, one by Mr Hyberry the hangman in May 1901; visits which signal the claims that are made on Jimmie by the black and the white worlds in which he has no place. The events of chapter 1 focus on Jimmie's initiation into tribal manhood, but the story begins with Jackie Smolders' visit shortly after Jimmie Blacksmith's marriage to a white girl: 'in June of 1900, Jimmie Blacksmith's maternal uncle Tabidgi – Jackie Smolders to the white world – *was disturbed* to get news that Jimmie had married a white girl in the Methodist church at Wallah' (1972/1978: 1). This beginning is a dialogic response to Clune's book, the mark of a disagreement:

> I did the research in bulk, and I read also Frank Clune's book on the Governor brothers – that's what started it all. I thought: Wow! I didn't agree with the book but I was sparked by it. There was a pattern there that Clune wasn't concentrating on – he was concentrating on police and pursuit aspects purely.
>
> (Keneally 1993: 191)

Within this first sentence are the seeds of most of the semantic oppositions and meanings that will dynamically, thematically and cohesively structure the rest of the novel. The opposition between black and white, the miscegenation of black by white, evident in the novel's naming practices (Tabidgi Jackie Smolders), the single and monologic identity of the Methodist Church which is 'never incommoded with the truth', the 'truth' of both worlds lived by Tabidgi, and the remarkable access of the white narrative voice to both – these are the elements that will structure the novel.

The first chapter is quite clearly divided into six segments which contrastively collocate the worlds of black and white, Easter and tribal initiation. The first is a framing segment, a heteroglossic black/white piece, structured recursively around Tabidgi's visit to Wallah with which it begins and ends. The second segment is a retrospective account of Jimmie's initiation into tribal manhood with the focus on black, the third contrasts this world with the white Methodist world of Mr Neville. The fourth returns to the black world, to Jimmie singing a tribal song in the wilderness after his initiation, the fifth recounts his heroic return to his people at Brentwood, the mission, the white world. The sixth is again a framing segment recounting his caning for truancy at the hands of the Methodist minister and returning to the black/white heteroglossia of the initial segment, contrasting the icons of Methodist schooling and the standard English voice of Mr Neville and the narrator with the learning of the Mungindi elders and the 'non-standard' Aboriginal speech of Wilf: 'for the truth of Mr Neville and the truth of Emu-Wren ran parallel. Mr Neville had his place, as did the poor-bugger-white-fella-son-of-God-got-nailed. "Cane teach yer to be good fella now," Wilf stated. "Don' let that stand in yer light"' (1972/1978: 6). This alternation of black and white functions to keep the two races distinct and apart, but it is framed by the assimilating and colonising white narrative voice. The corporeal trace here is of a whole cultural politics, and the pattern of black versus white contained by narrative assimilation persists throughout the novel. It is as categorical as the blackness of the media representations and the whiteness of Clune's. It is a romanticisation of Aboriginality, the innocence of tribal life, the passivity and promiscuity of tribal women, and an eroticisation of the murder story. These Aboriginal people are assumed, childlike, to have accepted all that they have been told by whites and to have simply accommodated to it. There is no sense of any resistance in this infantilisation and primitivisation of an indigenous people. It is also clear that the 'non-standard' Australian speech of these people is that of an underclass, intended to be read as 'non-standard'.

Jimmie's heroic return in chapter 1, his repositioning in a white narrative which remains insistently ignorant of the black story he also lives, parallels his return from another wilderness at the end of the novel. Again there is a conversion, a return to the church, in the bed of a nun, the ultimate feminisation of Jimmie, another denial and incorporation of otherness. The murders of the Newby women are represented explicitly and erotically, but also exotically, as an attempt on Jimmie's part to win back the manhood that has been denied him by white society: 'Jimmie admitted to his body a drunken judgmental majesty, a sense that the sharp-edged stars impelled him. He felt large with a royal fever, with rebirth. He was in the lizard's gut once more' (Keneally 1972/1978: 78). It is ironic, therefore, that the long pursuit of Jimmie, his capture, trial and hanging, should culminate in a particular construction of white Australian 'manhood', reborn into new nationhood at the end of the novel, and represented in all its glory at that other Easter icon of Australian mateship, the Sydney Royal Easter Show:

So the candy-floss was eaten in sunny April, the spring of the southern world. Men from Quirindi and Deniliquin rode mad bulls. Men from the cedar forests behind Nowra, Kempsey and Murwillumbah, dressed in athletic vests and white pants, raced each other at log-felling, and the summered biceps of a mettlesome gaucho-people flew in the high sun on the day of Christ's crucifixion.

(Keneally 1972/1978: 178)

The 'sweetness' of the final Easter scene is the sweetness of that final 'rebirth' which, in the novel, represents the ultimate cuckolding (the ultimate denial of identity and masculinity) of the black man by the white race.

Before this conclusion the reader is made to live the hallucinations of the wounded Jimmie, the doubts of the guilty Mr Neville, and the realities and identities of a number of disparate others, as the certainties of the world of chapter 1 fall apart textually and the narrative structure degenerates into a collage of fragments of text, indicating quite literally how our realities and identities are made intertextually of chunks of the texts (verbal or lived) that we have experienced or known. This textual fragmentation is, however, a deliberate narrative strategy to position the reader in readiness for the didactic and narrative resolution of this textual disorder in the final didactic coda to the novel – the Easter scene – where the narrative voice resumes control to tell us how the 'neatness' of the narrative structure and the momentary dissolution of that structure are to be read. White masculinity is questioned here, but the narrative structure of the novel remains iconic of the white man's control over, and colonisation of, the black man's story, even as Keneally tries (and to some extent succeeds) in telling it differently and in questioning the whole structure of which he and his story are part.

DISCOURSE, GENRE, DIALOGISM

In Texts 8.1 and 8.2, I have tried to represent graphically the sheer complexity of the generic, dialogic and discursive heteroglossia involved in Keneally's overcoded literary rewriting of the intertextual resources of the newspaper stories. My focus here is on the traces that are left in the text of the corporeality of the writing, traces of the dynamic process of developing the particles of meaning in the first sentence at the lexicogrammatical level through processes like lexical cohesion, conjunction, and the logical semantics of elaboration, addition and enhancement (Halliday 1985a), a process of making which maps clauses into clause complexes, clause complexes into larger units (discourse complexes), and these larger units into strategic 'moves' (what I have called segments above) and then generic units like chapters.

The intertextual discursive fields which frame this activity, the knowledge and the memory which is in the body, enable and constrain this development by specifying what cohesive patterns are possible, what narrative sequences may occur, what semantic oppositions are to be negotiated, what modes of conjunction are available and thus what kinds of moves can constitute a chapter. Halliday (1979) has argued that textual patterns assume a wave-like form in which paragraphs, and presumably larger units like moves, involve a nesting of wave-like structures, the 'waves' moving from speaker to hearer orientation. Voloshinov (1930/1973: 111) argued that paragraphs were analogous to exchanges in a dialogue and that the structure that resulted from making them was 'like a vitiated dialogue worked into the body of a monologic utterance'.

In Text 8.1, I have analysed the first move (segment) in chapter 1, marking its final sentence as both the conclusion to this move and the theme for the next move. The whole is the orientation in the genre that is the chapter, a strategic place to start and a strategy for beginning. Within it there are also clear generically marked sections – synopsis, orientation, record, re-orientation (Martin 1985a). Mapped dynamically on to these sections of the genre, however, are a number of differences in narrative voice, blurred by the use of free indirect speech as the mode of voice projection. The controlling narrative voice of the synopsis gives way to a hybrid Jackie/narrator voice in the orientation and the first record section. The next record section is marked by the heteroglossia of narrator/Dulcie, missionary voices. This is interrupted by the narrator/Jackie voice in '*But the deep truth was . . .*' and that voice continues through the next record section, across the re-orientation, until the narrative voice takes control again in the final sentence (paralleling the pattern in the novel as a whole).

Running down the righthand side of my figure are a set of disjunctive rhetorical patterns of parallelism and repetition, which are mapped on to the Jackie position, expressing the repeated anxiety about the white girl, the wedding, and the initiation tooth, but also (and at the same time) marking Keneally's continuing dialogue with Clune. Clune had argued that Aboriginal people were not concerned about their kinsmen marrying white women (Clune 1959: 27). That dialogue, or refusal, is projected on to the Jackie voice to give it Aboriginal authenticity (rather like the quoting of authorities in an academic article). The repeated lexical patterns function cohesively and rhetorically to mark the dialogism with Clune. This dialogism is realised grammatically in the ambivalence of the foregrounded Jackie voice even in the final two paragraphs, when the logical and anonymous modulations of the narrative voice reappropriate it: *It must be said that, It is necessary to take cognizance.*

At the same time, the whole text is marked by a paragraph organisation that is inherently dialogic, a series of cohesive exchanges which succeed one another in time until the argument comes full circle, ending where it began with Jackie Smolders' visit to Wallah. Each paragraph takes off at a local level from something previously said, or something that was simply 'around'. This is how textual goals and writer/reader dialogue are developed in the process of producing the text, probabilistically, in ways not set down

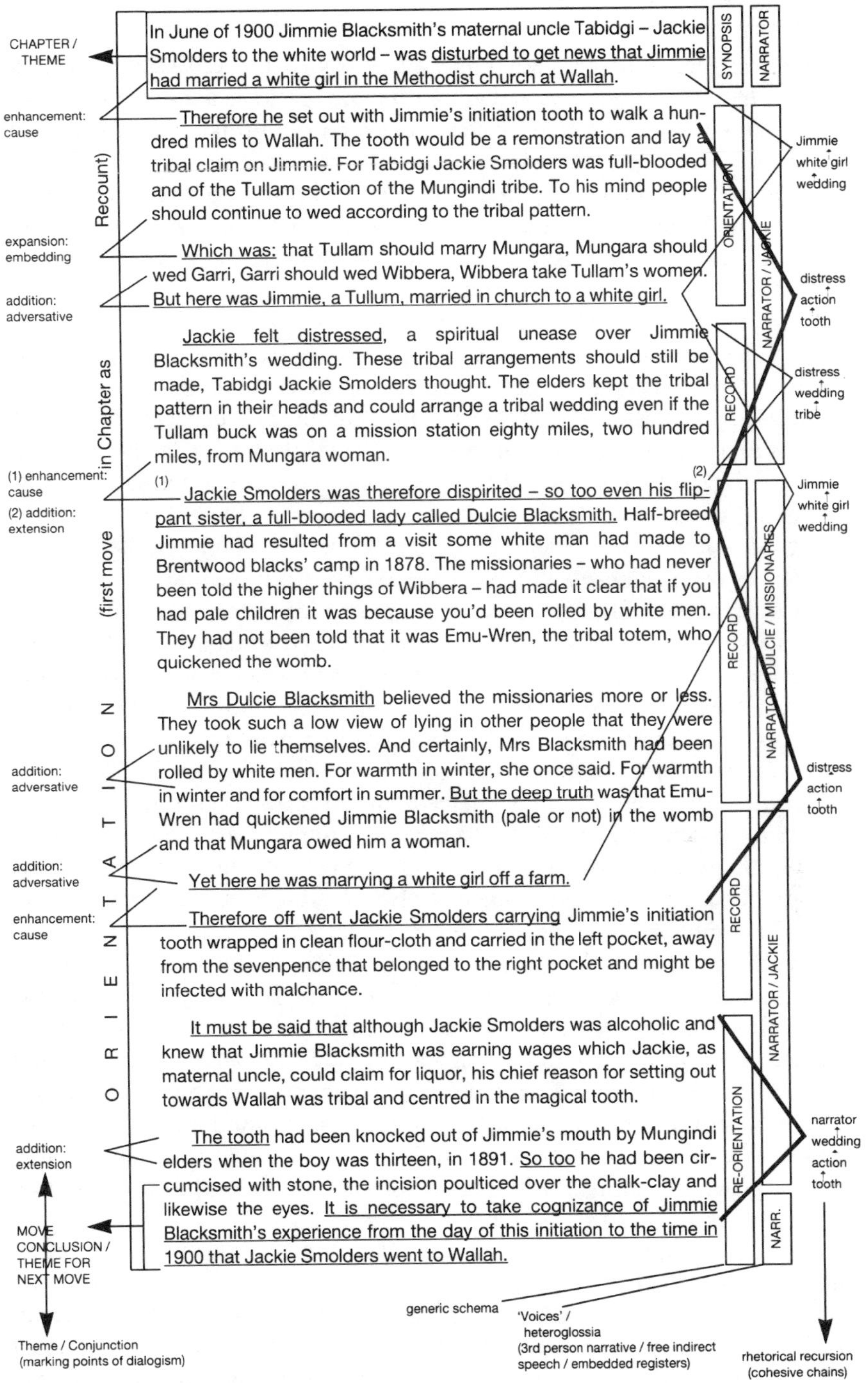

CHAPTER / THEME
SYNOPSIS
NARRATOR
In June of 1900 Jimmie Blacksmith's maternal uncle Tabidgi – Jackie Smolders to the white world – was disturbed to get news that Jimmie had married a white girl in the Methodist church at Wallah.
enhancement: cause
Therefore he set out with Jimmie's initiation tooth to walk a hundred miles to Wallah. The tooth would be a remonstration and lay a tribal claim on Jimmie. For Tabidgi Jackie Smolders was full-blooded and of the Tullam section of the Mungindi tribe. To his mind people should continue to wed according to the tribal pattern.
expansion: embedding
Which was: that Tullam should marry Mungara, Mungara should wed Garri, Garri should wed Wibbera, Wibbera take Tullam's women.
addition: adversative
But here was Jimmie, a Tullum, married in church to a white girl.
Jackie felt distressed, a spiritual unease over Jimmie Blacksmith's wedding. These tribal arrangements should still be made, Tabidgi Jackie Smolders thought. The elders kept the tribal pattern in their heads and could arrange a tribal wedding even if the Tullam buck was on a mission station eighty miles, two hundred miles, from Mungara woman.
(1) enhancement: cause
(2) addition: extension
(1)
(2)
Jackie Smolders was therefore dispirited – so too even his flippant sister, a full-blooded lady called Dulcie Blacksmith. Half-breed Jimmie had resulted from a visit some white man had made to Brentwood blacks' camp in 1878. The missionaries – who had never been told the higher things of Wibbera – had made it clear that if you had pale children it was because you'd been rolled by white men. They had not been told that it was Emu-Wren, the tribal totem, who quickened the womb.
Mrs Dulcie Blacksmith believed the missionaries more or less. They took such a low view of lying in other people that they were unlikely to lie themselves. And certainly, Mrs Blacksmith had been rolled by white men. For warmth in winter, she once said. For warmth in winter and for comfort in summer. But the deep truth was that Emu-Wren had quickened Jimmie Blacksmith (pale or not) in the womb and that Mungara owed him a woman.
addition: adversative
Yet here he was marrying a white girl off a farm.
enhancement: cause
Therefore off went Jackie Smolders carrying Jimmie's initiation tooth wrapped in clean flour-cloth and carried in the left pocket, away from the sevenpence that belonged to the right pocket and might be infected with malchance.
It must be said that although Jackie Smolders was alcoholic and knew that Jimmie Blacksmith was earning wages which Jackie, as maternal uncle, could claim for liquor, his chief reason for setting out towards Wallah was tribal and centred in the magical tooth.
addition: extension
The tooth had been knocked out of Jimmie's mouth by Mungindi elders when the boy was thirteen, in 1891. So too he had been circumcised with stone, the incision poulticed over the chalk-clay and likewise the eyes. It is necessary to take cognizance of Jimmie Blacksmith's experience from the day of this initiation to the time in 1900 that Jackie Smolders went to Wallah.
MOVE CONCLUSION / THEME FOR NEXT MOVE
ORIENTATION (first move in Chapter as Recount)
ORIENTATION
RECORD
RECORD
RECORD
RE-ORIENTATION
NARRATOR / JACKIE
NARRATOR / DULCIE / MISSIONARIES
NARRATOR / JACKIE
NARR.
Jimmie white girl wedding
distress action tooth
distress wedding tribe
Jimmie white girl wedding
distress action tooth
narrator wedding action tooth
Theme / Conjunction (marking points of dialogism)
generic schema
'Voices' / heteroglossia (3rd person narrative / free indirect speech / embedded registers)
rhetorical recursion (cohesive chains)

Text 8.1: Discourse, Genre, Dialogism

An attempt to show graphically how generic schema, generic recursion, thematic conjunction, lexical cohesion, heteroglossia, and rhetorical recursion are simultaneously mapped onto this section of the text.

in advance. There are, thus, a number of explicit conjunctive links between paragraphs, and within paragraphs, which mark the logical and ordered narrative argument of the text. They are marked on the lefthand side of the figure.

There are other cohesive patterns in each section of the text which these dialogic and generic strategies shape, contain and structure as they map their structures and meanings across them. Those cohesive patterns are marked throughout by the socially ratified and evaluated dichotomies of black/white, masculine/feminine, primitive/cultured, rational/irrational, which Keneally actually fails to shift in his appropriation and projection of imagined Aboriginal meanings into the text. Once again, 'there is a politically fraught substitution of the voice of the middle-class intellectual for that of the subject of popular or indigenous culture' (Frow 1995a: 59; see also above p. 77). In this text, the white world appears to be constructed from an Aboriginal perspective as merely intrusive, disruptive of tribal patterns. It is limited to a small set of collocating lexical items – *rolling, alcohol, wages, sevenpence, church* and *illness/malchance*. This lexical snapshot of colonialism at work appears to be also a linguistic intrusion, in that these words are constructed as part of an Aboriginal register which is alienated (half white, half black), primitive and illogical: *tribal patterns, totems, initiations, teeth, stone, clay, magic, hundred mile walk* and *deep truth*. This rather paternalistic construction of primitiveness undermines the argument with Clune and the construction of Jackie as a resistant colonial subject. This lexis is in a sense the corporeal trace of a whiteness masquerading as Aboriginality. Something similar happens with the representation of the *rolling* of Dulcie Blacksmith by some *white man*, and the *marriage* of the result, Jimmie Blacksmith, a *half-breed* to a *white girl*. Here the discourses of race and gender come together in the illicit taking and antisocial exchange of women realised through a grammar, a semantics, which does not enable the telling in any other terms (of, for example, a black or white woman *giving herself*, a black man not having to acknowledge the fractions that constitute his ancestry). The black world – despite its prevalence here lexically and the emphasis on *its* social obligations and requirements, the apparent telling from its point of view – is not actually *realised* at all. Given the modulation of Jackie Smolders' beliefs (what he sees as obligations) – e.g. *should wed, should marry* – which are 'unreal' proposals grammatically, and the contrast with the 'real' propositions of *had married, was married* – as narrated events, his *distress* is and must remain that of the marginalised/powerless minority in this discourse. It is the voice of a white, masculine world which, in the end, will direct proceedings as privileged insider in the worlds, even the heads, of both women and Aboriginals.

The dialogic position then changes, the generic strategies alter, but the statements of the discourses of race and gender are hardly scratched by these efforts at semogenesis. It is the neatness of the incongruence between the voice which controls, the register of logical conjunction and reasoned argument (*therefore, which was, therefore, but, certainly, therefore*) and the register of Aboriginality (*a tribal claim, the magical tooth, the higher things of Wibbera*) which constantly, intertextually, separates the worlds Keneally tries by projection to bring together, realising lexicogrammatically the fundamental binary oppositions which continue to structure his text-making.

This is clearer still in Text 8.2. Even in a highly crafted written text of this sort, the way the lexical patterns flow into one another has a choreographic character, marking the processual and dynamic nature of textual production. The written text is not nearly so remote from the strategies of casual conversation as linguists usually suppose. In this figure I have tried to look at these patterns again from the perspective of the wave-like motion through which the discursive field is shaped and organised in the movement from theme to rheme, from writer to reader orientation. This movement functions again, despite Keneally's dialogic intentions, to articulate the insider/outsider relations of the narrative projections and the black/white, feminine/masculine binaries of the discourses of race and gender.

I have analysed the theme/rheme relationships in the clauses of the text according to Halliday (1985a). Dependent clauses, whether hypotactic or embedded, are analysed separately for theme/rheme. In this text the theme/rheme patterns are nearly always co-extensive with the given/new patterns, so I have simply marked the lexical element in the rheme which carries the focus of the new by underlining. What follows the underlined (tonic) element is assumed, following Halliday, to be given. Halliday says:

> The theme is what I, the speaker, take as my point of departure. The given is what you, the listener, already know about or have accessible to you. Theme and rheme is speaker-oriented while given and new is listener-oriented. But both are of course speaker-selected.
>
> (Halliday 1985a: 278)

In a literary text which is always anticipating a reader, and dialogically responding to an absent interlocutor, part of the generic strategy must involve building the listener or the reader into the text – Eco's (1979) reader inscribed in the text. Thus, what is written as theme and/or given is *ipso facto* written both as where the narrator/speaker is at and as what is accessible to the reader. That is, the reader is constructed and mapped on to the narrative position. The narrator's starting point (and insider knowledge) becomes also the starting point for the compliant reader, but the narrator's conclusion in each clause is also inevitably where the reader is left, again positioned to work with, rather than against, the text. This, it seems to me, is the dynamic process through which corporeality is folded into texts and texts come to have effects on bodies. It is also, then, the way in which the habitus is formed so that the text becomes 'an active partner in the reality-making and reality-changing process' (Thibault 1987: 618). It parallels in the movement of the

THEME		RHEME (including new)
In June of 1900	#	Jimmie Blacksmith's maternal uncle Tabidgi – Jackie Smolders to the white world – was disturbed to get news
[that Jimmie	#	had married a white girl in the Methodist Church at Wallah]
Therefore he ↑ (enhancement:cause)	#	set out with Jimmie's initiation tooth to walk a hundred miles to Wallah
The tooth	#	would be a remonstration
and ↑		lay a tribal claim on Jimmie
For Tabidgi Jack Smolders (enhancement:cause)	#	was full-blooded
and ↑		of the Tullam section of the Mungindi tribe
To his mind	#	people should continue to wed according to the tribal pattern
[which was: ← (expansion:embedding) (postponed theme)		that Tullam should marry Mungara, Mungara should wed Garri, Garri should wed Wibbera, Wibbera take Tullam's women]
But here ← (addition: adversative) (postponed theme)	#	was Jimmie, a Tullam,
		married in church to a white girl.
Jackie	#	felt distressed,
		a spiritual unease over Jimmie Blacksmith's wedding.
*These tribal arrangements should still be made, (marked clausal theme)	#	Tabidgi Jackie Smolders thought
The elders	#	kept the tribal pattern in their heads
and		could arrange a tribal wedding
*even if the Tullam Buck ← (enhancement: condition)	#	was on a mission station eighty miles, to hundred miles, from Mungara woman.
Jackie Smolders	#	was therefore dispirited
so too even his flippant sister a full-blooded lady called Dulcie Blacksmith (extension: addition)	#	(marked theme, ellipted clause/rheme)
Half-breed Jimmie	#	had resulted from a visit [Some white man had made to Brentwood black's camp in 1878]
[some white man	#	had made to Brentwood black's camp in 1878]
The missionaries – [who had never been told the higher things of Wibbera]	#	had made it clear [that *if you had pale children it was *because you had been rolled by white men] (postponed theme, end-focus, end-weight)
They	#	had not been told
[that it	#	was Amu-Wren, the tribal totem, [who quickened the womb]]
Mrs Dulcie Blacksmith	#	believed the missionaries more or less
They	#	took such a low view of lying in other people
*that they	#	were unlikely to lie themselves
And certainly, Mrs Blacksmith	#	had been rolled by white men
for warmth in winter	#	she once said
for warmth in winter and for comfort in summer (cause: reason) (marked theme)	#	
But the deep truth ← (addition: adversative)	#	was [that Emu-Wren had quickened Jimmie Blacksmith (pale or not) in the womb and that Mungara owed him a woman]
Yet here he was ← (addition: adversative)	#	marrying a white girl off a farm
Therefore off went (cause: reason)	#	Jackie Smolders carrying Jimmie's initiation tooth

		[wrapped in clean <u>flour</u> cloth and carried in the <u>left</u> pocket, away from the sevenpence that belonged to the <u>right</u> pocket and might be infected with <u>malchance</u>
It must be said	#	*that <u>although</u> Jackie <u>Smolders</u> was <u>alcoholic</u> and knew *that Jimmie Blacksmith was earning wages [which <u>Jackie</u>, as maternal uncle, could claim for <u>liquor</u>] his <u>chief reason for setting out</u> towards <u>Wallah</u> was <u>tribal</u> and centred in the magical <u>tooth</u>. (postponed theme: end-focus, end-weight)
The tooth ◄	#	had been knocked out of Jimmie's mouth by Mungindi <u>elders</u>
*when the <u>boy</u> ↑	#	was thirteen, in 1891
So too he ◄ (extension: addition)	#	had been circumcised with <u>stone</u>
the incision	#	poulticed over the chalk-<u>clay</u>
and like<u>wise</u> the eyes	#	(ellipted clause/rheme)
It is necessary to take cognizance of	#	Jimmie Blacksmith's experience [from the day of this initiation to the time in 1900 that Jackie Smolders went <u>to Wallah</u>]

KEY TO TEXT 8.2

#	–	theme-rheme boundary
– – – –	–	theme in dependent clauses
underlined words	–	contrastive and tonic stress (focus of new in writing)
↑	–	marks a theme tied cohesively to an earlier theme
[ ]	–	embedded clauses
large arrows	–	mark dialogism in the text: the points where the rheme (and the focus of the new) is taken up as theme, often with explicit conjunction
*	–	dependent (hypotactic) clauses

Text 8.2: Dialogism, Theme and Embedding

eye, the hand, the body, from left to right, from clause to clause, the kind of sequenced patterns of reading between whole texts that Smith (1990) observes as constituting the social relations of ruling, dominant readings (or writings) always tending to silence marginal ones.

In Text 8.2 the thematised material can be traced down the lefthand side of the page. Theme *in* embedded and hypotactic clauses does not generally contribute to the thematic development of the text. Embedded and hypotactic clauses are, however, thematised. What is thematised in main clauses or in these fronted embedded and projected clausal themes (e.g. *these tribal arrangements should still be made*, fronted and projected from *Tabidgi Jackie Smolders' thought*) is Jackie Smolders' identity and beliefs in 1900, Dulcie Blacksmith's identity and beliefs in 1878 and 1900, the 'outsider' status of the missionaries with respect to those beliefs and, finally, the narrator's and reader's obligation to say and think what is constructed as rheme here and in the rest of the novel – *it must be said, it is necessary to take cognizance of*. These statements/propositions at the end of this orientation are generic of the contract established here between writer and reader such that their inscribed positions become indistinguishable.

It is projection from verbal and mental processes and nouns like *was disturbed, to his mind, thought, had not been told, had made it clear that, believed, the deep truth, it must be said*, and so on, the mapping of character and narrator voices onto the same lexicogrammar and the inscribing of the reader and Clune dialogically into the text, which 'makes' the heteroglossia of this text. It is specifically the conjunctive and deictic elements – *therefore he, for, which was, but here, so too even, yet here, therefore, off went* – which carry what Voloshinov called multiple 'intonations' and map the dialogism of multiple, overlapping and conflicting voices across the text.

Each of these elements takes off dialogically from the *new* element in a previous part of the text (see the arrows in Text 8.2), usually the previous clause complex. These items masquerade as moments in the enhancement or elaboration of Tabidgi Jackie Smolders' ruminations and responses to Jimmie's marriage to a white girl: *which was, even if, so too, so too*. They also mark moments in his fictive refusal of that event: *therefore, but here, but the deep truth was, yet here he was, therefore*. The dialogism is marked grammatically in each case by a movement from the new element in the rheme to an explicit form of conjunction between clauses and between clause complexes. These are the only cases in the text where a conjunctive thematic element picks up from the new in the previous clause. If you follow the arrows in Text 8.2 you see also the way the intertextual dialogue with Clune maps itself across and through Tabidgi Jackie's voice.

Other grammatical themes in this text are linked quite differently to the rest of the textual activity – by lexical cohesion, ellipsis or reference, or through additive or implicit conjunction with previous clause complexes. They are also linked to *given* thematic, not *new* rheme elements. Thus *The missionaries* as theme is cohesive lexically with *church, mission station, Brentwood black's camp.* There are other cohesive thematic chains like the following: *Jackie Smolders* (cohesive with rheme) – *he* – *Tabidgi Jackie Smolders* – *his mind* – *Jackie* – *Jackie Smolders* – *his . . . sister* – *Dulcie Blacksmith* – *Mrs Dulcie Blacksmith* – *Mrs Blacksmith.*

The final point I want to make here is about the material coded in embedded and projected clauses in rheme. Given the theme/rheme movement in the text, the rheme as news is what the reader is positioned to accept as news, and as unproblematically representational. But there is no 'reality' behind this text. There are only the traces of gendered bodies at work, of habitus and habituated and embodied practices. The lexicogrammar is almost entirely metarepresentational, a representation as meaning of words that were never spoken, thoughts that were never thought – except in the intertextual discursive fields in which white Australia constructs the realities it thinks are its others. If you run your eyes down the righthand side of Text 8.2 you will find realisations of most of the statements that constitute the elements of these discourses. One telling example will do to conclude this section: the clause complex that begins *It must be said.* What must be said here, narratively, are a collocation of projected and embedded articulations of stereotyped white beliefs about Aboriginality:

> *It must be said that . . . his chief reason . . . was tribal and centred in the magical tooth*
> (a projection from a projection, a making primitive, innocent and safe)

> although *Jackie Smolders was alcoholic*
> (a hypotactic clause of concession, conceding the effects of European colonisation, but containing this within the frame of the primitive setting-out)

> *and* knew *that Jimmie Blacksmith was earning liquor*
> (a projection of a knowing that is white knowing into Jackie's head)

> *which, Jackie, as maternal uncle, could claim for liquor*
> (postmodifier of the nominal *that Jimmie Blacksmith was earning wages* functioning to embed white stereotypes into the nominal group)

There is much more of this on the righthand side of Text 8.2. What is critical is that the material in embedded and projected clauses of this kind is 'unarguable' in terms of the mood structure (the organisation of the text as statements, questions, imperatives, and so on) (Halliday 1985a). That is, when we argue directly with a statement, we tend to argue with the material in the main clause and to take for granted as Ideas, Meanings, Phenomena, Things, the meanings that are coded as projections and embeddings (Halliday 1985a). So, in this case, we might say: 'Well, *must* it be said?', but we may well not argue about what has been said in this complex and choreographic way. The complexities of this dialogic logical structure are themselves persuasive and not easily open to argument. Thus it is that the making of this text, the generic and dialogic strategies for constructing discursive field in context, the arguments with racism and with Clune, nonetheless go on reproducing the ready-made chunks of white discourses on race and gender and class in partially hidden, ideological, gendered and crucially grammatical ways (Threadgold 1988). That making leaves traces of a white, masculine corporeality in the text which are not at all obvious to all readers and easily taken as universal ungendered truths. The anonymous note to the Fontana edition of the novel, linked intertextually with the film by the photograph of the filmic Jimmy Governor on the cover, declares that the novel 'is a most vivid recreation of the Blacksmiths' hunted lives'.

I have quite deliberately written about the grammar of the Keneally text in ways that have focused on the making, the processual and always probabilistic fashioning of the text, which always denies its status as finished product at the same time as it tries to articulate some of the resistances offered by the text to subsequent readings. Reading the grammar of the text does allow you to actually demonstrate the way the position of the enunciation (authorship) is folded into the enounced, the way that enfolded corporeality goes on debating intertextually with a context long past, the way that debate is marked by clear grammatical patterns in the text. It allows you to see how that enfolded corporeality comes also to be positioned in and by some of these intertextual histories, continuing to articulate a discourse of racism in an anti-racist text. You could not read it that way, however, without the kind of elaborate contextualisation I have been engaged in in these last two chapters, without understanding the grammatical patterns in text as always metonymically related to bodies and, through them, to contexts. Grammar is a small part of a textual apparatus for making realities and selves. Thus in part, what I have been trying to show above is that the structuring patterns of the text itself may be amazingly complex, may operate subliminally on readers in ways that are hard to resist or even to recognise. Keneally's is a crafted, overcoded text, a literary text, but there is little evidence in it that he was able, even as an educated, critical reader, to resist the structuring pressures of the newspaper texts he had been reading when he made the novel, or of the gendered white habitus which he embodied.

It is for this reason, it seems to me, that we need also to rethink some of the positions in recent cultural studies accounts of readership which are exploring in depth the reading formations which allow different and resistant readings in popular culture (Jenkins 1992; Ang 1996) so that we seem to have stopped thinking about the stabilities of particular formations and the incomprehension between formations (Tulloch and Lupton 1996). We have also forgotten the important matter of the resistances of the text and that those resistances also operate in high places. Thus we seem often to assume that the critical readings of 'high' culture (a category in which both Keneally's novel and Schepisi's film would have to be located) are somehow necessarily and institutionally critical and resistant to being positioned by dominant discourses or ideologies (to use an older terminology). This is one of the crucial reasons, it seems to me, why cultural studies must continue to read high culture, not in the old ways, but in its intersections and metonymic and corporeal relations to the popular. It is not only, as John Frow points out, that 'high' culture (intellectuals) construct imaginary versions *of* the popular, but also that intellectuals (and high culture) do not seem to recognise their own corporeal connections *to* the popular. When Schepisi wrote the screenplay for the film which was first shown in 1978, he also dialogued with Keneally, further romanticising Aboriginality. He was assisted in this by the cinematography of Ian Baker, the editorial work of Brian Kavanagh and the music of composer Bruce Smeaton, a collaborative process of remaking, rewriting as film. Baker's cinematography makes constant intertextual references to Australian and romantic epic and lyric modes, familiar landscape images with small Aboriginal figures inserted into a large canvas, interior shots that mimic and recall the work of painter Tom Roberts. There is a contradiction between the unpleasantness of Australian racism and a soft, Victorian romanticism (Turner 1989), supported intertextually by the music of the closing shot, for example, as white birds wheel symbolically to tumultuous music above the blue-green bush of the Australian countryside. None of these men is at all resistant to the neatness of Keneally's structuring of events or to his readings of Aboriginality. None of their rewriting in film manages to dislodge the discourses of race and gender which continue to be transmitted through the novel and now the film. And yet, the dialogism, the generic strategy to contest racism, remains apparent to readers of the film as it must be to readers of the novel. These rewritings, then, are partially successful in making white racism visible but they leave a good deal intact and they never question at all the sexism of the discourses with which racism has intersected historically, or the class relations in which their own intellectual positions are embedded.

CLUNE, KENEALLY, SCHEPISI: HUGE STABILITIES OF DISCOURSE

All three of these texts attempt – deliberately, polemically, in dialogue with one another, using different genres and media of expression – to make visible and audible, and therefore to challenge, the discourses of racism they perceive to be articulated in the media accounts of the Governor murders in 1900. They are therefore excellent examples of strategic and overcoded rewritings, and demonstrate all the attendant difficulties of that enterprise. I have listed below some of the groups of 'statements' from the intertextual discursive field which structures Keneally's embedded clauses. They are taken from the newspapers, the Clune and Keneally texts and the Fred Schepisi film of the Keneally novel. I have indicated in brackets in *which* of the four 'texts' the 'statements' about 'blacks' and women which constitute these discourses of race and gender occur. They occur verbally and visually. Each is already a bundle of interpersonal, textual and experiential meanings. They give some sense of the contradictions and incompatibilities in the elements that are able to be expressed, to be told, to be imaged, across all these genres and across all this time. In fact, all are constructed, transmitted, made from a white masculine position.

1   (All four texts)
  An aboriginal had no vote
  He was not allowed to own land
  Aboriginal reservations were under the control of missionaries
  They were a dying race
  Half-whites were classified as black
  Blacks were alcoholic and unreliable
  The best of them are likely to vanish at any time
  yer just git one of them into shape and they go off on bloody walkabout
  shots of two figures, dwarfed by landscape, running along ledge lined
    with dead trees

2   (Clune, Keneally, Schepisi)
  It was an offence to supply him with liquor
  They lived partly on rations supplied by the police
  shots of blacks' camp, drunkenness, whoring in film

3   (Clune, Keneally, Schepisi)
  He could be punished by laws which he had no hand in making
  One should make them Christians and leave them alone and let them die

Examples in 1, 2 and 3 above include relational processes involving the classification, identification and attribution of qualities to blacks as carriers and identified participants, material processes (actions, events) positioning blacks as recipients of white beneficence and as goals of white agency. The patterns of lexical cohesion all construct a negative interpersonal evaluation of black (*Aboriginal, black, dying, alcoholic*). Negatives (*no vote*) and modulations (*not allowed*) exclude black from the white world. The statements are all organised textually as third person. The 'I' of the enunciation is only apparently absent, coloured white by his absence and his objectifying and categorising discourse. This is true of all the examples below.

4   (Clune, Keneally)
  If you had a pale child you had been rolled by white men

(Keneally)
As far as Dulcie knew, the great lizard had smashed and swallowed him

(Clune, Keneally)
Cheap, wanton, luxurious black flesh
A flippant, giddy, full-blooded lady

The examples in 4 construct black femininity. They are all from the novel. Black women are absent from the newspapers and from Clune: *He* was not allowed to own land (*she* does not figure). The black feminine, the goal of the white phallus, the one who does not know, the carrier of negative objectifying attributes like *cheap, wanton*, whose knowing is constituted of myths and metaphors (*the great lizard*), is construed as passive and objectifiable in these accounts.

5 (Clune)
An educated, half-white, half-aboriginal
He was a half-caste who refused to accept the status of an outcast
the source of his white heritage and pride . . .
was the chief cause of the terrible protest that he made against racial
    discrimination

In 5, the positive evaluation of 'white' (cohesive in the text with *education, protest* and *refusal*) and the negative evaluation of 'black' in the cohesive pattern *half-aboriginal, half-caste, outcast* maintains the socially ratified values of the black/white dichotomy that structures this discourse even when Clune is dialogically attempting to subvert the discourse of the newspaper reports by refusing to call Jimmy Governor 'black' and crediting his desire for revenge to his 'white pride'.

6 (Media, Clune, Schepisi)
Jimmy's dark-skinned relatives *did not think* it a *disgrace* that their
    kinsman had married a white girl
The purity of their race had been too often sullied by the intercourse of
    their women with white men – outside marriage – for them *to feel* that
    the sanctified marriage of a half-white man with a full white woman was a
    shame

(Keneally)
Jimmie Blacksmith's maternal uncle . . . *was disturbed* to get news that
    Jimmie had married a white girl at the Methodist Church at Wallah –

(Keneally, Schepisi)
Jimmie was caned for truancy
No one resented it

In 6, the examples become more complex. They all involve a white male writer's projection through mental processes of what *he* thinks *blacks* think. Remember this was also a feature of the racist discourse in the newspapers. That is, black ideas and feelings, consistently presented as narrative facts, are equally consistently constructed as the grammatical and logical projection of white masculine beliefs. These are meanings of wordings that were never uttered or thoughts that were never thought. They represent at once the appropriation and the silencing of the voice of the racial 'other'.

7 (Media, Clune, Schepisi)
 She was probably a waif or a domestic
 She had no romance in her life
 Jimmy Governor was handsome, athletic, honest, sober, a steady worker,
  a fine horseman. Why shouldn't she fall in love with him?
 From a home for wayward girls in Sydney
 this one did not look pretty or individual enough to justify the adjective
 Most of the time she fretted about the house
 her mouth gaping adenoidally to serve Mrs Hayes
 (Representations of Gilda in the film)

8 (Keneally, Schepisi)
 Jimmie's criteria were home, heart, wife and land.
 He knew that love was a special fire that came down from God
 suspended between the loving tribal life and the European rapture from
  on high called falling in love
 I gotta start working so I kin get property
 A start had to be made somewhere with white women
 fucking scene in film, shot of white pantaloons, bare black legs, bonking
  noises

9 (Keneally, Schepisi)
 (Mr Neville had) often felt the distinctive pull of some slant-grinned
  black face
 It was not simply a matter of her being full and ripe (Jimmie of Mrs
  Healy/novel)
 her peculiar way of sitting still in the dray and breathing out into the
  morning a vapour of worship and submission to her husband (of Mrs
  Healy/novel, film)
 big, meaty, thick-pawed Newby girls
 Miss Graf was a big country girl herself
 she gave off a soft musk of delicacy and knew etiquette
 film segment of hewing and cutting of white women in Newby kitchen,
  pitcher, milk, white gowns, blood

Not only do white men lust after black flesh in these examples, but white women too are constructed consistently as the object of the male gaze, the goal of the colonised black other's desire for property and submission. *Full* and *ripe, meaty* and *thick-pawed*, these women are guilty of titillating that desire, of 'asking for it'. Similarly, the white woman who marries a black man has to be *wayward,* fretful, *her mouth gaping adenoidally.* No proper, full, ripe object of the white male gaze would do such a thing. The gendered stereotypes proliferate here. I have included the examples in 7 and 8 above because these statements offer some indication of the way discourses constrain the 'stories' that can be told. In this case, the gender field is mapped on to or extended into the field of heterosexual relationships, marriage, property and romance. This involves a degree of conflict with the discourses of race outlined above and cannot really be accounted for except in terms of intertextual dialogism. Faced with the need to 'explain' a white girl's marriage to a black man, Clune has first to construct white feminine in ways that devalue it (*waif, domestic*), then to construct half-caste masculine in positive 'white' terms (*sober, honest*), terms that are those of the romance field, and then to follow the discursive constraints on action sequences: *no romance ^handsome man^ feminine falls in love.* For Clune, the discourses involved here totally determine what story can be told and what stories (whatever they might have been) cannot be told, even when this involves the contradiction of negative 'black' being reconstructed as 'white', 'sober' and 'honest', in a 'story' with a decidedly Mills & Boon flavour. The same field-constrained 'story' is told by the defence lawyer at the Governor trial and by Keneally. Keneally adds to it the details of the undesirable nature of the only woman this black man can possess. Keneally and Schepisi have other stories as well, equally discursively constrained, of black men lusting after full, ripe white femininity, and of white men lusting after black flesh. This discourse is never questioned in any of these public rewritings.

The intersections of race, gender and class in 'stories' such as the above follow frequently from the cohesive and transitivity patterns, and from the narrative sequences that constitute the discourses outlined above. Narratives such as:

Blacks are always wandering off
Blacks cannot be trusted
Therefore blacks are murderers
　　　　　(the newspapers)

or

Women are irrational and childish
Women do not understand
Therefore women believe what men and missionaries tell them
　　　　　(Keneally's 'story' of black femininity)

are both more likely in this intertextual discursive field than other 'stories' and actively operate, as discursive constraints, in the construction of 'reality' in the newspaper and other texts.

As some indication of other stories that might have been told, it is worth briefly comparing the discourse of black/white relations constructed in Mudrooroo's (1988) very different generic and dialogic story.

1   They *stripped* yuh –
they *eye-fucked* yuh –
they *washed* you *down* with *stinkin* soap

2   A *shit-scared* heap of *shiverin* flesh
What were yuh? *Nuthin* man.

1 and 2 continue to construct Aboriginality as goal (of *eye-fucking, washing*) and as carrier (*shit-scared, nuthin*), but this time it is the subaltern who speaks. They, the agent of this *stripping* and *eye-fucking*, is *us*, seen from the position of the recipient of these activities.

3   The nomadic narrative

There comes a time
when y'uv ad enough of
yuh – senser/reaction   ad enough – mental process

em playin with yuh
em – agent/actor   material process   yuh – goal/affected

of em eying yuh off
em – observer/actor   material/behavioural process yuh – goal/affected

as if'n yuh were some animal
yuh – carrier   were – relational   animal – attribute

These clauses are all projected from *ad enough* of as meanings. It is very hard as a white reader to know what kinds of processes these are – mental anguish, embodied alienation, the brands on the body of white violence, 'the aggression' that 'might cause someone literally to fall apart' (Morrison 1993). This is the grammar of lived alienation, a habitus *we* do not live. When this 'other' speaks, as here, it does not sound at all like the infantilised and passive primitive of Keneally's imaginings. The nomadic character of the Aboriginal also comes to be seen as a reaction to intolerable racism, not merely the vagaries of primitive black nature. In this Aboriginal discourse, Aboriginal women, too, look different and belong in different stories:

1   (Of Ernie's mother)
She's sexy too

She was small yuh know
small an dark with long black air that went down to her waist
She was so beautiful

me mum – ow *strong* she was
an ow *she fought* to get a *widow's pension*
to *support* us kids
for the time *they left us* with er.

This small, sexy, beautiful Aboriginal woman, who fights white society with its own social services as they take her children in the name of the pernicious discourse of protection, bears little relation to the primitive tribal women rolled by white men in Keneally's novel. Mudrooroo also has very different things to say of the Standard English of Keneally's educated white voice, and of the Aboriginality which is marked, branded vocally, by being co-opted into that alienating whiteness of sound and manner:

But she's a *stunner* all right, *brown lush skin* sort of shiftin towards yuh.
A garden to wander through slowly,
but er voice as bin educated into that pose tone that sets these people away
from me in some distant land of limp ands and dismissal.

Jinda as *one of those educated voices that put me on guard straight away.*
Maybe it's because she's *from Sydney an that town breeds em ard.*

The same kinds of comment on Aboriginal use of white speech are made of men in the novel. They frequently enact a discourse of mimicry or camouflage – an Aboriginal speech which is expert in self-reflexively speaking in tongues or heteroglossia:

Ee begins an I notice *ee's changed is accent* so ee is close *to mimickin* the students.
That's what I mean about *livin in two worlds* an *learnin ow to camouflage yer speech an manners when it suits yuh.*

MRS FITZPATRICK: MAKING MEMORIES

I want to talk here about the making of different meanings, different readings of the events in 1900, about a common poetics, a cultural memory, about nomadic and productive readers at work in ways never entirely constrained by the social milieu or the dominant and public stories of the Jimmy Governor murders. My interview with Mrs Fitzpatrick, like the texts I will quote at the end of this chapter, has always been an 'index', 'rare and partial, like bubbles rising from the depths of water' (de Certeau 1984/1988: 172), of that common poetics, all those everyday and resistant ways of making meanings with texts and the lived body and experience that, as de Certeau says, have always been there but, usually not committed to writing, are hard to trace. They are not voices to romanticise.

I interviewed Mrs Fitzpatrick in 1989. Her 'memories' of the Governor murders are thoroughly intertextual, partly acquired from listening and through family oral traditions, but also 'mixed in' with recollections of newspaper clippings read and talked about, magazine stories, the yellowed copies of which have been handed down in the family for nearly a century, annotated family photographs of Kieran Fitzpatrick's headstone, of members of the family standing with Kieran's gun, beside the stump that once stood before his house, of the gap in the hills through which the Governors disappeared after killing him, of the typed copy of the story Ellis, the hawker, sent to a member of the family after he had given evidence at the Governor trial in Sydney. Her memories are also of her husband ('I married into this family'), and from, or supported by (I cannot know the sequencing), a number of fairly late accounts of the murders (she mentions the accounts in *People* (1975), *Western Magazine* (1978)). Very early in the interview, like Polly Porteous below, she actually begins to claim the story for her own family through her mother and the possibility that her mother's sister may have married the engineer who captured one of the criminals. Her lived experience of the Governor story, though, relates to a 'sentimental journey' she and her sister made, after her husband's death, to Wollar. On the way they stopped at Dubbo and happened to spend the night in a motel owned by descendants of the Mawbey family (the family the Governors murdered), who over dinner were telling their version of the Governor murders, thus demonstrating that the stories live on in other families, probably in yet different versions.

The Fitzpatrick family also owns a copy of Frank Clune's book, annotated in the margins where members of the family have disagreed with his version of events, traces of bodies at work. Mrs Fitzpatrick was angry that Keneally represented Jimmy Governor in ways that her family just did not believe were true.

She identifies Jimmy Governor with Ned Kelly, and comments that he was much better educated than the average white boy in the district, because they had to help on the farms while black children stayed on longer at school. She refuses my implicit assignment of 'prejudice' to the inhabitants of Wollar, pointing out that Jimmy Governor was 'very popular', and good-looking, but then telling me how the whites would turn on him and call him 'black-fella', and how they made him run with his boots on so he would not win the races. She makes a reference here to an article to support this, indicating that some of these 'family' memories may be textual memories, a mixing of texts. The family are still so confident that the blacks would not have deliberately harmed Kieran Fitzpatrick, their uncle (because he knew them and had been good to them), that their story is one of misunderstanding and panic, not murder. Mrs Fitzpatrick also gave me a story from the

National Times in which a schoolteacher, Miss Porteous, who taught Jimmie Governor, is reported as refusing to believe the Aboriginals would hurt her. This, too, may be part of the history of Mrs Fitzpatrick's memories.

Questioned about the family's apparent sympathy with a man who murdered one of their kin, she remains committed to what is clearly a profoundly believed story, that the Aboriginals would not have deliberately harmed Kieran, indeed that they did not mean to hurt anybody. Even their killing of the Mackay baby becomes a sympathetic killing – 'they didn't want to leave the baby to die' – and this 'reading' of events seems to rely on a belief that the Aboriginals had been very badly treated by the Mawbeys and others. Thus, in this family story, the Mawbey men are the villains. It is the question of the fenceposts not paid for that is the issue – 'the real crux of the situation was they had all these fence posts ready . . . ' (Interview: 17), and for the first time in the many tellings of this tale, a niggardly boss and white male racism (but this is this writer's reading, not hers) becomes the trigger for the murders.

Mrs Fitzpatrick's memories of the Jimmy Governor murders are a metarepresentation, just as overcoded (even if constructed as memory) as any of the texts mixed intertextually with them. It is also possible to hear, in her telling of them, how the value of an event lies in the way it fits into a discursive formation of other textual and intertextual events, how talk structures, assesses and authenticates the existence of the event, lodges it in cultural memory, makes it a part of a lived experience of family and history.

HISTORY AND ABORIGINAL TEXTS: MUDROOROO'S *DOIN WILDCAT*

Stephen Muecke (1992), in the same book that records the stories of Pigeon the bushranger referred to above, discusses the difficulties of writing Aboriginal history, distinguishing between the doing of that in the Standard English and 'mandated' forms of the academy and (as we have seen in the case of Keneally) the literary establishment, and the 'authentification' of Aboriginal history by Aboriginal voices who speak as one 'who was there'. After reading the black and white versions of the Pigeon story (1992: 75), Muecke suggests that it might be possible 'To use the oral tradition in the construction of a different kind of writing', that this 'would be another rhetorical device . . . ' for writing and rewriting Aboriginal history. Muecke argues that it might, indeed, be possible to displace the 'absent author' syndrome (a literary or filmic emphasis on third person narrative) 'in favour of the textual strategy of the implication of writer and reader positions in a process of specific deployment of stories with changing rhetorical effects in current arenas of public debate' (1992: 75).

He is speaking here about the strategies used by Mudrooroo in *Doin Wildcat: A Novel Koori Script* (1988). The 'oral speech', the Aboriginal

English, that Mudrooroo uses in his novel is the same speech that is constructed as 'non-standard' in Keneally. But this time it is valued and spoken from an Aboriginal perspective, a perspective which also regularly forces the reader (particularly the white reader) to confront the deafness of her own Standard English discursive forms and genres, and to understand how these forms and genres regularly and violently silence the voice of Aboriginal experience, its oral language, its lived realities.

The novel *Doin Wildcat* is one of a trilogy in which the same narrative, the story of a young Aboriginal man and his early encounters with the law and with various facets of white society, is constantly retold, rewritten and reconstructed, from different and often conflicting perspectives, by that Aboriginal grown old, recently released from gaol after serving twenty-three years for the accidental murder of a white policeman. In gaol he wrote the novel, the filming of which this novel is all about. Identities are fluid, constantly changing, as they reappear in different versions of the narrative. The story, in this novel, is about the way a white film-maker 'steals the aboriginal's script', the film script (of the novel we are reading), by rewriting it in ways that again appropriate Aboriginality for a white world. The speaking subject in this novel – black, educated through the experience of the violence of the law – is doubly divided from himself, doubly displaced, ventriloquist, able to mimic because he lives the discourses of the master, a monolingual master who cannot hear or read his stories and languages, and who constantly recuperates them, makes them safe by reappropriating them into his white narratives and worlds.

This double displacement is in fact a place from which to confront not only white histories of Aboriginality, but white formalisms, white genres and forms of the novel (Mudrooroo 1990) and from which to negotiate the power of white linguistic capital. The novel is written in what the sociolinguist would call 'non-standard' English, Aboriginal English, but the non-standard speaker in this novel is multilingual, able to 'read' and deconstruct the monolingual blindness of the guardians of Standard English, its powerful genres and their violently recuperative tendencies. What the novel deconstructs as it represents are the powerful hierarchies of race, class and gender inherent in all textual processes. Nowhere is this politics of deconstruction and re-presentation (rewriting) more poignant than in the re-presentations of the narrativity of legal process in the novel. This is the one example that I will explore here in detail.

At 15, the by-now already 'institutionalised' (1988: 87) hero of the novel is let loose on a society he has few means to deal with. The narrative he tells is of agency and lack of agency. Victim of a white world which not only cannot, but will not, hear his story, he learns to identify with a new community. Streetwise, he steals to clothe himself with an identity, he makes himself a self in the milk-bar world where he is ultimately arrested for doing just that. In custody, he confides the details of this narrative to his probation officer

('Ee wanted me to talk about meself, an I obliged im' [89]) who, asked to
give evidence in court, 'does the dirty on me' (88). It is worth comparing the
details of the two narratives which confront the reader in the novel – two
incommensurable constructions of differently lived and understood realities:

> *I get outa Swanview, or rather am pushed out* when I reach fifteen.
> Naturally by then I can't fend for meself, and so they get the Catholic
> Welfare to elp me. They get me a job an a place to stay in an ouse that
> specialises in puttin up coloured people. There's a couple more stayin
> along with me, but after the ome an bein outa that ome, I think there
> must be somethin more to the outside. I get outa that place, find meself
> another one across the tracks on the wild side of town, *an then the job
> gets rid of me,* an I've to use me wits to survive. It's pretty easy but *I ate
> bein on me own.* Then one night I wander into the Royal Milk Bar, *an feel
> a bit at ome.*
>
> (87)

The probation officer's story, as courtroom evidence, constructed in the
novel by the speaker of the narrative above, is a classic example of the way
the discourse of the other is regularly reclaimed for normative public discourse by institutional practices like the law. The probation officer is that
kind of expert reader who has learned to distrust the evidence of the eyewit-
ness (Smith 1990: 120) and is practised precisely in normalising (and thus
misreading) unruly and 'non-standard' discourses:

> ROBINSON: *Unfortunately there is little that can be said for this boy.*
> The Child Welfare Department has had nothing but trouble from
> him since his release from Swanview Boys' Home. At the age of nine
> he was sent there for breaking and entering a number of stores in
> the town in which he was then living with his mother. *The family to
> put it mildly were a bunch of drifters.* Reports show that he was not
> unintelligent, and he was quite good at school . . . I found him a
> job   and   accommodation   but   he   left   these   almost
> immediately . . . *He is of aboriginal descent, on his mother's side,
> and I believe that this goes a long way towards explaining his behav-
> iour.*
>
> (89)

The significance of the narrative incompatibility of these two accounts, of
the deafness of the public version to the private and individual and here very
specifically black and juvenile one, is made yet clearer in the narrator's
account of the cross-examination, a speech genre not known at the best of
times for its propensity to listen to what it does not already know:

> MAGISTRATE: *You say in your statement that you do not believe in
> God?*

'Yeah that's right'. (A nudge from Robinson makes me remember the sir.)
'Yes, that's right, sir!'
MAGISTRATE: *And so you have no time for such things as the bible and oaths made before God, and this court?*
'No I don't . . . Sir!'
MAGISTRATE (with a smile):   And so, we may presume that you'll swear to tell the truth on your honour?
What is ee gettin at? I shrug, but another nudge from Robinson makes me realise that ee wants an answer. Well, what else to say, but 'Yes, Sir!'.
MAGISTRATE: Well, we'll have to take that on good faith won't we?
Is words scare me, frighten me to ell an back. *They out to get me, an suddenly I don't want to be got. I blurt out just like the frightened kid I am inside: 'Sir, couldn't find no job. No matter what ee says, couldn't find no job. Ad no money either. Ad to pay me rent, ad to eat, ad nuthin to live on, or for!'*
MAGISTRATE: Mr Robinson was there for you to appeal to. Did you?
'Im! Ee wouldn't elp me if I was dyin.'
MAGISTRATE: And these articles of clothing that are on the table. I suppose you were going to sell them for food and shelter?
'Me own gear was dirty and outa fashion. Me mates expect me to dress sharp.'
MAGISTRATE: Oh . . . Now remember you have given me your word of, of honour to tell the truth. This is very important. *Do you feel any remorse for the crimes you have committed?*
'Dunno what that is. I was ungry, the rent was due, and I needed some dough.'
MAGISTRATE: I think we have heard more than enough. Mr Robinson will you come here please.

(89; my italics)

Mudrooroo's juxtaposition of these different realities in this novel is specifically and self-consciously political, a politics of reading and of rewriting. His own position as educated Aboriginal in a white world makes him as author a powerful deconstructive mimic and rewriter. His novels are now becoming part of that small group of canonical texts set as part of the final-year English Literature curriculum in many Australian states, as is Keneally's. The political implications of the reading and teaching of a fictional text like this one in Australian schools cannot be underestimated. The powers for the recuperation of Mudrooroo's deconstruction of institutionalised literary and linguistic power are, of course, enormous in that context, and in some ways its inclusion in the curriculum might be seen as a mode of reappropriation, but the text itself is remarkably resistant to the recuperative powers of public discourse on a number of levels simultaneously (linguistic, literary, narrative and generic).

It is through the careful interweaving of conflicting narratives that Mudrooroo is able to 'voice' and 'make heard' what the white narratives themselves cannot hear, cannot read, cannot speak. Reading him in sequence after Keneally, the film, Clune and the newspapers, it is hard not to read them as what this novel is all about – the stealing of the Aboriginal script by white Australia – but the novel's plurality of endings, the one the narrative voice tells us happened, the one his novel tells, the one the director makes of the novel, and the one he makes to get out of gaol, steal that script back by rewriting (his)tory:

DIRECTOR: This'll make the movie man. Beautiful, real beautiful. They'll love these bush scenes in the states . . . Poetry and sympathy for the underdog are where it's at, and that means the Australian bush for sure

. . .

ERNIE [TO NARRATOR]:   Well, yuh ended it wrong yuh did. All yuh got is another blackfella ending up in jail

. . .

[NARRATOR:]   So what do yuh do? Inside all yer life or give in a little – a lot – to get out. That book was me ticket to the outside brudda. It ad to please em, so the ending was a appy one for em. Little Jacky so sorry for shooting the policeman – . . .

(Mudrooroo 1988: 112–13)

CODA: NARRATIVE, MEMORY, IDENTITY

In mid-1996 the question of just to what extent Mudrooroo has told white Australia what it wants to hear has emerged as part of a series of debates around authorship and identity in the Australian context. These debates have been intimately connected to the questions of postcoloniality and diaspora that cultural studies and social theory have been investigating (Chow 1993; Young 1995). Perhaps the first and most outraged discovery of a signature that was not authentic was the case of Helen Demidenko, a young woman whose first novel, ironically called *The Hand That Signed the Paper*, won a prestigious literary prize. The young novelist had constructed herself as the child of Ukrainian parents so that the novelistic account of terrible wartime deeds, of Ukrainians killing Jews for the Nazis, had the apparent value of testament and authenticity. A truly literary fracas resulted from the disclosure that the young woman was not Ukrainian at all but an 'ordinary' Australian and the charges of anti-Semitism were legion. The case produced a whole industry of Demidenko commentaries, including several books, as the media and literary establishments and the publishing industry capitalised on the scandal.

The issues here are of diaspora and identity, of proper and improper identity, and of the signature that does not authenticate, of the ownership of histories, of an invalid, not-habituated corporeality enfolded into a text, and masquerading there as ethnic, other, minority, when in fact it is none of these things. Indeed, what appears here to be a corporeal trace of authorship turns out to be only a discursive trace (from stories, records, other books), an imaginary body again produced by a white intellectual, indeed two imaginary bodies: that of the author (a different performance of the self) and that of the narrative. And again one sees how texts and bodies produce one another, fold into one another.

Much more recently, Mudrooroo's Aboriginal identity has been questioned. Indeed, so has the authenticity of the conclusion of the novel I quoted at the end of the last section of this chapter. In an article called 'Identity Crisis' by Victoria Laurie, Mudrooroo is quoted as commenting on the 'help' he received from Dame Mary Durack who edited and introduced his first novel, *Wildcat Falling*, in 1965:

> In an interview in May with HQ magazine, Mudrooroo said Durack had 'changed [the novel] quite a bit – she wanted a happy ending and humanity in the eyes of the cop and so on.' He described the novel's reception thus: 'Until then, Aborigines were known for indifferent watercolours, and now one . . . had written a novel'.
>
> (*Australian Magazine*, 20–1 July 1996: 31)

It is clear from the paternalistic tones of Dame Mary Durack's introduction to that novel that she at least had constituted the young Colin Johnson as part Aboriginal and also it seems that she had 'stolen his script', constituting yet another imaginary version of Aboriginality. This is supported in a quote from Durack's daughter in the same article: 'He started writing and sent Durack the draft of *Wildcat Falling*. Millett [Durack's daughter] claims her mother gave him all kinds of help . . . It needed heavy editing and she pulled it into shape to make it publishable' (p. 31).

It seems that Australia's first Aboriginal writer may well have been the partial construction of another well-meaning white intellectual, an editor this time. Yet there is not much question that Colin Johnson, now Mudrooroo, grew up a dark-skinned youth in racist Australia. The histories recorded in *Doin Wildcat* and the Wildcat trilogy are his lived histories; ones that marked and branded the body folded into these texts. Australian history still bears the mark of the 'stolen generation' of mixed-race Aboriginal children taken away from their families to assimilate them into white society. Mudrooroo's siblings were certainly taken into child welfare's care, and he spent much of his early life in a boys' home, separated from that family, and then in Fremantle Gaol. In that context, as the writer of the article points out, he 'became', if he was not already, Aboriginal. There is a grandfather of probably 'negro' origin. It was in Fremantle Gaol that Dame Mary Durack met him:

The 'coloured boy' of indeterminate origins had become an angry young black man, hardened by poverty, family separation and jail, an experience shared by so many of his Aboriginal inmates. 'Many of Us Mob', he writes in his recent book, 'have served gaol sentences, and it is in the prisons of Australia that many of Us Mob develop a consciousness of nationwide Indigenality which is overtly political.'

(*Australian Magazine*, 20–1 July 1996: 31)

It seems that if Mudrooroo has been living an improper, illegal Aboriginality all this time, it is the institutions and the imaginary of white Australia that has produced that Aboriginality. Mudrooroo himself has refused to be drawn into the family, media, and now Aboriginal, interest in his ancestry. ' "Indigenality" rests on heredity and descent, he writes, "[but] includes a learnt portion, and to stress degrees of "blood" is in effect playing the [white] Master's game, which is always one of dealing with possession, legality, paternity and caste' (*Australian Magazine*, 20–1 July 1996: 32).

Some white commentators have been only too ready to declare Mudrooroo a 'career aborigine' (Beatrice Faust, *Weekend Australian*, 'Focus', 3–4 August 1996: 8), neglecting the details of his biography as one letter to the editor pointed out. Interestingly the letter also refers to Keneally:

Will Ms Faust now refer to Thomas Keneally as a 'career Roman Catholic'?

To suggest that Mudrooroo has assumed an Aboriginal identity in order to further his career ignores the facts of his biography.

As Ms Faust points out, his first novel was published in 1965 – hardly a time at which a person derived cultural kudos or prestige from being Aboriginal.

(Tom Morton, 'Mudrooroo's Career', *Australian*, 7 August 1996: 12)

Historical memory is often very short and racism does not go away with time. On the same page of the *Australian* as this letter was another written by Ruby Langford Ginibi, an Australian Aboriginal woman writer. She writes as follows:

He was the first published Aboriginal writer, so who are these people who are bent on pulling him down? . . . [H]e is one of the most proficient writers of our Koori stories and poetry, and one whom I regard as a spiritual brother.

So, if his own family disowns him, I'll claim him as one of mine! You see, he lived in my country (Bundjalung country) . . . and I took him to see my people . . . and I say this, that he couldn't write the way he does if he is not Aboriginal. You see, we Kooris, Nyoonga, murris, and all Aboriginal people, have for too long been written about by misinformed white people . . . Sure, he was taken from his mother at an early age, nearly 30,000 stolen half-caste kids taken in Western Australia . . . So bully for Mudrooroo in becoming an author to write about the oppression we have not recovered from yet!

(Ruby Langford Ginibi, 'The Right to be a Koori Writer', *Australian*, 7 August 1996: 12)

For Ruby Langford Ginibi, as for Mudrooroo, authenticity is in the body, the corporeality, of the lived experience of Aboriginality. That is the position of enunciation that she reads as folded into Mudrooroo's texts. This absolutely irrevocable folding of whiteness into blackness (and of blackness into whiteness) in the history of Australia is something that must be acknowledged even if it is difficult to theorise and describe. We are all implicated. The possibility of the third person narrative voice is no longer available.

Mudrooroo is not the only one whose identity is fractured, multiply positioned, incapable of being neatly contained by the opposition between black and white. Kay Ferres' (1995) work on Rosa Praed's autobiography and the light it sheds on the Hornet Bank massacre in mid-nineteenth-century Australia is linked to this question of hybrid and diasporic blackness and whiteness. This massacre, like the Governor murders, was one in which Aboriginals killed white settlers, raped and murdered white women. At least, that is the white reading. Ferres writes:

My object is to show that the lines of difference are not always clear cut: that dissenting voices, heard in the moments of contestation, are later muffled, and ambivalence resolved through the circulation of stereotypes of black, masculine savagery and white, feminine vulnerability. A doubled reading will be in process here: on the one hand, I am reading in the spaces of Praed's autobiographical writing to uncover the uncertainties which threaten official discourses of otherness; at the same time, I want to open up a space in my own practice, between a deconstruction of differences and a strategic essentialism (Spivak 1988), in order to suggest how de Lauretis' 'feminist understanding' might be incorporated in historical narratives so that dissenting voices can be heard.

(Ferres 1995: 141–2)

Ferres argues that what Praed's narrative allows is the making visible again of the Aboriginal women who were the sexual objects of the Fraser men and the interventions of Martha Fraser, their widowed mother, who understood the serious consequences her sons' sexual conduct could have (1995: 149). In this context the rape of white women can be seen not as 'bestial excess' but as 'retribution for the failure to honour obligations' (1995: 149). The elision of white masculine sexuality as a factor in colonisation is, Ferres argues, disallowed by Rosa Praed's text which 'reinserts the mangled bodies of the

Fraser women into history' (1995: 151) in ways which promote insistently gendered readings of colonial events.

This account, like mine of the Governor murders earlier, 'cannot altogether dispense with the polarisation of black and white, but it can show how lines of difference are drawn through multiple sites of power' (Ferres 1995: 156). It suggests that hybridity and sexuality are regularly written out of colonialist history and that feminist work might write these things back in and write the stories differently. But it also suggests that there are many other voices, many other stories, not neatly black or white, that might have been heard or that might be heard now about the Governor murders.

The texts that I will leave you with are ambivalent, the traces of many different corporeal realities, traces of what the public records in the Governor case could not hear, would not accommodate, traces the case continues to produce. They are the grammatical, textual and corporeal traces of Australian men and women, whose identities and subjectivities are constant rewritings, renegotiations, made of family memories, texts, reading practices and conversations, all of these part of the ambivalent conversations the public and published stories tidy up, elide, silence. They are suggestive of differences in reading formations, lived experience, habitus and position of enunciation. They are not all of a piece. Black and white corporealities are folded ambivalently through all of them. Two (at least) are indicative of the powers of pedagogy to both position and empower. These are the very recent texts by Jamie Baxter and Polly Porteous. Both are positioned in various ways by the intertextual materiality of the stories they know of the Governor murders, stories they have come to know at school and university. Both young women also shape that knowledge generically, folding a certain immediate corporeality and the trace of different communities, different reading formations, into the histories and selves they make as they write.

I would like to leave you with these self-questioning and assertive voices, together with a different discursive space in which we may begin to understand how family and social memories, the realities that are lived by the body, contribute to the making of culture and how subjectivity is formed through 'gendered' and radicalised racial difference – a space in which to understand the networks that connect the body, memory, language, pedagogy, politics, the literary, the legal, and the popular which is in us all.

1 *S. G. Ellis, hawker, August 1900*

We trusted those blacks and they reciprocated. I often camped near them with my hawker's van and they were always anxious for me to do so . . . Nothing was ever molested and I had no fear of it ever being molested.

. . . In passing I quote one of their weird beliefs, 'Pointing the bone'. They form a corroboree, which means that a number of their wise men form a circle. The head man acquired a dry kangaroo shank bone . . . Then the condemned man whom they want to torture is tapped on the shin bone . . . No doctor can cure him. With a little education they think they have a whiteman's knowledge. With their own bushcraft on top of that, of which they are very conceited, with some indiscreet white man's flattery, they rate themselves superior to the inexperienced white man.

I told them this pointing of the bone business was silly . . . and invited them to try it on me. Jimmy refused, saying that he would not kill me as I was his friend and he liked me . . . That altered my opinion of them and I saw they were not to be played with.

The full blooded aboriginal can be taken out of the camp as an infant into a good living white family and the aboriginal nature never departs, this has been proved to the regret of many pioneering white families.

2 *Fitzpatrick interview, 23 September 1989*

MRS F: – it was all in our minds and we went on out to Dubbo and went to the zoo – 'n we were very disappointed in that – but we were driving around Dubbo looking for a motel to check in for the night and we just picked one that looked alright an' we just – we got into the office – and who should the licensee of the motel be but Mawbey –

TT: Oh really?

MRS F: – and – we went into dinner that night – it was the weekend – so they had lots of guests coming – there was sort of a – someone in the family was getting married – or a very close friend – I'm not sure which – because we were only overhearing this – we sat at our table – and they had all these guests there – and here they are telling all these guests about this – this –

TT: You're kidding?

MRS F: No – no – I'm not – telling them all about this massacre – and everything –

TT: Talk about coincidence – and so that was still being told among the family –

MRS F: Oh yes – they told all those people that night – and my sister and I were nearly having a fit – sitting a few feet away from them you see – so anyway the next morning I went into the office – I told him who I was – and um – because I was – at that stage – I wanted to ring Wallar – to tell Millie – this elderly lady – that we were coming –

Page 10

MRS F: Now the family have always contended that because Kyrien was friendly with them and wouldn't – you know – said they wouldn't harm him –

Page 17

MRS F: – the point that makes us so mad is that – not so mad but – it's irritating – to find people who – who were so ready to put him down –

('They' above is the Governors. 'Him' is Jimmy.)

3 *Jamie Baxter, Year 9, Robinvale Secondary College, 1992 Education Booklet for Koori Students*

Jimmy Governor reminded white Australians in the cities that there were still aborigines in their land . . . There were not many of them left, they thought, and they would soon die out. Those who still existed lived far away from cities, on reserves and missions. They were useful workers, even if they were rather lazy, and liked to go walk about now and then. Jimmy Governor showed aborigines would not go away so easily. As he said when he was captured 'I have made a name for myself'.

So aborigines were treated very bad back in the old days. Thank God it isn't like that now.

4 *Polly Porteous, Sydney University Law Student, personal letter, November 1995*

There's one new interesting discovery I made. One of the articles in your materials (Eric Rolls in the *National Times*) refers to a 'Miss Porteous' who taught Jimmy Governor at school. I looked up my family tree and I think I've located this 'Miss Porteous'. My father's great-great-grandfather was Andrew Porteous. In the 1860s he was 'Protector of Aborigines' (filth!) in Langham, Victoria. He apparently learned the aboriginal dialects in the area – and recorded them. He was also a bit of a land-owner (and probably very conservative). Anyway he had two daughters and some sons too. As is typical, the family tree doesn't record any details about these two daughters. However the family had moved to NSW when Andrew died in 1868 (I think). So it is quite probable that the 'Miss Porteous' who claimed to be unfearful of any attacks on herself by Jimmy Governor (because she reckoned according to the article, that she and Jimmy got along well) is Andrew Porteous' daughter.

And the story goes on . . .

The impresario that stages this patriarchal drama is called 'culture', itself the production of an emergent European society; the conflictual structures generated by its imbalances of power are consistently articulated through points of tension and forms of difference that are then superimposed upon each other; class, gender and race are circulated promiscuously and crossed with each other, transformed into mutually defining metaphors that mutate within intricate webs of surreptitious cultural values that are then internalised by those whom they define. Culture has always carried these antagonistic forms of inner dissonance within it . . .

The structure of pidgin – crudely, the vocabulary of one language superimposed on the grammar of another – suggests a different model from that of a straightforward power relation of dominance of colonizer over colonized.

(Young 1995: xi–xii, 5)

Bibliography

Althusser, L. (1971) *Lenin and Philosophy and Other Essays*, trans. B. Brewster, London: New Left Books.

——(1971/1977) 'Ideology and Ideological State Apparatuses (Notes Toward an Investigation) (January–April 1969)', in *Lenin and Philosophy and Other Essays*, trans. B. Brewster, London: New Left Books.

Ang, I. (1991) *Desperately Seeking the Audience*, London/New York: Routledge.

——(1995) 'I'm a Feminist but . . . "Other" Women and Postnational Feminism', in B. Caine and R. Pringle (eds) *Transitions: New Australian Feminisms*, Sydney: Allen & Unwin.

——(1996) *Living Room Wars: Rethinking Media Audiences for a Postmodern World*, London/New York: Routledge.

Austin, J. L. (1976) *How to do Things with Words*, William James Lectures delivered at Harvard University, 1955, ed. J. O. Ormson and M. Sbisa, London/Oxford/New York: Oxford University Press.

Bakhtin, M. (1981) *The Dialogic Imagination: Four Essays by M. M. Bakhtin*, ed. M. Holquist, trans. C. Emerson and M. Holquist, Austin: University of Texas Press.

——(1986) *Speech Genres and Other Late Essays*, ed. and trans. V. W. McGee, C. Emerson and M. Holquist, Austin: University of Texas Press.

Bal, M. (1985) *Narratology: Introduction to the Theory of Narrative*, trans. Christine van Boheemen, Toronto: University of Toronto Press.

Barthes, R. (1953/1968) *Writing Degree Zero*, trans. A. Lavers and C. Smith, New York: Hill & Wang.

——(1957/1973) *Mythologies*, trans. A. Lavers, London: Granada Publishing Limited.

——(1964/1967) *Elements of Semiology*, trans A. Lavers and C. Smith, New York: Hill & Wang.

——(1979) 'The Death of the Author', and 'Introduction to the Structural Analysis of Narratives', in R. Barthes, *Image–Music–Text: Essays Selected and Translated by Stephen Heath*, Glasgow: Fontana/Collins.

——(1986a) 'To Write: An Intransitive Verb?', in *The Rustle of Language*, trans. R. Howard, Oxford: Basil Blackwell.

——(1986b) 'Writing Reading', in *The Rustle of Language*, trans. R. Howard, Oxford: Basil Blackwell.

Bartkowski, F. (1988) 'Epistemic Drift in Foucault', in I. Drummond and L. Quinby (eds) *Feminism and Foucault: Reflections on Resistance*, Boston: Northeastern University Press.

Bartky, S. L. (1988) 'Foucault, Femininity, and the Modernisation of Patriarchal

Power', in I. Drummond and L. Quinby (eds) *Feminism and Foucault: Reflections on Resistance*, Boston: Northeastern University Press.

Bazerman, C. (1988) *Shaping Written Knowledge: The Genre and Activity of the Experimental Article in Science*, Madison: University of Wisconsin Press.

Benhabib, S. (1987) 'The Generalized and the Concrete Other', in S. Benhabib and D. Cornell (eds) *Feminism as Critique*, London: Polity, pp. 77–95.

Bennett, T. (1983/1993) 'Texts, Readers, Reading Formations', in P. Rice and P. Waugh (eds) *Modern Literary Theory: A Reader*, London: Edward Arnold.

Benveniste, E. (1966) *Problèmes de Linguistique Générale*, Paris: Gallimard.

Berger, P. and Luckmann, T. (1966) *The Social Construction of Reality: A Treatise in the Sociology of Knowledge*, New York: Doubleday.

Bernstein, B. (1971) *Class, Codes and Control 1: Theoretical Studies Towards a Sociology of Language*, Primary Socialization, Language and Education, London: Routledge & Kegan Paul.

——(1975) *Class, Codes and Control 3: Towards a Theory of Educational Transmissions*, Primary Socialization, Language and Education, London: Routledge & Kegan Paul.

——(1990) *The Structuring of Pedagogic Discourse*, vol. 4, *Class, Codes and Control*, London/New York: Routledge.

Birch, D. and O'Toole, M. (1988) *Functions of Style*, London/New York: Pinter.

Blakemore, C. (1973) 'The Baffled Brain', in R. L. Gregory and E. H. Gombrich (eds) *Illusion in Nature and Art*, New York: Scribner's.

Bohemia, J. and McGregor, B. (1995) *Nyibayarri: Kimberley Tracker*, Canberra: Aboriginal Studies Press.

Bourdieu, P. (1980/1990) *The Logic of Practice*, trans. R. Nice, Cambridge: Polity Press.

——(1991) *Language and Symbolic Power*, ed. J. B. Thompson, Cambridge: Polity Press.

Braidotti, R. (1990) 'The Problematic of the "Feminine" in Contemporary French Philosophy: Foucault and Irigaray', in T. Threadgold and A. Cranny-Francis (eds) *Feminine/Masculine and Representation*, Sydney: Allen & Unwin.

Braudel, F. (1958) *On History*, London: Fontana.

Buchbinder, D. (1994) *Masculinities and Identities*, Melbourne: Melbourne University Press.

Burton, D. (1982) 'Through Dark Glasses, Through Glass Darkly', in R. Carter (ed.) *Language and Literature*, London: Allen & Unwin.

Butler, J. (1990) *Gender Trouble: Feminism and the Subversion of Identity*, New York/London: Routledge.

——(1992) 'Contingent Foundations: Feminism and the Question of "Postmodernism"', in J. Butler and J. W. Scott (eds) *Feminists Theorise the Political*, New York/London: Routledge.

——(1993) *Bodies That Matter: On the Discursive Limits of 'sex'*, New York/London: Routledge.

Caine, B., Grosz, E. A. and de Lepervanche, M. (1988) *Crossing Boundaries: Feminisms and the Critique of Knowledges*, Sydney: Allen & Unwin.

Calvino, I. (1982) *If on a Winter's Night a Traveller*, London: Picador.

Cameron, D. (1985) *Feminism and Linguistic Theory*, London: Macmillan Press.

——(1995) *Verbal Hygiene*, London/New York: Routledge.

Cameron, D. and Frazer, E. (1987) *The Lust to Kill*, Cambridge: Polity Press.

Castle, J. and Pringle, H. (1993) 'Sovereignty and Sexual Identity in Political Cartoons', in S. Magarey, S. Rowley and S. Sheridan (eds) *Debutante Nation: Feminism Contests the 1890s*, Sydney: Allen & Unwin.

Cazden, C., John, V. and Hymes, D. (eds) (1972) *Functions of Language in the Classroom*, New York: Teacher's College Press.

de Certeau, M. (1984/1988) *The Practice of Everyday Life*, Berkeley/Los Angeles/London: University of California Press.

——(1986) *Heterologies: Discourse on the Other*, Manchester: Manchester University Press.

Chow, R. (1991) 'Violence in the Other Country: China as Crisis, Spectacle and Woman', in C. T. Mohanty et al. (eds) *Third World Women and the Politics of Feminism*, Bloomington: Indiana University Press.

——(1993) *Writing Diaspora: Tactics of Intervention in Contemporary Cultural Studies*, Bloomington/Indianapolis: Indiana University Press.

Clune, Frank (1959) *Jimmy Governor*, London: Horwitz Publications.

Coates, J. (1986) *Women, Men and Language*, Cambridge: Cambridge University Press.

Coates, J. and Cameron, D. (eds) (1988) *Women in Their Speech Communities*, Harlow: Longman.

Connell, R. W. (1995) *Masculinities*, Sydney: Allen & Unwin.

Cornell, D. (1995) *The Imaginary Domain: Abortion, Pornography and Sexual Harassment*, New York/London: Routledge.

Cornell, D., Rosenfeld, M. and Carlson, D. G. (eds) (1992) *Deconstruction and the Possibility of Justice*, London: Routledge.

Deleuze, G. (1986/1988) *Foucault*, ed. and trans. S. Hand, Minneapolis: University of Minnesota Press.

Deleuze, G. and Guattari, F. (1980/1987) *A Thousand Plateaus: Capitalism and Schizophrenia*, trans. Brian Massumi, Minneapolis: University of Minnesota Press.

Demidenko, H. (1994) *The Hand That Signed the Paper*, Sydney: Allen & Unwin.

Derrida, J. (1967/1976a) 'Linguistics and Grammatology', in *Of Grammatology*, trans. Gayatri Chakravorty Spivak, Baltimore/London: Johns Hopkins University Press, pp. 27–73.

——(1967/1976b) *Of Grammatology*, trans. Gayatri Chakravorty Spivak, Baltimore/London: Johns Hopkins University Press.

——(1978) 'Structure, Sign and Play in the Discourse of the Human Sciences', in J. Derrida, *Writing and Difference*, Chicago: University of Chicago Press.

——(1980) 'La Loi du Genre' ('The Law of Genre'), *Glyph* 7: 176–232.

——(1988) *Limited Inc*, trans. S. Weber, Evanston, IL: Northwestern University Press.

van Dijk, T. (1990) Editorial, *Discourse and Society* 1, 1: 1–14.

——(1995) Editorial, 'Esoteric Discourse Analysis', *Discourse and Society* 6, 1: 5–6.

Dixon, R. (1995) *Writing the Colonial Adventure: Race, Gender and Nation in Anglo-Australian Popular Fiction 1875–1914*, Cambridge: Cambridge University Press.

Dobbs, B. J. (1975) *Foundations of Newton's Alchemy or 'The Hunting of the Green Lion'*, Cambridge: Cambridge University Press.

Eagleton, T. (1990) *The Ideology of the Aesthetic*, Oxford: Basil Blackwell.

Eco, U. (1967/1986) *Travels in Hyperreality*, San Diego/New York/London: Harcourt Brace Jovanovich.

——(1979) *A Theory of Semiotics*, Bloomington: Indiana University Press.

——(1981) *The Role of the Reader*, London: Hutchinson.

Edelsky, C. (1977) 'Acquisition of an Aspect of Communicative Competence: Learning What it Means to Talk Like a Lady', in S. Ervin-Tripp and C. Mitchell-Kernan (eds) *Child Discourse*, New York: Academic Press.

Elam, D. (1994) *Feminism and Deconstruction: Ms. en Abyme*, London/New York: Routledge.

Ellis, S. G. (1900) *The Breelong Tragedy, Fitzpatrick Family Papers*, August 1900.

Fairclough, N. (1989) *Language and Power*, London: Longman.

——(1992a) *Discourse and Social Change*, Cambridge: Polity Press.

——(1992b) 'The Appropriacy of "Appropriateness"', in N. Fairclough (ed.) *Critical Language Awareness*, London/New York: Longman.

——(1992c) 'Discourse and Text: Linguistic and Intertextual Analysis Within Discourse Analysis', *Discourse and Society* 3, 2: 193–217.

——(1995) *Critical Discourse Analysis: The Critical Study of Language*, London/New York: Longman.

Ferres, K. (1995) 'Losing Sight of Jenny: Sex, Race and Gender in Rosa Praed's Wild Bush Childhood', in P. van Toorn and D. English (eds) *Speaking Positions: Aboriginality, Gender and Ethnicity in Australian Cultural Studies*, Melbourne: Victoria University of Technology.

Fesl, E. M. D. (1993) *Conned!*, Brisbane: University of Queensland Press.

Finch, L. (1993) *The Classing Gaze: Sexuality, Class and Surveillance*, Sydney: Allen & Unwin.

Firth, J. R. (1957) *Papers in Linguistics 1934–51*, London: Oxford University Press.

Flax, J. (1993) *Disputed Subjects: Essays on Psychoanalysis, Politics and Philosophy*, New York/London: Routledge.

Fleming, M. (1995) 'Women and the Public Use of Reason', in J. Meehan (ed.) *Feminists Read Habermas: Gendering the Subject of Discourse*, New York/London: Routledge.

Foucault, M. (1966/1973) *The Order of Things: An Archaeology of the Human Sciences*, New York: Vintage Books.

——(1969/1972) *The Archaeology of Knowledge*, trans. A. M. Sheridan Smith, London: Tavistock Publications Limited.

——(1970/1971) 'The Discourse on Language', Appendix, *The Archaeology of Language*, London: Basil Blackwell.

——(ed.) (1973/1975) *I, Pierre Rivière, Having Slaughtered My Mother, My Sister and My Brother . . .: A Case of Parricide in the 19th Century*, Lincoln, NE/London: University of Nebraska Press.

——(1975/1982) *Discipline and Punish: The Birth of the Prison*, trans. Alan Sheridan, Harmondsworth: Penguin.

——(1976/1980) *The History of Sexuality*, vol. 1, *An Introduction*, New York: Vintage Books.

——(1978) 'Politics and the Study of Discourse', *Ideology and Consciousness* 3: 7–26.

——(1980) *Power/Knowledge: Selected Interviews and Other Writings, 1972–77*, London: Harvester Press.

——(1982) 'Afterword: The Subject and Power', in H. L. Dreyfus and P. Rabinow, *Michel Foucault: Beyond Structuralism and Hermeneutics*, Sussex: Harvester Press.

——(1984/1985) *The Use of Pleasure*, New York: Pantheon Books.

Fowler, A. (1982) *Kinds of Literature: An Introduction to the Theory of Genres and Modes*, Oxford: Clarendon Press.

Fraser, N. (1995) 'What's Critical About Critical Theory?', in J. Meehan (ed.) *Feminists Read Habermas: Gendering the Subject of Discourse*, New York/London: Routledge.

Frow, J. (1982) 'The Chant of Thomas Keneally', *Australian Literary Studies* 10: 291–9.

——(1995a) *Cultural Studies and Cultural Value*, Oxford: Oxford University Press.

——(1995b) 'A Note on Legal Semiotics', *Social Semiotics* 5, 2: 183–9.

Gallop, J. (1995) *Pedagogy: The Question of Impersonation*, Bloomington/Indianapolis: Indiana University Press.

Gatens, M. (1989) 'Woman and Her Double(s): Sex, Gender and Ethics', *Australian Feminist Studies* 10: 33–48.

——(1991) 'Corporeal Representations in/and the Body Politic', in R. Diprose and R. Ferrell (eds) *Cartographies: Poststructuralism and the Mapping of Bodies and Spaces*, Sydney: Allen & Unwin, pp. 79–87.

——(1996) *Imaginary Bodies: Ethics, Power and Corporeality*, London/New York: Routledge.

Gibson Cima, G. (1993) *Performing Women: Female Characters, Male Playwrights and the Modern Stage*, Ithaca/London: Cornell University Press.

Goodrich, P. (1991) *Reading the Law: A Critical Introduction to Legal Method and Techniques*, Oxford: Basil Blackwell.

Goodrich, P. and Hachamovitch, Y. (1991) 'Time Out of Mind: An Introduction to the Semiotics of the Common Law', in P. Fitzpatrick (ed.) *Dangerous Supplements: Resistance and Renewal in Jurisprudence*, London: Pluto Press.

Goodwin, C. (1994) 'Professional Vision', *American Anthropologist* 96, 3: 606–33.

Graycar, R. and Morgan, J. (1990) *The Hidden Gender of the Law*, Sydney: The Federation Press.

Greimas, A. G. (1987) *On Meaning: Selected Writings in Semiotic Theory*, trans. P. J. Perron and F. H. Collins, Minneapolis: University of Minnesota Press.

Grenville, K. and Woolfe, S. (1993) *Making Stories: How Ten Australian Novels Were Written*, Sydney: Allen & Unwin.

Grimshaw, P., Lake, M., McGrath, A. and Quartly, M. (1994) *Creating a Nation*, Victoria: McPhee Gribble Publishers.

Grosz, E. A. (1989) *Sexual Subversions: Three French Feminists*, Sydney: Allen & Unwin.

——(1994) *Volatile Bodies: Toward a Corporeal Feminism*, Sydney: Allen & Unwin.

——(1995a) *Space, Time and Perversion: The Politics of Bodies*, Sydney: Allen & Unwin.

——(1995b) 'Labors of Love: Analyzing Perverse Desire (An Interrogation of Teresa de Lauretis's *The Practice of Love*)', in *Space, Time and Perversion: The Politics of Bodies*, Sydney: Allen & Unwin.

Haar, M. (1977) 'Nietzsche and Metaphysical Language', in D. Allison (ed.) *The New Nietzsche: Contemporary Styles of Interpretation*, NY: Delta.

Habermas, J. (1981) *The Theory of Communicative Action: Reason and the Rationalisation of Society*, trans. T. McCarthy, 2 vols, Cambridge: Polity Press, vol. 1.

Hall, S. (1986) 'Cultural Studies: Two Paradigms', in Richard Collins et al. (eds) *Media, Culture and Society: A Critical Reader*, London: Sage.

Halliday, M. A. K. (1978) *Language as Social Semiotic: The Social Interpretation of Language and Meaning*, London: Edward Arnold.

——(1979) 'Modes of Meaning and Modes of Expression: Types of Grammatical Structure, and Their Determination by Different Semantic Functions', in D. J. Allerton, E. Carney and D. Holdcroft (eds) *Function and Context in Linguistic Analysis: A Festschrift for William Haas*, Cambridge/London: Cambridge University Press, pp. 57–8.

——(1983) 'On the Ineffability of Grammatical Categories', in A. Manning, P. Martin and K. McCalla (eds) *The Tenth LACUS Forum*, Columbia, SC: Hornbeam Press, pp. 3–18.

——(1985a) *An Introduction to Functional Grammar*, London: Edward Arnold.

——(1985b) *Language, Context and Text: Aspects of Language in a Social-Semiotic*

Perspective, Geelong: Deakin University Press (republished by Oxford University Press in 1989).
——(1985c) *Spoken and Written Language*, Geelong: Deakin University Press.
——(1987) 'Language and the Order of Nature', in N. Fabb, D. Attridge, A. Durant and C. McCabe (eds) *The Linguistics of Writing: Arguments between Language and Literature*, Manchester: Manchester University Press, pp. 135–54.
Halliday, M. and Hasan, R. (1976) *Cohesion in English*, London: Longman.
Halperin, D. (1995) *Saint-Foucault: Towards a Gay Hagiography*, New York: Oxford University Press.
Hamilton, P. (1993) 'Domestic Dilemmas: Representations of Servants and Employers in the Popular Press', in S. Magarey, S. Rowley and S. Sheridan (eds) *Debutante Nation: Feminism Contests the 1890s*, Sydney: Allen & Unwin.
Haraway, D. (1991a) *Simians, Cyborgs and Women: The Reinvention of Nature*, London: Free Association Books.
——(1991b) 'A Cyborg Manifesto: Science, Technology, and Socialist-Feminism in the Late Twentieth Century', in D. Haraway, *Simians, Cyborgs and Women: The Reinvention of Nature*, London: Free Association Books, pp. 149–82.
Hartsock, N. (1987) 'The Feminist Standpoint: Developing the Ground for a Specifically Feminist Historical Materialism', in S. Harding (ed.) *Feminism and Methodology*, Bloomington: Indiana University Press, pp. 157–80.
Harvey, D. (1989) *The Condition of Postmodernity: An Enquiry into the Origins of Cultural Change*, Oxford: Basil Blackwell.
Hasan, R. (1985) *Linguistics, Language and Verbal Art*, Geelong: Deakin University Press.
Hauptmeier, H. (1987) 'Sketches of Theories of Genre', *Poetics* 16: 397–430.
Hayles, N. K. (1989) 'Chaos as Orderly Disorder: Shifting Ground in Contemporary Literature and Science', *New Literary History* 20, 2: 305–22.
Heath, S. B. (1983) *Ways with Words: Language, Life and Work in Communities and Classrooms*, Cambridge: Cambridge University Press.
Henriques, J., Hollway, W., Urwin, C., Couze, V. and Walkerdine, V. (1984) *Changing the Subject: Psychology, Social Regulation and Subjectivity*, London/New York: Methuen.
Hjelmslev, L. (1943/1961) *Prolegomena to a Theory of Language*, trans. F. J. Whitfield, Madison: University of Wisconsin Press.
Hofstadter, D. R. (1980) 'On Formally Undecidable Propositions of TNT and Related Systems', in *Gödel, Escher, Bach: An Eternal Golden Braid*, Harmondsworth: Penguin Books.
Holland, P. (1992) *What is a Child? Popular Images of Childhood*, London: Virago Press.
hooks, bell (1994) *Outlaw Culture*, New York: Routledge.
Hornadge, Bill (ed.) (1974) *Old Dubbo Gaol*, Dubbo: Old Dubbo Gaol Restoration Committee.
Huddleston, R. D. (1971) *The Sentence in Written English*, Cambridge: Cambridge University Press.
Huggins, J. (1993) 'Pretty Deadly Tidda Business', in S. Gunew and A. Yeatman (eds) *Feminism and the Politics of Difference*, Sydney: Allen & Unwin.
Hughes, G.E. and Cresswell, M.J. (1973) *An Introduction to Modal Logic*, Oxford: Oxford University Press.
Hunter, I. (1988) *Culture and Government: The Emergence of Literary Education*, London: Macmillan.
——(1994) *Rethinking the School: Subjectivity, Bureaucracy, Criticism*, Sydney: Allen & Unwin.

Hymes, D. (1967) 'Models of the Interaction of Language and Social Setting', *Journal of Social Issues* 23: 8–28.

Irigaray, L. (1974/1985) *Speculum of the Other Woman*, trans. G. C. Gill, Ithaca, NY: Cornell University Press.

——(1977/1985a) *This Sex Which is Not One*, trans. C. Porter and C. Burke, Ithaca, NY: Cornell University Press.

——(1977/1985b) 'Commodities Among Themselves', in L. Irigaray, *This Sex Which is Not One*, trans. C. Porter and C. Burke, Ithaca, NY: Cornell University Press.

Jakobson, R. (1956/1985) 'Metalanguage as a Linguistic Problem', in *Selected Writings*, vol. 7, *Word and Language*, The Hague: Mouton, pp. 113–21.

——(1957/1971a) 'Shifters, Verbal Categories and the Russian Verb', in (1971) *Selected Writings*, vol. 2, *Word and Language* , The Hague: Mouton.

——(1957/1971b) 'Two Aspects of Language and Two Types of Aphasic Disturbances', in (1971) *Selected Writings*, vol. 2, *Word and Language*, The Hague: Mouton, pp. 239–59.

——(1958/1981) 'Linguistics and Poetics', in (1981) *Selected Writings: Poetry of Grammar and Grammar of Poetry*, ed. S. Rudy, The Hague: Mouton, pp. 18–51.

Jameson, F. (1984) 'The Politics of Theory: Ideological Positions in the Postmodernism Debate', *New German Critique* 33: 33–65.

Jenkins, H. (1992) *Textual Poachers: Television Fans and Participatory Culture*, New York/London: Routledge.

Johnson, C. (1987) *Long Live Sandawara*, Melbourne: Hyland House.

Kamler, B., Maclean, R., Reid, J-A. and Simpson, A. (1994) *Shaping Up Nicely: The Formation of Schoolgirls and Schoolboys in the First Month of School, A Report to The Gender Equity and Curriculum Reform Project*, Department of Employment, Education and Training, Canberra, Geelong: Deakin University Press.

Keneally, Thomas (1972/1978) *The Chant of Jimmie Blacksmith*, Pymble, Australia: Fontana Collins.

——(1982) 'My Fiction and the Aboriginal', in G. Amirthanayagam (ed.) *Writers in East–West Encounter: New Cultural Bearings*, London: Macmillan.

——(1993) *The Chant of Jimmie Blacksmith*, in K. Grenville and S. Woolfe (eds) *Making Stories: How Ten Australian Novels Were Written*, Sydney: Allen & Unwin.

Kirkby, D. (ed.) (1995) *Sex, Power and Justice: Historical Perspectives on Law in Australia*, Melbourne: Oxford University Press.

Knapman, C. (1993) 'Reproducing Empire: Exploring Ideologies of Gender and Race on Australia's Pacific Frontier', in S. Magarey, S. Rowley and S. Sheridan (eds) *Debutante Nation: Feminism Contests the 1890s*, Sydney: Allen & Unwin.

Knoespel, K. (1989) 'Newton in the School of Time: The Chronology of Ancient Kingdoms Amended and the Crisis of Seventeenth Century Historiography', *The Eighteenth Century: Theory and Interpretation* 30, 3: 19–41.

Knorr-Cetina, K. D. (1981) *The Manufacture of Knowledge*, Oxford: Pergamon.

Kress, G. (1985) *Linguistic Processes in Sociocultural Practice*, Geelong: Deakin University Press.

Kress, G. and van Leeuwen, T. (1990) *Reading Images*, Geelong: Deakin University Press.

Kress, G. and Threadgold, T. (1988) 'Towards a Social Theory of Genre', *Southern Review* 21, 3: 215–43.

Kristeva, J. (1970) *Le Texte du Roman*, The Hague/Paris/New York: Mouton.

——(1973) 'The System and the Speaking Subject', *Times Literary Supplement*, 12 October 1973: 1249.

——(1974/1984) *Revolution in Poetic Language*, trans. M. Waller, New York: Columbia University Press.

Kuhn, T. S. (1962/1974) *The Structure of Scientific Revolutions, International Encyclopedia of Unified Science* vol. 2, no. 2, Chicago: University of Chicago Press.

Labov, W. (1972) *Language in the Inner City: Studies in the Black English Vernacular*, Philadelphia: University of Pennsylvania Press.

Labov, W. and Fanshel, D. (1977) *Therapeutic Discourse: Psychotherapy as Conversation*, New York: Academic Press.

Labov, W. and Waletsky, J. (1967) 'Narrative Analysis: Oral Versions of Personal Experience', in June Helm (ed.) *Essays on the Verbal and Visual Arts*, Seattle: University of Washington Press, pp. 12–44.

Lake, M. (1993) 'The Politics of Respectability: Identifying the Masculinist Context', in S. Magarey, S. Rowley and S. Sheridan (eds) *Debutante Nation: Feminism Contests the 1890s*, Sydney: Allen & Unwin.

Lakoff, R. (1975) *Language and Women's Place*, New York: Harper & Row.

de Lauretis, T. (1984) *Alice Doesn't: Feminism, Semiotics, Cinema*, Bloomington/Indianapolis: Indiana University Press.

——(1987) *Technologies of Gender: Essays on Theory, Film and Fiction*, Bloomington/Indianapolis: Indiana University Press.

——(1994) *The Practice of Love: Lesbian Sexuality and Perverse Desire*, Bloomington/Indianapolis: Indiana University Press.

de Lauretis, T. and Heath, S. (eds) (1985) *The Cinematic Apparatus*, New York: St Martin's Press.

Lee, A. (1993) 'Whose Geography? A Feminist-Poststructuralist Critique of Systemic "Genre"-Based Accounts of Literacy and Curriculum', *Social Semiotics* 3, 1: 131–56.

van Leeuwen, T. (1987) 'Generic Strategies in Press Journalism', *Australian Review of Applied Linguistics* 10, 2: 199–220.

Lemke, J. (1985) 'Ideology, Intertextuality, and the Notion of Register', in J. D. Benson and W. S. Greaves (eds) *Systemic Perspectives on Discourse*, Norwood, NJ: Ablex, vol. 1.

—— (1988) 'Discourses in Conflict: Heteroglossia and Text Semantics', in J. D. Benson and W. S. Greaves (eds) *Systemic Functional Approaches to Discourse: Selected Papers from the 12th International Systemic Workshop*, Norwood, NJ: Ablex.

Lévi-Strauss, C. (1963) *Structural Anthropology*, trans. C. Jacobson and B. Grundfest Schöpf, New York: Basic Books.

——(1969) *The Elementary Structures of Kinship*, Boston: Beacon Press.

Lloyd, G. (1989) 'Woman as Other: Sex, Gender and Subjectivity', *Australian Feminist Studies* 10: 13–22.

Longacre, R. E. (1974) 'Narrative Versus Other Genres', in R. Brend (ed.) *Advances in Tagmemics*, Amsterdam/London: North-Holland.

Lotman, J. M. (1979) 'The Origin of Plot in the Light of Topology', trans. J. Graffy, *Poetics Today* 1, 1–2: 161–84.

Luke, C. (1989) *Pedagogy, Printing and Protestantism: The Discourse on Childhood*, Albany: State University of New York Press.

——(1992) 'Feminist Politics in Radical Pedagogy', in C. Luke and J. Gore (eds) *Feminisms and Critical Pedagogy*, New York: Routledge, pp. 25–53.

——(1994) 'White Women in Interracial Families: Reflections on Hybridization, Feminine Identities, and Racialized Othering', *Feminist Issues* 14, 2: 42–91.

Lyotard, Jean-François (1979/1984) *The Postmodern Condition: A Report on*

Knowledge, trans. G. Bennington and B. Massumi, Manchester: Manchester University Press.
McCarthy, T. (1995) ' "Battered Woman's Syndrome": Some Reflections on the Invisibility of the Battering Man in Legal Discourse, Drawing on R. v Raby', *Australian Feminist Law Journal* 4: 153–76.
McConnell-Ginet, S. (ed.) (1980) *Women and Language in Literature and Society*, New York: Praeger.
Macdonell, D. (1986) *Theories of Discourse: An Introduction*, Oxford: Basil Blackwell.
McHoul, A. and Grace, W. (1993) *A Foucault Primer: Discourse, Power and the Subject*, Melbourne: Melbourne University Press.
Magarey, S., Rowley, S. and Sheridan, S. (eds) (1993) *Debutante Nation: Feminism Contests the 1890s*, Sydney: Allen & Unwin.
Malinowski, B. (1923) 'The Problem of Meaning in Primitive Languages', Supplement 1, in C. K. Ogden and I. A. Richards (eds) *The Meaning of Meaning*, London: Routledge & Kegan Paul.
Manuel, F. E. (1974) *The Religion of Isaac Newton*, Oxford: Clarendon Press.
Marcus, S. (1992) 'Fighting Bodies, Fighting Words: A Theory and Politics of Rape Prevention', in J. Butler and J. W. Scott (eds) *Feminists Theorize the Political*, New York and London: Routledge.
Markley, R. (1991) 'Complex Dynamics: Literature, Science and Postdisciplinarity', *Poetics Today* 12, 2: 335–46.
Martin, J. R. (1985a) *Factual Writing: Exploring and Challenging Social Reality*, Geelong: Deakin University Press.
——(1985b) 'Text and Process: Two Aspects of Human Semiosis', in W. S. Greaves and J. O. Benson (eds) *Systemic Perspectives on Discourse: Selected Theoretical Papers from the 9th International Systemic Workshop*, Norwood, NJ: Ablex, pp. 248–74.
——(1991) 'Intrinsic Functionality: Indications for Contextual Theory', *Social Semiotics* 1, 1: 99–162.
Matejka, L. (ed.) (1978) *Sound, Sign and Meaning: Quinquagenary of the Prague Linguistic Circle*, Ann Arbor: University of Michigan.
Mathesius, V. (1911) 'On the Potentiality of the Phenomena of Language', in J. Vachek (ed.) (1964) *A Prague School Reader in Linguistics*, Bloomington: Indiana University Press.
Meehan, J. (ed.) (1995) *Feminists Read Habermas: Gendering the Subject of Discourse*, New York/London: Routledge.
Mellencamp, P. (1990) *High Anxiety: Catastrophe, Scandal, Age, Comedy*, Bloomington/Indianapolis: Indiana University Press.
Mercer, C. (1992) 'Regular Imaginings: The Newspaper and the Nation', in Tony Bennett, Pat Buckridge, David Carter and Colin Mercer (eds) *Celebrating the Nation: A Critical Study of Australia's Bicentenary*, Sydney: Allen & Unwin.
Metz, C. (1981) *The Imaginary Signifier*, Bloomington: Indiana University Press.
Miller, J. (1992) *More Has Meant Women: The Feminisation of Schooling*, Institute of Education, University of London: The Tufnell Press.
——(1996) *School for Women*, London: Virago.
Mills, S. (1995) *Feminist Stylistics*, London/New York: Routledge.
Morgan, W. (1994) *Ned Kelly Reconstructed*, Cambridge: Cambridge University Press.
Morris, M. (1988) *The Pirate's Fiancée: Feminism Reading Postmodernism*, London/New York: Verso.
Morrison, T. (1993) 'Afterword', in *The Bluest Eye*, London: Picador.

Mudrooroo Narogin (1965) *Wildcat Falling*, Introd. Stephen Muecke, Foreword Mary Durack, Sydney: Angus & Robertson.

——(1988) *Doin Wildcat: A Novel Koori Script*, Melbourne: Hyland House.

——(1990) *Writing from the Fringe: A Study of Modern Aboriginal Literature*, Melbourne: Hyland House.

Muecke, S. (1992) *Textual Spaces: Aboriginality and Cultural Studies*, Kensington: NSW University Press.

Mukarovsky, J. (1977) *The Word and Verbal Art: Selected Essays*, ed. and trans. J. Burbank and P. Steiner, New Haven/London: Yale University Press.

Mulvey, L. (1989a) 'Changes: Thoughts on Myth, Narrative and Historical Experience', in *Visual and Other Pleasures*, Bloomington/Indianapolis: Indiana University Press.

——(1989b) 'Visual Pleasure and Narrative Cinema', in *Visual and Other Pleasures*, Bloomington/Indianapolis: Indiana University Press.

Norris, C. (1992) *Uncritical Theory: Postmodernism, Intellectuals and the Gulf War*, Amherst: University of Massachusetts Press.

O'Toole, M. (1994) *The Language of Displayed Art*, London: Leicester University Press.

Pasolini, P. P. (1991) 'Aspects of a Semiology of Cinema', in K. Cohen (ed.) *Writing in a Film Age*, Colorado: University Press of Colorado.

Pateman, C. (1988) *The Sexual Contract*, Cambridge: Polity Press.

Pateman, C. and Gross, E. (1986) *Feminist Challenges: Social and Political Theory*, Sydney: Allen & Unwin.

Paulson, W. R. (1988) *The Noise of Culture: Literary Texts in a World of Information*, Ithaca: Cornell University Press.

Pêcheux, M. (1975/1982) *Language, Semantics, Ideology*, trans. H. Nagpal, London/Basingstoke: Macmillan.

Peirce, C. S. (1931–58) *Collected Papers*, Cambridge: Harvard University Press.

Pheng, C. (1994) 'Sexual Difference, Cultural Difference – Body and History in Gallop', in J. Julius Matthews (ed.) *Jane Gallop Seminar Papers*, Humanities Research Centre Monograph 7, Canberra: The Australian National University.

Podgórecki, A. (1973) ' "Second Life" and its Implications', mimeo.

Poynton, C. (1985) *Language and Gender: Making the Difference*, Geelong: Deakin University Press.

——(1990) 'The Privileging of Representation and the Marginalising of the Interpersonal: A Metaphor (and More) for Contemporary Gender Relations', in T. Threadgold and A. Cranny-Francis (eds) *Feminine/Masculine and Representation*, Sydney: Allen & Unwin.

——(1993) 'Grammar, Language and the Social: Poststructuralism and Systemic-Functional Linguistics', *Social Semiotics* 3, 1: 1–22.

Praed, R. (1885) *Australian Life: Black and White*, London: Chapman & Hall.

Pribram, D. (1988) *Female Spectators: Looking at Film and Television*, London/New York: Verso.

Prior, A.N. (1967) *Past, Present and Future: A Study of Tense Logic*, Oxford: Oxford University Press.

Probyn, E. (1993) *Sexing the Self: Gendered Positions in Cultural Studies*, London/New York: Routledge.

Propp, V. (1928/1968) *Morphology of the Folk Tale*, ed. L. A. Wagner, Austin/London: University of Texas Press.

Radway, J. (1984) *Reading the Romance: Women, Patriarchy and Popular Literature*, London/New York: Verso.

Reynolds, H. (1982) *The Other Side of the Frontier: Aboriginal Resistance to the Invasion of Australia*, Harmondsworth: Penguin.
——(1995) *Fate of a Free People*, Ringwood: Penguin Books.
Ricoeur, P. (1978) *The Rule of Metaphor: Multi-Disciplinary Studies of the Creation of Meaning in Language*, trans. R. Czerny (with K. McLaughlin and J. Costello), London/Henley-on-Thames: Routledge & Kegan Paul.
——(1986) *Lectures on Ideology and Utopia*, ed. G. H. Taylor, New York: Columbia University Press.
Rolls, E. (1978) 'The Hunt for Jimmy Governor', *National Times*, 2–7 January: 5–10.
Rossi-Landi, F. (1973) *Ideologies of Linguistic Relativity*, ed. T. A. Sebeok, *Approaches to Semiotics* vol. 4, The Hague: Mouton.
——(1977) *Linguistics and Economics*, The Hague: Mouton.
Rowse, T. (1993) *After Mabo: Interpreting Indigenous Traditions*, Melbourne: Melbourne University Press.
Scholes, R. (1979) *Fabulation and Metafiction*, Urbana: University of Illinois Press.
Scott, J. (1988) *Gender and the Politics of History*, New York: Columbia University Press.
Sebeok, T. A. (ed.) (1960) *Style in Language*, Cambridge, MA: MIT Press.
Schepisi, F. (1978) *The Chant of Jimmie Blacksmith*, screenplay by Fred Schepisi (from the novel by Thomas Keneally), director of photography Ian Baker, produced and directed by Fred Schepisi.
Silverman, K. (1983) *The Theory of Semiotics*, New York: Oxford University Press.
Silverstein, M. (1979) 'Language Structure and Linguistic Ideology', in P. R. Clyne, W. F. Hanks and C. L. Hofbauer (eds) *The Elements: A Parasession on Linguistic Units and Levels*, Chicago: Chicago Linguistic Society, pp. 192–247.
Smith, D. E. (1987) *The Everyday World as Problematic: A Feminist Sociology*, Boston: Northeastern University Press.
——(1990) *Texts, Facts and Femininity: Exploring the Relations of Ruling*, London/New York: Routledge.
Spariosu, M. (1989) *Dionysus Reborn: Play and the Aesthetic Dimension in Modern Philosophical and Scientific Discourse*, Ithaca: Cornell University Press.
Spivak, G. (1983) 'Displacement and the Discourse of Woman', in M. Krupnik (ed.) *Displacement, Derrida and After*, Bloomington: Indiana University Press.
——(1988) 'Subaltern Studies: Deconstructing Historiography', in *In Other Worlds*, London: Routledge.
——(1989) 'Feminism and Deconstruction, again: Negotiations', in G. Spivak (1993) *Outside in the Teaching Machine*, New York/London: Routledge.
Summers, A. (1975) *Damned Whores and God's Police: The Colonization of Women in Australia*, Ringwood: Penguin Books.
Swales, R. (1990) *Genre Analysis: English in Academic Settings*, Cambridge: Cambridge University Press.
Thibault, P. J. (1984) 'Narrative Discourse as a Multi-Level System of Communication: Some Theoretical Proposals Concerning Bakhtin's Dialogic Principle', *Studies in 20th Century Literature* 9, 1: 89–117.
——(1987) 'An Interview with Michael Halliday', in R. Steele and T. Threadgold (eds) *Language Topics: Essays in Honour of Michael Halliday*, Amsterdam: Benjamins, vol. 2, pp. 601–27.
——(1991) *Social Semiotics as Praxis: Text, Social Meaning Making, and Nabakov's Ada*, Minneapolis/Oxford: University of Minnesota Press.
Threadgold, T. (1986) 'The Semiotics of Halliday, Voloshinov and Eco', *American Journal of Semiotics* 4, 3: 107–42.
——(1987) 'Rossi-Landi's Higher Dialectical Level: Some Observations on

Linguistic Alienation, Relativity and Ideology', *Il Protagora: Rivista di Filosofia e Cultura Fondata da Bruno Widmar (Il Protagora: Review of Philosophy and Culture Founded by Bruno Widmar)* 27, series 1V, 11–12: 81–98.

——(1988) 'Language and Gender', *Australian Feminist Studies* 3: 41–70.

——(1989) 'Paradigms of Culture and Semiosis: Grammatics for Cryptogrammars or Metalanguage for the Ineffable?', in Walter A. Koch (ed.) *Evolution of Culture – Evolution der Kultur, Proceedings of the International and Interdisciplinary Symposium*, 19–23 September 1988, Loveno di Menaggio, Italy, Bochum: Brockmeyer.

——(1990) 'Introduction', in T. Threadgold and A. Cranny-Francis (eds) *Feminine/Masculine and Representation*, Sydney: Allen & Unwin.

——(1991) 'Legal Practice in the Courts: Discourse, Gender and Ethics', *Australian Journal of Law and Society* 7: 39–70.

——(1993a) 'Genre', in *Encyclopedia of Language and Linguistics*, Edinburgh: Pergamon/Aberdeen University Press, vol. 3, pp. 1408–11.

——(1993b) 'Structuralism and Semiotics, Literary', in *The Encyclopedia of Language and Linguistics*, Edinburgh: Pergamon/Aberdeen University Press, vol. 8, pp. 4359–4373.

——(1994) 'Re-Writing Law as Postmodern Fiction: The Poetics of Child Abuse', in J. Neville Turner and P. Williams (eds) *The Happy Couple: Law and Literature*, Sydney: The Federation Press.

——(1995) 'Regulative Fictions: Translations and Performing Subversions', Keynote Address delivered at the International Conference of The Law and Humanities Institute and the Australian Law and Literature Association, Berkeley, California, September (to be published in 1996 in *Law/Text/Culture*).

——(1996) 'Everyday Life in the Academy: Postmodern Feminisms, Generic Seductions, Rewriting and Being Heard', in C. Luke (ed.) *Feminisms and Pedagogies of Everyday Life*, New York: SUNY Press.

Tulloch, J. and Lupton, D. (eds) (1996) *Television, Aids and Risk*, Sydney: Allen & Unwin.

Turner, G. (1989) 'Art Directing History: The Period Film', in A. Moran and T. O'Regan (eds) *The Australian Screen*, Victoria, Australia: Penguin.

Voloshinov, V. N. (1930/1973) *Marxism and the Philosophy of Language*, trans. L. Matejka and I. R. Titunik, New York/London: Seminar Press.

Wayne, V. (1991) *The Matter of Difference: Materialist Feminist Criticism of Shakespeare*, New York/London: Harvester Wheatsheaf.

Weedon, C. (1987) *Feminist Practice and Poststructuralist Theory*, Oxford: Basil Blackwell.

Weir, A. (1995) 'Toward a Model of Self-Identity: Habermas and Kristeva', in J. Meehan (ed.) *Feminists Read Habermas: Gendering the Subject of Discourse*, New York/London: Routledge.

Whorf, B. L. (1956) *Language, Thought and Reality: Selected Writings of Benjamin Lee Whorf*, ed. J. B. Carroll, Cambridge, MA: MIT Press.

Wiggershaus, R. (1995) *The Frankfurt School*, Cambridge: Polity Press.

Williams, R. (1980) *Problems in Materialism and Culture*, London: Verso.

Wright, J. (1993) 'Regulation and Resistance', *Social Semiotics* 3, 1: 23–54.

Yeatman, A. (1987) 'The Politics of Child Abuse', Paper presented to conference on The Social Context of Child Abuse, sponsored by the South Australian Office of the Government Management Board and Department of Premier and Cabinet, 1 December 1987.

——(1990) *Bureaucrats, Technocrats, Femocrats: Essays on the Contemporary Australian State*, Sydney: Allen & Unwin.

——(1993) 'Voice and Representation in the Politics of Difference', in S. Gunew and A. Yeatman (eds) *Feminism and the Politics of Difference*, Sydney: Allen & Unwin.

Yell, S. (1990) 'Gender, Class and Power: Text, Process and Production in Strindberg's *Miss Julie*', in T. Threadgold and A. Cranny-Francis (eds) *Feminine/Masculine and Representation*, Sydney: Allen & Unwin.

——(1993) 'A Critical Linguistic Study of Conversational Texts in the Contemporary Novel', Unpublished PhD thesis, University of Sydney.

Young, R. J. C. (1995) *Colonial Desire: Hybridity in Theory, Culture, Race*, London/New York: Routledge.

Index